BERLITZ®

DISCOVER
AUSTRALIA

Ken Bernstein

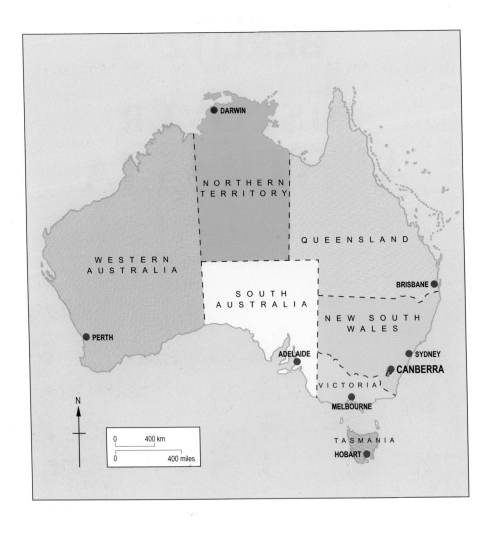

Contents

Covering a Continent:
Planning the Trip of a Lifetime

Seeing an entire island on holiday may sound feasible, but not when it's Australia. Deciding where to go and what to see in a limited time may be the hardest part of your journey; don't skimp on the advance planning. You'll have to compromise, weighing the time and funds available, the season, your special priorities, and your choice of gateway city—one of the really big decisions. But why settle for one gateway? Why not begin your visit in, say, Sydney and depart from Perth? Or arrive at Darwin, and head home from Melbourne? It often costs no more.

For simplicity, this guide follows the geographical reality of Australia's states and territories. Although there's no visible difference between the red deserts of the Northern Territory or those of Western Australia, it's convenient to consider them in the context of the political frontiers. And even though Broken Hill, NSW, is easier to reach from neighbouring South Australia than from Sydney, you'll find it in this book, as on the map, under New South Wales. But aside from such eccentricities, the way history and chance carved Australia into states comes fairly close to a manageable division into sightseeing regions.

Discover Australia makes no claims to encyclopedic coverage. But it does aim to include most places a visitor from afar is likely to find interesting: more, indeed, than you could see in months of intensive travel. And we assume you're trying to see as much as you can in the time available. The sights *omitted* are usually of parochial interest, or simply too hard to reach to justify a side-trip.

In one of its big, alluring brochures, the Australian Tourist Commission concedes with understatement, "Not all visitors will have the time to explore completely this vast continent." The commission thus devises a series of itineraries of 14, 21 and 28 days,

Dressed for the desert climate, tourists retreat from the perimeter of Ayers Rock.

AUSTRALIA

TIMOR SEA

ARAFURA SEA

CORAL SEA

SOUTH PACIFIC OCEAN

TASMAN SEA

INDIAN OCEAN

SOUTHERN OCEAN

Great Barrier Reef

Gulf of Carpentaria

Arnhem Land

Great Sandy Desert

Great Australian Bight

Nullarbor Plain

Bass Strait

WESTERN AUSTRALIA

NORTHERN TERRITORY

SOUTH AUSTRALIA

QUEENSLAND

NEW SOUTH WALES

VICTORIA

TASMANIA

Great Dividing Range

MacDonnel Ranges

Flinders River
Roper River
Fitzroy River
Fortescue River
Ashburton River
Gascoyne River
Murchison River
Murray River
Cooper Creek

Lake Eyre

Mount Olga
Ayers Rock

DARWIN
Jabiru
Nhulunbuy (Gove)
Katherine
Borroloola
Wyndham
Broome
Port Hedland
Camarvon
Geraldton
PERTH
Fremantle
Bunbury
Albany
Esperance
Kalgoorlie
Woomera
Coober Pedy
Alice Springs
Tennant Creek
Mount Isa
Normanton
Cooktown
Port Douglas
Cairns
Townsville
Proserpine
Mackay
Rockhampton
Noosa
BRISBANE
Surfers Paradise
Toowoomba
Lightning Ridge
Bourke
Broken Hill
Dubbo
Bathurst
Katoomba
SYDNEY
CANBERRA
Port Augusta
ADELAIDE
Bendigo
Ballarat
MELBOURNE
Devonport
Launceston
Port Arthur
HOBART

N

0   400 km
0   400 miles

Dry Lake
▲ Mountain
Land above 500m (1,640ft)

starting in one of the principal gateways and ending up in another. Itinerary 2 can be tacked on to Itinerary 1 if time allows, and so on. The permutations seem infinite. Your own plan will depend on your time-and-money budget and your tastes.

Whatever you do, don't make a city-by-city itinerary as if you were "doing" Europe or sharing the businessman's fate. The capital cities are worthy attractions, but what really makes Australia different is the rest—the natural glories, the mystery and colours of even the most desolate bushland. Find the balance between the towns and the Outback. You don't have to drive for days, or rough it, to sample the wilds; as soon as you leave the suburbs you'll have the feeling of wide open spaces.

An obvious way to organize your trip is to emphasize your own interests or hobbies. Scuba-divers prefer the Great Barrier Reef, while geologists are happier in the gold-fields. History buffs can follow in Captain Cook's wake, or catch up on colonial architecture. You could even spend several weeks doing nothing more strenuous than wine-tasting. For visitors in pursuit of such itineraries, we offer a generous sample of ideas, mostly offbeat, in our **Leisure Routes** chapter.

All the capital cities are close to beaches, so it's tempting to squeeze a couple of swims into your busy schedule. If it's winter Down Under you might substitute a bit of skiing, unless you go to the tropics—of which Australia has no shortage. The weather you can expect is more complicated

*M*ap of Australia.

than a look at the world map might indicate.

When to Go

Any day of the year you can find perfect sunny weather somewhere in Australia. You just have to be in the right place at the right time. In a word, avoid the tropical north's uncomfortably hot rainy season, which is also the cyclone season. Otherwise, Australia is the driest of continents, though you might not think so on a chilly, gloomy winter day in Sydney or Melbourne.

The southern, temperate areas of the country have four seasons—at opposite times from the northern hemisphere's schedule. Summer is December to February, with hot days everywhere (except Tasmania, which has a climate more like Britain) and mild nights in all the nation's capital cities but Darwin. Winter in the south (June to August) is cool with more of a chance of rain marring the sunny stretches; snow covers the southern mountains. In the desert at the heart of Australia, winter is the most comfortable season.

For the detailed city-by-city statistics, see the charts below. However, averages provide only the most general guidance, always subject to drastic variations. That should inspire you to stay in Australia as long as you can, to give the averages time enough to average out.

*I*n a fertile zone of South Australia, the scene is peeling trees with farm buildings to match (following spread).

Travel Basics

Australia's efficient, heavily travelled domestic airlines serve all the cities and many obscure towns as well. Getting around by air is fast and comfortable but relatively expensive in most cases. Overseas visitors have a privileged position, benefiting from various "bargain" fares. Check before you leave home, lest you miss out on one of the special deals, which are inviting even though they involve seemingly arbitrary restrictions on routing and stopovers. While the major national and regional airlines fly the latest jets, the small regional companies operate propjet aircraft that recall the more adventurous days of aviation. It's all part of the Australian adventure.

For independent travellers there's no substitute for a car. It confers the privilege of choosing an itinerary on a whim, stopping anywhere that looks interesting, exploring the byways—and packing as haphazardly as you please. Australia's roads are good, in many cases better than you'd expect in difficult conditions. Highway 1, which circumnavigates the continent, is now paved all the way. In the most heavily travelled parts of the road network—between Sydney and Melbourne, for example—there are well landscaped divided highways. Secondary roads may be narrower than you're accustomed to, and they tend to dwindle eventually, perhaps hundreds of kilometres later, into unpaved surfaces. Although service stations and motels can be extremely far apart in the Outback, the main roads are well supplied with every amenity. Renting a car is straightforward, either

reserving one before you leave home or arranging it on arrival. Also for rent are four-wheel-drive vehicles, campervans and motorhomes.

Intercity coaches are a money-saving alternative way of seeing the country. Service on the big national routes is fast, rather luxurious, and well organized thanks to computer reservations. There are various bargain passes, for instance two weeks or a month of unlimited travel for a fixed price. Some of these are available only if purchased in advance, before you arrive in Australia. Yet another alternative is the coach tour, of which there are endless varieties, from the out-and-back daytrip to a two-night excursion all the way up to a month or two on the road.

Trains come farther down the list because the choices are more limited and the speed is unimpressive. But riding on a legendary train like the Ghan or the Indian-Pacific is a great adventure, which is reason enough for many travellers. Advance reservations—a year in advance, if you want—are essential for the best-known trains. They are air-conditioned, with sleeping compartments, showers, dining cars and every comfort. Other than the famous trains, rail travel in Australia is less glamorous, with utilitarian intercity and commuter trains.

When you arrive wherever you're going, you can stay in utter luxury—posh hotels in the cities and resorts meet the most exacting international standards—or on a strict economy regime. The choice of accommodation is wide: hotels of all standards, motels (on the road or in town), service flats, country pubs, youth hostels, camping

Where a train ride becomes an adventure: the legendary Ghan approaches Alice Springs.

sites, bed-and-breakfast establishments and farmhouses that accept paying guests. It's reassuring to have a confirmed booking in advance. This becomes absolutely essential during Australian school holidays, when the entire nation seems to be on the move. Each state has its own schedule, varying each year. You can get a calendar from Australian tourist offices.

Discover Australia is arranged by states, each chapter starting with the capital city gateway and then fanning out. We begin where Australia itself began, at Sydney Cove. After a side-trip to the federal capital, Canberra, we continue beyond New South Wales in an anticlockwise direction: from Brisbane in Queensland all around the country until Melbourne in Victoria. Our coverage winds up with the continent's lovely green footnote, Tasmania. Of course, you can read it, and travel it, in any order you like.

Where? Where?

Many place names on the Australian map have a certain charm, a childlike singsong sound. Most of these delights are said to be derived from Aboriginal words or descriptions. Here are a few, in alphabetical order, to savour as you say them:

Bungle Bungle range, WA
Burra Burra, SA
Curl Curl Beach, NSW
Cutta Cutta Caves, NT
Jim Jim Falls, NT
Mitta Mitta, Vic.
Wagga Wagga, NSW
Woy Woy, NSW
My my!

Climate

The seasons, of course, are upside down: winter runs from June to August and Christmas comes in summertime. But it's much more complicated than that, for Australia covers so much ground, from the tropics to the temperate zone.

From November to March, it's mostly hot, or at least quite warm, everywhere. In the north this period brings the rains, which can wash out roads and otherwise spoil vacation plans. In the south the nights, at least, are mild.

April to September is generally ideal in the tropics and central Australia—clear and warm. Occasional rain refreshes the south, which can become quite chilly, with skiable snow in the southern mountains.

By way of regional superlatives, Darwin is the state capital with the

Average Maximum and Minimum Temperatures Across Australia in Celsius (Farenheit)

	J	F	M	A	M	J	J	A	S	O	N	D
Sydney												
max.	26	26	25	22	19	17	16	18	20	22	24	25
	(79)	(79)	(77)	(72)	(66)	(63)	(61)	(64)	(68)	(72)	(75)	(77)
min.	18	19	17	15	11	9	8	9	11	13	15	17
	(64)	(64)	(63)	(59)	(52)	(48)	(46)	(48)	(52)	(55)	(59)	(63)
Brisbane												
max.	29	29	28	26	23	21	20	22	24	26	28	29
	(84)	(84)	(82)	(79)	(73)	(71)	(68)	(72)	(75)	(79)	(82)	(84)
min.	21	21	19	17	13	11	9	10	13	16	18	20
	(69)	(71)	(66)	(63)	(55)	(52)	(48)	(50)	(55)	(61)	(64)	(68)
Alice Springs												
max.	36	35	32	28	23	20	19	22	26	30	33	35
	(97)	(95)	(90)	(82)	(73)	(68)	(66)	(72)	(79)	(86)	(92)	(95)
min.	21	21	17	12	8	5	4	6	10	15	18	20
	(71)	(71)	(63)	(57)	(46)	(41)	(39)	(43)	(50)	(59)	(64)	(68)
Perth												
max.	30	30	28	24	21	19	18	18	20	22	25	27
	(86)	(86)	(82)	(75)	(71)	(66)	(64)	(64)	(68)	(72)	(77)	(81)
min.	18	19	17	14	12	10	9	9	10	12	14	16
	(64)	(66)	(63)	(57)	(54)	(50)	(48)	(48)	(50)	(54)	(57)	(61)
Hobart												
max.	22	21	20	17	14	12	12	13	15	17	18	20
	(72)	(71)	(68)	(63)	(47)	(54)	(54)	(55)	(59)	(63)	(64)	(68)
min.	12	12	11	9	7	5	4	5	6	8	9	11
	(54)	(54)	(52)	(48)	(45)	(41)	(39)	(41)	(43)	(46)	(48)	(52)

Cowboys, real or self-styled, come to see the Alice Springs camel derby.

highest average hours of sunshine, but it also gets the most rain. Adelaide has the lowest average rainfall of all capital cities. Far to the south, Hobart is the coolest capital; its climate is similar to Britain's. But statistics indicate that the cities of Australia bask in more sunshine than any others in the world.

Statistics can lie or at least distort reality, but for your general guidance, some average daily maximum and minimum temperatures, month by month are shown in the table.

Time Differences

Australia is so big it needs three time zones to follow the sun: Eastern, Central and Western. These are delineated by state boundaries. Awkwardly, Central time is only half an hour earlier than Eastern, and daylight saving time occurs (but not in all states) in the northern hemisphere's winter. Here is the outlook for the period from March to October when Australia is on standard time:

Los Angeles	4.00 a.m.
New York	7.00 a.m.
London (GMT+1)	12.00 noon
Perth	7.00 p.m.
Adelaide-Darwin	8.30 p.m.
Sydney-Melbourne	9.00 p.m.

15

Getting to Australia

By Air

Flights from Asia, North America and Europe chiefly go to Sydney and Melbourne, but Australia has seven other international airports. Apex and other special fares reduce the expense of travelling such great distances. Only a knowledgeable travel agent can unravel the intricacies of these advance-booking fares, the prices depending on season and even the day of the week you choose to fly. Look into round-the-world fares as well. Travel agents also have information on a big range of package tours available—fly-drive arrangements, rail or bus tours, camping vacations and safaris.

Getting to Australia by any route is a long haul. Average journey times: New York–Sydney 25 hours, Los Angeles–Sydney 19 hours, London–Sydney 24 hours, London–Perth 18 hours, Johannesburg–Perth 11 hours. If jet lag is a factor, consider breaking the flight for a day or two at one of the stops along the way; in most cases this doesn't affect the price of the air ticket.

Airports

The principal gateways are Melbourne, Sydney, Brisbane, Cairns, Darwin and Perth. Sydney's Kingsford Smith airport is the busiest. Other international airports serve Adelaide, Hobart and Townsville. The domestic air network is very well developed, and even smallish towns usually have comfortable, efficient terminals. The big airports have the full range of restaurants, bars, newsstands, souvenir shops, post offices and banks, and, in the case of Melbourne, a motel on the premises. The international airports have duty-free shops for both arriving and departing passengers. Free baggage carts are available.

Arriving passengers can travel from airport to town by taxi or bus. In most cities, an airport bus service goes to and from the door of major hotels. Travel time ranges from 20 minutes (Perth and Darwin) to 30 minutes (Sydney). Note that the domestic and international terminals are a bus ride apart in Sydney and, more drastically, Perth.

Check-in time for departing passengers on domestic flights is 30 minutes before the scheduled flight time; international passengers should check in at least 90 minutes in advance.

By Sea

Australian ports feature in the itineraries of a number of cruise ships. You can fly to, say, Bali or Fiji and embark on the liner there, sailing to Australia, then flying off from any Australian city, or resuming the cruise around the world if you choose. Travel agents have cruise line schedules and brochures long in advance.

Customs, Entry and Exit Regulations

All visitors except New Zealanders need valid passports and visas to enter Australia. Travel agencies and Australian consulates can provide visa application forms. The completed form, along with the passport and an identity photo, must be filed with the consulate. There is no charge for a visa.

Main Duty Free Allowances

Into:	Cigarettes		Cigars (grams)		Tobacco (grams)	Spirits (litres)		Wine (litres)
Australia	200	or	250	or	250	1	or	1
Canada	200	and	50	and	900	1.1	or	1.1
Eire	200	and	50	or	250	1	and	2
New Zealand	200	or	50	or	250	1.1	and	4.5
S. Africa	400	and	50	and	250	1	and	2
UK	200	or	50	or	250	1	and	2
USA	200	and	100	and	*	1	or	1

*A reasonable quantity

Only after a visa has been issued should you buy your air ticket.

Travellers who are issued the normal short-term visitor visa are formally warned that it precludes getting a job or undertaking formal studies while in Australia, much less becoming a permanent resident. However, travellers aged 18 to 25 can apply for a working holiday visa, normally valid for six months, permitting casual employment to top up the holiday budget. Unaccompanied children under 18 must have the written consent of a parent or guardian.

Entry Formalities

On the last leg of your flight to Australia you'll be asked to fill in a voluminous customs form, swearing that you are not trying to import foreign foodstuffs, weapons, drugs or other forbidden articles. The check-list runs to 15 categories of prohibited items. There is also an immigration form.

Even before you've disembarked from the aircraft you'll become aware of Australia's sensitivity about its unique environment, isolated from overseas pests and diseases. As seated passengers close their eyes, the cabin is thoroughly sprayed to kill any insect stowaways. Once in the terminal you go through Quarantine, then Customs and Immigration. If you're arriving in Australia after a stop in an area where yellow fever is endemic, you must show a valid vaccination certificate. You'll have to show your return or onward ticket, and you may have to prove that you have sufficient funds to last out your planned stay. All the paperwork is bound to slow down the arrival procedure.

Duty-free

The chart above shows the main duty-free items you may take into Australia and, when returning home, into your own country.

Exit Formalities

Leaving Australia, each passenger aged 12 or more must pay a $20 departure tax. (If you've run out of cash by then, major credit cards are accepted.) Children under 12 must obtain an exemption sticker from the Departure Tax counter at the airport, and proof of age is required. One final bit of business to keep the bureaucratic wheels turning: a departure form to fill in for the immigration authorities.

Money Matters

Currency

Since 1966, when pounds, shillings and pence were abandoned, the monetary unit has been the Australian dollar (abbreviated $ or $A), divided into 100 cents. There are coins of 1, 2, 5, 10, 20 and 50 cents, $1 and $2; they show the Queen's head on one side and native animals on the reverse side. Banknotes come in denominations of $5, $10, $20, $50 and $100; the dimensions of the notes increase according to their face value. But it doesn't necessarily follow with coins—beginners confuse the $2 coin with the two-cent piece. You can bring with you as much Australian or foreign currency as you wish, and on departure you can take away $5,000 in local currency.

Changing Money

Exchange rates fluctuate daily. Traveller's cheques and foreign currency may be changed at most banks in Australia with a minimum of fuss. Normal banking hours are 9.30 a.m. to 4.00 p.m. Monday to Thursday, and till 5.00 p.m. Friday. In addition, in big cities the main downtown banks are open for foreign currency transactions as early as 8.00 a.m. and as late as 6.00 p.m. Some states charge a small tax for each transaction. Many hotels will change money at all hours, but the rate tends to be unfavourable.

Credit Cards

The well-known international charge cards are recognized by car rental companies, airlines, hotels, and, in general, in most places tourists go; look for their signs displayed at the entrance to a store or restaurant.

18

Getting Around

Car Rental

For seeing the Australian countryside at your own pace there's no substitute for a car. Brisk competition among the

Outback trips can challenge car and driver; some car hire firms levy extra charges for remote itineraries.

international and local car rental companies means you can often find economical rates or special deals, for instance unlimited mileage or weekend discounts. Rates are considerably higher if you announce that you plan to drive in remote country areas; the car owners are acutely sensitive to the wear-and-tear problem. In general, it's worth shopping around. But be careful—some companies impose a metropolitan limit on vehicles. Check first, as your insurance won't be valid outside the designated area.

Just as you can enter Australia at one gateway and leave at another, you can pick up a car in one city and return it elsewhere. Interstate arrangements are commonly available from the big firms, which also offer the convenience of offices at airports.

In busy locations you can rent anything from a super-economy model or a four-wheel-drive vehicle to a limousine with or without chauffeur. Campervans and caravans (trailers) are available, though most are reserved far in advance for school holiday periods.

To rent a car you'll need a current driver's licence. The minimum age is 21, or in some cases 25. Third-party insurance is automatically included; for an additional fee you can also sign up for collision damage and personal accident insurance.

If you're planning a long stay and a lot of travel, consider buying a car and selling it when you're done. It can be a complicated and risky business for anyone, even an expert on used cars. However, a Sydney firm, Mach 1 Autos, has pioneered a seemingly fail-safe plan. It guarantees to buy back, at agreed prices, cars it has sold. If three or four people are travelling together, the scheme works out to a big saving.

Driving in Australia

In common with Britain and many Asian countries, Australia drives on the left. If you're not accustomed to it, you'll have to fight your reflexes all the time; be specially vigilant when setting forth at intersections, and after a break.

Australian roads are good, considering the size of the country and the problems of distance, terrain and climate. Although the most populous regions have ever more freeways (expressways or motorways), some of them beautifully landscaped, most roads are two-lane highways which are often overcrowded at busy times.

In country areas you'll notice cars usually have imposing extra bumpers designed to deflect kangaroos or other animals apt to wander onto the road. Cars may also have wire-mesh screens to protect the windshield from gravel and stones launched by other vehicles on unpaved roads.

Regulations

Drive on the left and ovetake on the right. Drivers and passengers must wear seat belts. In some states there are on-the-spot fines for transgressors.

The speed limit in cities and towns is normally 60 kmh (about 35 mph). In the country, the limits differ from state to state, also depending on the quality of the road; it's either 100 or 110 kmh (60 or 65 mph).

Driving under the influence of alcohol or drugs is a serious offence. Spot checks are made, with breath tests. In most states the limit on alcohol in the blood is 0.05 per cent, meaning in practice that three drinks will probably take you over the top.

City Driving

Heavy traffic and parking problems afflict some downtown areas. Parking meters and "no standing" zones proliferate. For longer stays parking garages are the answer, but these, too, fill up. Melbourne's trams (streetcars) cause intriguing traffic problems. At a number of busy intersections, if you want to turn right you must do so from the *left* lane after the trams have passed, and when the cross-street light has turned green. Everywhere in Victoria, you should know that the car turning right has priority in the event that two cars heading in opposite directions are planning to turn at an intersection.

Outback Driving

(*See* also Survival Essay, pp. 259–262.) Check thoroughly the condition of your car and be sure you have a spare wheel. Find out about the fuel situation in advance and leave word as to your destination and anticipated arrival time. Always have plenty of water aboard. Fill up the fuel tank at every opportunity, for the next station may be a few hundred kilometres away. Some dirt roads are so smooth you may be tempted to speed, but conditions can change abruptly; also, soft shoulders and clouds of dust are problems when other vehicles pass. Be extra cautious of road trains, consisting of three or four huge trailers barrelling down the highway towed by a high-powered truck. Pass one, if you dare, with the greatest of care.

Fuel

Many filling stations are open only during normal shopping hours, so you may have to ask where out-of-hours service is available. Petrol in most garages comes in super, unleaded-regular and unleaded-super grades and is dispensed by the litre. Many stations are self-service.

Road Signs

Signposting is generally good, especially along heavily travelled roads. Tourist attractions and natural wonders are signalled by white-on-brown direction signs. To drive into the centre of a city, simply follow the signs

*Y*ou don't have to know the language, or go far afield, to be warned about the kangaroo menace.

marked "City". But leaving a city is less straightforward: exit routes are often signposted with the assumption that every driver has local experience, so you may require a good map and some advance planning. All distances are measured in kilometres. Although most road signs are the standard international pictographs, many use words. Some of these will confuse even English-speakers:

Amphometer	**speed-measuring device**
Crest	**steep hilltop limiting visibility**
Cyclist hazard	**dangerous for cyclists**
Dip	**severe depression in road surface**
Hump	**bump or speed obstacle**
Safety ramp	**uphill escape lane from steep downhill road**
Soft edges	**soft shoulders**

Domestic Flights

Air traffic is exceptionally well developed, with more than 14 million passengers a year flying the domestic airlines across Australia's vastness. For years, two companies—Ansett Airlines and the state-owned Australian Airlines—competed on most of the important routes in a price cartel. The airline industry was deregulated in 1990 and for a time new companies transformed the market with reduced fares. But the innovative independent Compass Airlines crashed at the end of 1991. Regional airlines, including dozens of commuter companies, round out the busy aerial network. It's wise to book in advance, particularly during the busy school holiday periods. Tourists from overseas are entitled to discounts on air tickets, but the packages may involve rigid itineraries.

Trains

Intercity train travel in Australia can be a great adventure—so fascinating for rail buffs that reservations may be hard to come by. The legendary trains involve desert journeys between Adelaide and Alice Springs (22 hours on the Ghan) and between Sydney and Perth (65 hours aboard the Indian-Pacific). Nowadays modern air-conditioned trains with sleeping compartments, showers, dining cars and club cars cover these gruelling routes in comfort. Advance reservations—up to 12 months in advance—are especially recommended for the Indian-Pacific linking ocean to ocean, as well as certain long-distance routes in Queensland. On a more prosaic level, trains cover shorter-range interstate and commuter runs. Ask your travel agent about money-saving rail passes, in first or economy class, for foreign tourists.

Intercity Buses

Luxurious air-conditioned express coaches, often equipped with everything from toilets to television, link all the main population centres. For unhurried travellers who want to see Australia close up, at a reasonable price, the main coach companies offer special deals, for instance two weeks or a month of unlimited mileage at fixed rates. Some of the packages must be purchased before arriving in Australia. It's a 24-hour bus trip from Sydney to Adelaide, 27 hours Cairns–Brisbane, and 21 hours Darwin–Alice Springs.

*A*ir travel in all its modes is highly developed all over Australia. These scuba-diving fans swoop in to a raft anchored on the Great Barrier Reef.

Local Transport

In the big cities you can hail a **taxi** on the street if its roof sign reads "Vacant". Otherwise you can go to one of the cab stands, usually found at shopping centres, transport terminals and big hotels. You can also phone for a taxi. Meters indicate the fare plus any extras, such as waiting time. A courtesy note: Australians usually sit next to the taxi driver; if you don't, you might be considered unfriendly.

Local **bus** service tends to be concentrated during business hours; in many towns it tapers off after dark. To encourage car drivers to avoid downtown traffic and parking problems, some cities provide free buses from the periphery. There are also special tickets valid for unlimited public transport travel for two hours or a whole day.

Melbourne is proud of its **trams** (streetcars), which provide an efficient grid of downtown and suburban lines. The tracks, running down the middle of the street, are also used effectively by emergency vehicles. Melbourne also has an **underground** railway system (subway), as do Sydney and Brisbane. Sydney's **monorail** scenically links the central city and Darling Harbour.

Ferries

Ferries are a vital part of life in Sydney, where so many commuters cross the harbour. The ferries, concentrated at Circular Quay, also provide cheap outings for sightseers.

Bicycle Hire

With clearly marked bicycle lanes, Australian cities are attuned to cyclists, and the sparsely travelled roads beyond metropolitan areas are very inviting. Bicycle rental companies are found in all main cities and resorts. Alternatively, you can sign up for all-inclusive tours involving transport to and from a scenic area (where bikes are provided), accommodation, food and the services of a local guide.

Hitchhiking

Although discouraged by the authorities (and banned in Queensland), hitchhiking is fairly commonplace in Australia, even in isolated spots where prospects are few. Successful practitioners recommend you show a sign with your destination clearly marked. It helps to choose a place, usually on the outskirts of a town, where cars go slowly and can pull over safely.

Guides and Tours

Local guided tours are organized in all parts of the country, even in some small towns where few tourists venture. Brochures are available at your hotel or the local tourist office. Long-distance coach tours are very popular among Australians as well as foreign visitors. The coach drivers generally contribute a running commentary rich in facts and folksy humour. In a country as big as Australia, some day-tours take more than 12 hours to get out and back. On tours of two or more days, the main meals are included in the price, along with accommodation in hotels or motels along the way. A variety of two- and three-week tours cover substantial chunks of one or two states. Round-Australia coach tours, which touch every mainland state, can go on for nearly two months.

A more expensive alternative, an air tour, covers much more territory and gives another perspective. For the rushed traveller, there are many advantages to a day-trip to the Great Barrier Reef or Ayers Rock. Longer tours, of up to 14 days, include accommodation, most meals, and sightseeing tours on land.

Tourist Information Offices

Some overseas offices of the Australian Tourist Commission (ATC):
USA: 489 Fifth Ave., 31st Floor, New York, NY 10017; tel. (212) 687-6300. 150 N. Michigan Ave., Suite 2130, Chicago, IL 60601; tel. (312) 781-5150. Suite 1200, 2121 Avenue of the Stars, Los Angeles, CA 90067; tel. (213) 552-1988.
Canada: Suite 1730, 2 Bloor Street West, Toronto, Ontario M4W 3E2; tel. (416) 925-9597.
UK: Gemini House, 8–10 Putney Hill, Putney, London SW15; tel. (081) 780-1424.
New Zealand: 15th Floor, Quay Towers, 29 Customs Street West, Auckland 1; tel. (09) 79 9594.
Singapore: 17th Floor, United Square, 101 Thompson Road, Singapore 1103; tel. (65) 255-4555.
Hong Kong: Sun Plaza Suite 604–5, Canton Road, Tsimshatsui, Kowloon, Hong Kong; tel. 311 1555.
Japan: Sankaido Building, 8th Floor, 9–13 Akasaka 1-chome, Minato-ku, Tokyo 107; tel. (03) 582-2191.

Within Australia, each state operates its own tourist authority, with branch offices abroad and in most other capital cities. Each office is full of booklets, maps and information, and can help you with arrangements for travel and accommodation.

Maps

State and local tourist offices give away useful maps of their areas. For more detailed maps, check at newsstands and bookstores. Car hire companies often supply free city directories showing each street and place of interest. For driving beyond the cities you'll want to buy an up-to-date map of the region. Entering the Outback, in addition to a good map you'll need local advice on new developments and seasonal problems.

Disabled Visitors

People with special needs get sympathetic treatment in all areas of Australian life but only the newer buildings are equipped with wheelchair ramps and other facilities. It's always best to give advance notice of your requirements to hotels, airlines, etc. For information about the places geared to people with special needs, write to the Australia Council for Rehabilitation for the Disabled (ACROD), PO Box 60, Curtin, ACT 2605. Tel. (062) 82 4333.

Children

Between the beaches and the bush, the kangaroos and the koalas, Australia

will keep children amused and amazed. In addition to the natural beauties and oddities, the man-made attractions rate highly: boat excursions, vintage trains, imaginative amusement parks and "hands-on" museums.

New latitudes bring new problems. Be sure to supervise children at the beaches, where tides, sharks or poisonous jellyfish may be a menace. In the Outback, dangers can range from poisonous snakes and spiders to man-eating crocodiles. Seek local advice. In the great outdoors in general, and especially in the tropics, too much sun can be debilitating. Sun screen and extra rations of liquids are essential. On the "plus" side, sanitation is carefully maintained everywhere.

If your hotel can't find someone to take care of your child, look in the yellow pages of the telephone directory under *Babysitters*.

Splashing in the surf at Bondi Beach: carefree fun, but mind the flags and the advice of the lifeguards.

Health and Medical Care

Standards of hygiene are high throughout Australia and, in fact, you can drink the tap water anywhere—unless a notice specifically warns otherwise. However, there are hazards in the countryside, starting with the threat of too much sun. Skin cancer has become a serious concern in sun-loving Australia; protective cream is essential, even on cloudy days. Poisonous snakes and spiders lurk in many places, and bathers must beware of sharks and, in certain seasons and areas, dangerous

26

jellyfish. Crocodiles are a genuine menace in the north. Also, watch where you walk on the beaches, some of which—notably around Sydney—have become polluted.

Australia has excellent medical services, with highly trained doctors and fully equipped modern hospitals, but the fees are high. Visitors are advised to arrange in advance for insurance to cover any medical or hospital costs on the trip. Your hotel can call a doctor if you become ill, or you can get a list of approved doctors from your embassy, high commission or consulate.

If you have a doctor's prescription from your own physician at home it cannot be filled by an Australian pharmacy unless you have it endorsed by a local doctor. As well as prescription drugs, Australian chemists sell toiletries, cosmetics and home remedies. In all the big cities at least one pharmacy operates 24 hours a day.

Embassies and Consulates

The embassies or high commissions of about 70 countries are established in Canberra, the national capital. They have consular sections dealing with passport renewal, visas and other formalities. Many countries also maintain diplomatic outposts—full-time or honorary—in the larger cities, which can be useful for citizens in difficulty. Sydney alone has more than 40 consulates. To find the address of your consulate, look in the white pages of the telephone directory under *Consuls* or in the yellow pages under *Consulates and Legations.*

Consulates can be extremely helpful in emergencies but they can't get you a job or an airline ticket or act as your lawyer or banker.

Accommodation

Australia welcomes the traveller with every kind of accommodation from five-star palaces as lavish as any hotel in the world to austere economy-class rooms. There are 400,000 beds to go around in the graded hotels and motels alone. The luxury end of the spectrum is sumptuous in all respects—the rooms and suites and the associated lobbies, lounges, restaurants, boutiques, saunas and spas. Five-star hotels have 24-hour room service as well as multiple restaurants. Even in budget-priced hotel and motel rooms you can expect a private shower or bath and toilet, a telephone, a TV set, a small refrigerator, and coffee- and tea-making equipment (and free instant coffee, tea bags and milk). In most areas air-conditioning or at least a ceiling fan is provided.

There's no limit to the level of luxury a hotel or motel can attain, and either type can be anywhere—along the highway or right downtown. A fine line distinguishes hotels from motels. The only sure difference is that a hotel has a bar open to the public—indeed, the most modest ones have little else to offer. "Hotel" and "pub" are synonymous. If a motel has a bar, it's usually strictly for the guests. So you cannot judge a hostelry by what it calls itself.

Private hotels, often small guest houses, do not have a licence for

alcohol. There are bed and breakfast establishments—private homes taking paying guests—in towns or out on the farm. The farm stays usually include all meals; guests who want to take the rural experience to its limit can pitch in with the farm work, too.

An alternative housing idea in the big towns and resort areas: self-catering apartments with one, two or three bedrooms, maid service and fully equipped kitchens, convenient for longer stays. (Many refuse one-night bookings, particularly at peak periods.)

Overseas offices of the Australian Tourist Commission have listings of hotels and motels. You can reserve accommodation through your travel agent, the nearest offices of the international and Australian hotel chains, or your airline. Within Australia, the state tourist bureaus, domestic airlines and hotel chains offer instant, free bookings. If you arrive out of the blue, local tourist offices have desks for last-minute reservations.

Accommodation may be hard to find when Australians themselves go travelling, by the million, during school holidays. These are staggered state by state except for the year-end period when schools everywhere close. Offices of the Australian Tourist Commission have charts of the school holiday schedule more than a year in advance.

Camping
Australians are avid campers, and you'll find campsites dotted all over

*T*ravellers weary of modern hotels can opt for a touch of history and character.

the areas frequented by tourists. The sites tend to be jammed on school holidays. They have at least the basic amenities, and in some cases much more. Aside from roomy tents with lights and floors, some installations have caravans (trailers) or cabins for hire. Showers, toilets, laundry facilities and barbecue grills are commonly available. Sheets and blankets can often be hired. The national parks generally have well-organized camping facilities; to camp beyond the designated zone you must ask the rangers for permission. There are coach tours for campers, or you can hire a campervan or motorhome (*see* also CAR HIRE).

Youth Hostels

Young backpackers can find cheap lodgings in more than 150 youth hostels across Australia. You should have a membership card from the Youth Hostel Association in your home country. Information may be obtained from the Australian Youth Hostel Association, 60 Mary Street, Surry Hills, NSW 2010; tel. (02) 212 1266.

Alternative accommodation at extremely economical rates: backpacker hostels unaffiliated with the YHA can be found in many towns as well as country and resort areas. Standards and facilities vary greatly. There are several chains of backpacker hostels, and detailed directories are available.

Restaurants

Eating Out

Self-effacing Australians might deny there is any such thing as "cuisine" in their country, but the visiting gourmet will soon know better. The stereotype of a meat-pie-and-beer diet is as outdated Down Under as pounds, shillings and pence. You can eat very well in all the cities and often in the countryside; in fact almost any time and place the spirit and the budget choose. There's no secret about the success of Australian cooks: they exploit the wonderful wholesomeness of the natural resources. Thanks to the climate and the abundance of grazing lands, oceans and farms, the lean beef, milk-fed lamb, fresh seafood and vegetables are mouthwatering, all the year round.

And if you want to gild the lily with an exotic sauce, the immigrant community has contributed a repertoire of spices and subtleties to satisfy sophisticated requirements. A smattering of foreign food has filtered down to the most insular Aussies; the blackboard of a backwoods café may well list as local specialities moussaka and spaghetti bolognese, or something as bizarre as "dim sims with chips". At the other end of the scale, some of Australia's top chefs have plunged into deep eclectic waters, putting, say, Chinese and French flavours on the same plate. It makes for adventurous dining, and it's definitely called "cuisine".

You'd better be very hungry. In most eateries the size of the portions match the continent's dimensions, which may help to explain some of the potbellies you'll notice straining T-shirts. This is ironic when you consider the gaunt profiles of the first settlers, who barely endured when the crops failed and the livestock died or wandered into the bush. Survival rations were issued; stealing food became a capital offence. As the settlers struggled against famine, the Aborigines, Stone Age hunter-gatherers, watched with detachment. Their own traditional diet was crammed with proteins and vitamins, thank you.

Eating Exotica

The Northern Territory offers the most opportunities for the tourist to taste bush tucker—the wild berries, vegetables, herbs and other natural foods the continent's original inhabitants thrived on. You can sample a fabled Aboriginal delicacy, witchetty grubs, the larvae of beetles and moths found in trees

Some of the sheep submitting to the discipline of these clever little dogs may wind up in mutton stew.

and roots. In the bush they are eaten baked at best, raw if necessary. Some brave visiting gourmets say witchetty grubs have a sweetish, nutty taste. Otherwise, Aborigines favour staples like roast wallaby, snake or lizard, preferably with a garnish of various grasses, fruits, seeds and spices.

In spite of its abundance, kangaroo is on few menus these days, due to various conservationist pressures and perhaps sneaking regrets about consuming the national symbol. It's legal, though, in restaurants in South Australia, Tasmania, the Northern Territory and Canberra. If you're craving unfamiliar meat for the adventure of it, consider buffalo steak—marinated, highly seasoned, and tender as good beef. Or try the camel stew, which tastes like a stronger version of lamb stew. Or crocodile cutlets, a reptilian equivalent of slightly fishy chicken.

On the Menu

Breakfast can be as basic as pastry and coffee or as elaborate as a buffet of fruits, eggs, meats and breads, as marshalled by the big hotels. If your early morning appetite is voracious enough to tackle some Outback atmosphere, many a café can rustle up steak and eggs or lamb chops and eggs. You'll also be offered breakfast oddities like spaghetti on toast or baked beans on toast. All of which takes us more than halfway to lunch.

Fish and seafood. From fish and chips on the run to a candlelit restaurant's lobster extravaganza, the harvest of Australia's tropical and temperate oceans offers the food-lover great variety and promise. Among the fine fish adorning the menu: delicious snapper (sometimes still spelled the German way, Schnapper), similar to sea bream; meaty John Dory, smallish flounder and bigger sole (they all have an odd configuration: both eyes on the same side, like a Picasso face); bony but flavoursome whiting (no relation to the English whiting); and the tropical game-fish called trevally. Then there's barramundi, which means "big scales" in an Aboriginal language. This "giant perch" is found in both fresh and salt water; game fishermen in the north take "barra" of up to 15 kg (33 lb) and consumers relish its tender fillets. Along the Barrier Reef they even eat red emperor, a fish so gorgeous it might take a snorkeller's breath away. Another curiosity: Tasmania *breeds* ocean trout and Atlantic—that's right, Atlantic—salmon. Try it smoked.

News from the shellfish front is all good. Australia claims to be the world's largest exporter of lobster and prawns, but they've saved a few for you. Grilled or thermidored, lobster makes any occasion more festive. Prices are less forbidding when it comes to steamed mussels or fried prawns. You'll also meet some of the lobster's freshwater cousins, known locally as yabbies. Treat yourself to other succulent seafood specialities like Sydney rock oysters, as delicious as any in the world, and Brisbane's famous Moreton Bay bug, a crustacean to gloat over, and mud crabs, gloriously meaty.

Meat eaters revel in the high quality and hefty portions served in Australia. The choice, though, seems to boil down to grilled steaks and roast lamb or lamb chops, especially in the less elaborate restaurants. Meat pies are produced with regional differences; in Adelaide the crusty delight evolves into the beloved floater, a meat pie afloat in green pea soup. A cultural note about steak: no matter what kind you order it will arrive well-done unless

---

For Fish Fans

Not much farther than a fly-caster's throw from Darling Harbour, the Sydney Fish Market at Pyrmont is one of Australia's most fascinating lures for gourmets. More than 100 varieties of freshly landed fish and seafood are on show, and selling like, well, hotcakes. Sydney's top chefs wouldn't dream of planning their menu for the day until they've taken part in the big Dutch auction, which starts at the fisherman's hour of 5.20 a.m. If you can get there before 8.00 a.m. you'll probably catch some of the computerized action.

Visitors who just can't wait to sample the wares can try the market's sushi bar.

you explain that you want it "rare". If you feel strongly about this, emphasize that you want it "blue" or it may be incinerated. Otherwise, nothing but good can be said about Australian beef. If you're up to it, try carpetbag steak (stuffed with oysters). Apart from beef and lamb you'll find pork in the form of chops, roast, or spare ribs, and chicken. You may also come across a distinctly Australian mixed salad, combining slices of cold meat and cheese with vegetables. All sorts of meat are conducive to outdoor barbecuing, and everybody knows how Australians love their "barbie". Some pubs and restaurants have outdoor eating and cooking facilities; you can choose a steak and grill it yourself.

Vegetables, uncommonly fresh, add flavour, wholesomeness and variety to the largely meat-and-potato diet. If your taste buds have been benumbed by the banality of mass-produced vegetables elsewhere, you're in for

Vegetarians, too, can enjoy themselves in Australia's meat-and-potatoes environment.

pleasant surprises. But a cloud hangs over the Australian vegetable patch: overcooking, a hard habit to break.

Fruit is plentiful and delicious, taking full advantage of the country's generous spectrum of climatic zones. For example, fresh orange juice is available year-round. The temperate zones provide apples, cherries, plums and berries, while the tropics account for avocados, bananas, papayas (or pawpaws), passionfruit, pineapples and mangoes. Australia claims two great "inventions" in the fruit department: the Granny Smith apple and the William pear.

Desserts. Calorific cakes and fruit pies come in many tempting flavours. Also very rich is a favourite Australian dessert, the light and fluffy pavlova, a

Sandwiched between two big buildings in Sydney, a Chinese restaurant adds to the city's ever more cosmopolitan cuisine potential.

meringue concoction traditionally topped with kiwi fruit. It is named after Anna Pavlova, an immortal of the early 20th-century Russian ballet, who seems to have made a big impression when she visited Australia on a world tour. Also in the celebrity department, peach melba, with ice-cream and raspberry sauce, was dedicated to Melbourne's eponymous opera diva. The fruit-flavoured ice-creams are delicious on their own.

Cheese benefits from a wave of innovation. The familiar cheddars have been joined by salty ewe's-milk cheeses and cheeses blended of cow's and goat's milk. From many parts of the country come pleasing impressions of Brie, Camembert, Gruyère, Gorgonzola and Gouda. King Island, between Tasmania and the mainland, capitalizes on its sea-splashed grasslands to produce superrich, runny Bries and Camemberts.

Foreign Food

Gastronomical changes of pace are so readily available around Australia that you'll never get in a rut. Almost no town is too small to have a foreign restaurant or two to feed the ethnic population and increasingly adventurous locals. In metropolitan areas the Australian melting pot cooks up some first-class foreign specialities. Melbourne claims to have the third biggest Greek population in the world (after Athens and Salonika), so you don't have to look very far to find some authentic *taramasalata, dolmades* and *souvlaki.* Sydney is so cosmopolitan you can choose from dozens of cultural strains, yielding anything from

---

Revolvers

If you like to mix sightseeing with dining out, zoom up to one of Australia's revolving restaurants. A tour of the horizon's towering vantage points for gourmets:

Sydney: Centrepoint, Market Street; Australia Square, George Street.

Canberra: Telecom Tower, Black Mountain.

Surfers Paradise: Four Winds, 2807 Gold Coast Highway.

Perth: St Martins Tower, St George's Terrace.

Hobart: West Point Casino.

*S*ampling the local wines at the "cellar door" figures among the favourite Barossa Valley pastimes.

Thailand's sweet-and-sour *mee grob*, even if you don't know their names; chopsticks are optional. At lunchtime, east and west meet hungrily in Chinese *dim sum* restaurants with their vast array of dumplings, buns and snacks, also known as *yum cha* (meaning simply "to drink tea" in Cantonese). Japanese, Indian and Korean restaurants round out the Asian line-up.

Drinking

Australian Wines
Even the old-world wine snobs have to agree that something "rather nice" is being bottled Down Under. Objectively, the merest *vin du pays* in Australia is more than potable and the top of the line is truly distinguished. The secret is a happy blend of advantages: the sun-roasted vineyards, the flexibility and expertise of the winemakers, and the last word in technology.

Admittedly, until fairly recent times most Australian wine was as rough and ready as a stockman's idea of an aperitif. But inspired winemakers have worked hard and invested heavily to

Arab *pita* and *falafel* to Russian *blini*. Darwin is noted for its high percentage of immigrants and transients, so you can choose from various shades of Chinese cuisine plus Indonesian, Malaysian and all manner of European styles. Yesterday's boat people are now dishing up lettuce-wrapped Vietnamese spring rolls. Several cities have self-service establishments offering "Chinese and Asian Smorgasbord". For a moderate set fee you can pile your plate as high as you like with Shanghai sautéed prawns and

> **Drinking Glossary**
> Australian consumers of *booze* and *grog* use a specialized vocabulary. A few practical expressions to tide you over:
> *Bottle shop.* Liquor store or off-licence where bottles are sold to take away.
> *BYO.* "Bring your own" bottle invitation from unlicensed restaurants.
> *Cuppa.* A cup of tea, if it should come to that.
> *Esky.* Portable insulated cooler to carry beer and the like, to beach or barbecue.
> *Shout.* Buying a round of drinks in a pub.
> *Tinnie.* A can of beer.

raise standards to more than respectable levels. Even the humble "kangarouge" that comes in a cardboard box (known as a cask) is comparable to the quality of carafe wine in a French bistro, or an Italian trattoria's *fiasco*.

Australians used to be such fanatical beer drinkers that wine was considered a minority pleasure, for the élite and for immigrants from wine-loving latitudes. Nowadays, about 600 wineries keep busy supplying a nation that drinks twice as much wine per head as Americans or Britons. What's left over—something like 40 million litres (9 million gal)—is exported to more than 80 countries. The most enthusiastic importing nations are Sweden, Britain and the United States.

Although Australia's modern wine era began as recently as the 1960s, the industry actually got its start thanks to the founder of the New South Wales colony, Captain Arthur Phillip. One of the first projects he ordered in 1788 was the planting of vines at Sydney Cove. Because of factors like the damp and the sea breezes, the site (now part of Sydney's Botanic Gardens) was quite wrong for growing grapes, and the experiment failed. But in 1791 1 ha (3 acres) of vines were successfully planted a few miles inland.

Rum, not wine, became the favourite drink under Governor Phillip's successor. Free-enterprising army officers enjoyed a monopoly on the staggeringly profitable sales of rum, and abuses were reported to London. So Captain William Bligh, the original hardliner of Bounty fame, was despatched to clean up Australia. Governor Bligh, who never made a lot of

friends, was deposed in the Rum Rebellion of 1808, a mutiny led by one of the first wine-growers, John Macarthur. Another pioneering vintner was Gregory Blaxland, a prosperous settler who exported red wine to England. He is better known as one of a team of explorers who in 1813 first crossed the Blue Mountains to reach the rich pasturelands of the interior.

When Australians got around to appreciating their own production, the demand was strongest for fortified wines like port and sherry. Much later the populace opened its heart to the kind of still wines that complement a meal—the refreshment of a cool white, the satisfaction of a robust red. (A great catalyst was an Australian invention of the 1970s—the bag-in-box winecask or soft-pack, which made wine cheap and convenient for everyone, even people unaccustomed to vintages and corkscrews.) And then, in recent years, the experts moved in to upgrade the average wine and propel the best into the big leagues.

Labels and Vintages

For connoisseurs of European wines, accustomed to official appellations and all that, Australia is a bewilderment. European terminology on the labels can be innocently deceptive, perhaps prompting the visiting snob to thunder, "How dare you call this a Rhine Riesling!" A Cabernet from New South Wales is likely to taste quite different from the South Australian equivalent, which, in turn, is a far cry from its French namesake. Australia imposes none of those regional restrictions delimiting districts where certain grapes may be grown, so anything goes,

depending on the grower's whim and the potential of the soil and climate. The consumers take it all in their stride, and although many of them are knowledgeable about wine, few are pretentious. In egalitarian Australia, the only "class" difference is that the "masses" buy their wine by the cask (two-, four- or five-litre cartons) costing less than beer, and the "ruling class" chooses relatively expensive bottles. Happily, the price of a thoroughly acceptable bottle of Australian wine is quite reasonable by world standards.

You needn't look for vintages. In most cases they are irrelevant, for year in and year out the crop and climate are equally good. The specific region, too, can be vague. Wines are named either generically (Burgundy or Moselle, for instance) or more often according to the pedigree of the grape (say, the noble Pinot Noir or Chardonnay). Blending to taste is common. The varietal names can get

The desert blooms near Alice Springs, where irrigation permits the production of red and white wines.

complicated, for instance when Cabernet-Sauvignon is blended with Shiraz to become Cabernet-Shiraz. Look for Cabernet-Merlot blends and Semillon-Sauvignon Blanc.

Wine is produced in every Australian state, even at the extremes in rainy Tasmania and the baking Northern Territory (where the only vineyard belongs to a small "château" on the edge of Alice Springs). The biggest producer is South Australia, of which the best-known wineries are found in the beautiful Barossa Valley and the Southern Vales. In New South Wales the most important wine-producing region is the Hunter Valley. In Victoria the Goulburn Valley and Murray

Valley are strongest. And Western Australia's Swan Valley and Margaret River areas have made their mark. Touring the Australian equivalent of châteaux is a rewarding pastime, featuring tastings at the "cellar door". Many of the vineyards just happen to be in accessible, picturesque regions that are well supplied with charming hotels and restaurants.

In quality and quantity, Australian wine production has never been in a stronger position. Generic wines like Claret and Burgundy are giving way to varietal names or brand names. White wine outsells red, with sweetish sparkling wines particularly popular. The nation's vineyards also provide rosé and, by way of fortification, sherry, port, vermouth and brandy... and some splendid Tokay and Muscat dessert wines.

"The Amber Fluid"

Those hot Australian summers call for beer and more beer, a thirst that seems only slightly assuaged the rest of the year. Regardless of the season, the brew has to be cold enough to freeze the teeth and taste buds. The icy temperature is so vital that real fans demand deep-frozen glasses, or enclose their cold "tinnies" in insulated holders to defend them from the heat of the atmosphere and the drinker's hands.

For some years the world has been let in on the secret of Australian beer, which is widely exported. Foster's lager, based on a tradition more than a century old, has been the most highly publicized brand abroad, selling in 80 countries. Other beers generate pronounced regional loyalties—for instance Swan Lager in Western Australia, Toohey's in New South Wales and Castlemaine XXXX (called simply "four-ex") in Queensland.

Australian beer, in the pilsner or lager stream, is stronger than its nearest equivalent in the US or Britain, though some European brews contain even more alcohol. Australia also follows the trend toward so-called "light" beers, with considerably lower alcohol content. Connoisseurs look for speciality beers, with names as exotic as Brass Monkey, Bullshead, Dogbolter, and Redback (named after a poisonous spider). Other unusual beers

Cheery beer fanciers greet passersby from within a Sydney pub. Australians are among the world leaders in per capita consumption of beer.

are the pride of boutique breweries, so small they may be just outside the back door of a pub.

When the barman asks, "What's yours, mate?" you may be at a loss for words. The size of a draught beer varies according to the state you're in, geographically. You'll come across a middy, a schooner, a pot, a five and a stubby. When in doubt, simply ask for a beer. You can't go wrong.

Other Refreshments
Teetotallers, or anyone in the mood for a change from wine and beer, can experiment with the country's fruit drinks. They come canned in inventive combinations of flavours, for instance a mixture of orange and passionfruit juices. Less vitamin-laden, all the familiar fizzy soft drinks are available. And, if you run out of thirst-quenching ideas, you *can* drink the water.

Billy Tea
Tourists on excursions into the hinterland are introduced to the mystique of billy tea, a macho version of the traditional pick-me-up. The water has to be boiled over a camp-fire in a metal can. Tea leaves (tea bags if the tourists aren't looking) are brewed, with perhaps a eucalyptus leaf added for Outback flavour. Then the pail is whirled several times in a demonstration of centrifugal force that's supposed to settle the tea, which is served in enamel mugs.

The standard accompaniment is bush damper, unleavened bread produced by burying the "oven" (an iron pot) in the glowing ashes of the camp-fire.These elementary biscuits, served hot, can be greatly enhanced if the luxuries of butter and jam are at hand.

Shopping

Whether you're looking for Aboriginal art, gems, classy fashions, or a koala doll stuffed with a music box that plays *Waltzing Matilda*, you'll enjoy the shopping in Australia. The good taste may have its ups and downs, but shopping in almost any of the towns is rich in gratifying surprises. The variety is impressive. You won't find many bargains, though; the production costs are too high.

In most cities, browsers and window-shoppers congregate along the downtown pedestrian malls. Department store chains like David Jones, Grace Bros., and Myer provide a dependable cross-section of what's available. And the central-city arcades and courts are crammed with boutiques handling everything from high fashion to silly souvenirs.

Shopping hours usually run nonstop from 8.30 or 9.00 a.m. to 5.00 or 5.30 p.m., Monday to Friday, and Saturday mornings until noon (until 5 p.m. in Sydney and Melbourne). One night a week, either Thursday or Friday depending on the city, the stores stay open until about 9.00 p.m. In some places, tourist needs are catered for on Sundays, as well.

The price structure is as simple as life in an earlier age: the price is on the tag (haggling is generally unknown), and there's no value added tax to worry about. Most stores honour the major international credit cards.

Where to Shop
In **Sydney** the skyscrapers are built atop subterranean shopping arcades; the principal pedestrian plaza, Martin

*A*mong *the charms of shopping in Sydney: the atmosphere in carefully restored Victorian-era arcades with their boutiques.*

Place, is not a shopping mall at all but a perfect place to relax between sorties. For some atmospheric shopping try the restored Queen Victoria Building or arcades from the same era—the Strand Arcade and the Imperial Arcade. A fashionable new shopping mall, Sky Garden, has up-market boutiques in a spacious modern atmosphere, with restaurants on the glass-roofed top floor. And there are vast suburban shopping complexes.

In **Melbourne** the main shopping streets are Collins and Bourke, with the Bourke Street Mall the heart of the matter. The "Paris end" of Collins Street is very posh. Some Melbourne arcades are historic architectural sites. Melbourne fashion spreads to the suburbs—Richmond's Bridge Road and the all-round elegance of Toorak Road.

The essence of shopping in **Adelaide** is Rundle Street Mall. The equivalent in **Perth**, traffic-free Hay Street Mall, extends to parallel streets; charming London Court imitates Tudor England. **Brisbane's** Queen Street Mall has fashion, flower stalls and food; the Myer Centre here is called the largest city-centre retail development in Australia.

In the resorts, the sun might inflate the prices but the beachwear and leisure fashions will match your mood.

What to Buy

The possibilities are at least as voluminous as your budget. With temptations as diverse as mass-produced knick-knacks and true works of art, it all depends, as anywhere else, on your taste and your bank balance. Here's a brief survey, in alphabetical order, of

the distinctive shopping opportunities to keep in mind as you travel across Australia. In a country so big and varied, the regional differences are worth keeping in mind; if you see something you like, buy it, for you may not find it elsewhere.

Aboriginal arts. The first example of the regional effect: the Northern Territory and North Queensland are likely places to come across a good cross-section of authentic works of art as well as boomerangs, didjeridoos (drone pipes) and trinkets. Farther from the source, though, you can find Aboriginal products in specialist stores all over the country. Outback artists produce traditional paintings on bark, the subjects and style recalling the prehistoric rock paintings: kangaroos, emus, fish, snakes, crocodiles, and impressions of tribal ceremonies. Other Aboriginal painters use modern materials to produce canvases in a style that looks uncannily like some abstract-expressionist work, yet recounting Dreamtime legends and rituals. If the themes are old, the economics are contemporary; the price tags on paintings easily go into four figures. Fine workmanship is also seen on some of the painted wood sculptures of animals and birds. You'll see large, brightly decorated didjeridoos, wind instruments made from tree-trunks hollowed out by obliging termites. More portably, there are clap-sticks for percussion accompaniment. Aboriginal craftsmen also produce decorated wooden shields and, inevitably, boomerangs. The better boomerangs, hand carved and painted, can be quite expensive. Aboriginal craftsmen also create rather pricey trinkets such as baskets and place-mats from pandanus leaves.

Antiques might seem a fruitless field in a country as young as Australia, but some worthy colonial pieces turn up: furniture, clocks, jewellery, porcelain, silverware, glassware, books and maps. Some dealers specialize in non-Australian antiques, for instance Chinese ceramics or Japanese screens. In Sydney the Paddington district is full of antique shops. Melbourne's antique centre is High Street, Armadale.

Arts and Crafts. Outdoor markets in the cities and in the big resorts brim with bright ideas, from modern hand-painted pottery to garden furniture and gnomes. Among the local colour you'll also find home-made jams and folk remedies for man and beast. The venues are as various as Melbourne's Queen Victoria Market and Brisbane's riverside.

Books. Every bookstore in the country has shelves full of "Australiana"—giftworthy books about everything from the nation's history and geography to the animals, birds and insects. In addition, this might be the time and place to catch up with Australian literature, with authors as eminent as Thomas Keneally and David Malouf—or Clive James.

Diamonds. In sheer volume, Australia outsparkles all the world's other diamond producers, thanks to the whopping strikes in the isolated Kimberley region of Western Australia. The cut-and-polished results of this bonanza—precious stones in yellow, brown or white, but especially pink—are sold at jewellers in the major cities. The Argyle sales force is trying to improve the image of brown gems, giving them the fashionable names of champagne or cognac diamonds.

Duty-free shopping is highly organized throughout Australia, not just at airports but in the cities. Some downtown duty-free stores claim to have lower prices and greater variety than the airport shops. If you're in the market for a Japanese stereo rig or camera, not to mention the familiar spirits and perfume options, the competition among duty-free firms has made Australia an interesting marketplace. You have to produce your air ticket and passport at the duty-free store. You mustn't open the packages before you leave the country; on your departure you have to show them to the customs agent. Thanks to the almighty computer, he'll be looking for you.

Fashions. Australian fashion designers get high marks for their relaxed, sometimes eccentric styles and rousing colours; they most often use natural fabrics. This is a good place to pick up resort and casual fashions, though the prices are almost always at high-season peaks. The swimwear, pareus, shorts and T-shirts come in novel patterns, likely to excite admiration at other latitudes. A most unusual design in fancy shirts is sold at the historic Hyde Park Barracks in Sydney: pin-stripes with, at the bottom, the broad arrow symbol of a prisoner of King George III.

Hats. Once you buy one of the cowboy-style hats that protect Australian stockmen from sun and rain, you may have to go the whole hog and invest in the entire get-up. Or go home in a digger hat, the kind with a chin-strap and

one side of the brim up, as worn by "Breaker" Morant and his ANZAC mates. Then there is the jokey cork hat, with dangling wine corks to discourage the attentions of those vexatious Outback flies.

Kangaroo-skin products include toy kangaroos and koalas and other such souvenirs, some of them quite silly. The cheapest stuffed kangaroos and koalas, sometimes wrapped in patriotic Australian packaging, are imported. Or you can buy a kangaroo skin to use as a small rug or a wall decoration—or tell your friends it's a hunting trophy.

Opals lie embedded in the most ordinary rocks until somebody stumbles on them. Australia produces the great majority of all the world's opals. Precious opals come in three sorts, primarily from fields in three states. Coober Pedy, in South Australia, the continent's biggest opal field, produces the white, or milky, opal. In the Out-

Not exactly Asprey's or Cartier's, this jewellery shop in Alice Springs sells precious and less precious stones.

back of Queensland, around Quilpie, the reward is the so-called boulder opal, with brilliant colours and patterns. Finally, Lightning Ridge in New South Wales is the source of black opals (more blue than black), the most expensive of all. You could go to the opal fields to find a stone of your own, simply noodling through the hills of rejected pebbles. However, it's easier to buy an opal at one of the specialist stores in any of the cities. Opals, considered among Australia's best buys, are sold unset or as finished jewellery. The big jewellery shops can arrange tax-free purchase for foreign visitors, but you will have to pay duty when you arrive back home.

Outback clothing. Australian city folk sometimes like to affect the kind of fashions the stockmen (cowboys) wear, and you, too, might want to try a bit of ruggedness-by-association. There are flannel shirts, moleskin (a durable form of cotton) trousers, kangaroo-hide belts, oilskin coats to withstand any squall, and low- or high-heeled boots to strut in.

Paintings and prints. Inspired by Australian panoramas and colours, contemporary artists distinguish themselves in both realistic and abstract modes. They are on show in commercial galleries in many areas, but the biggest concentration is in the capitals.

For souvenir shoppers who have finally run out of ideas, a T-shirt emporium is usually close at hand.

Sydney galleries are clustered in the central shopping district and in Paddington. In Melbourne try the City, Toorak Road, and High Street, Armadale. They'll handle the packing, insurance and shipping for you.

Pearls. For more than a century the tepid seas off Broome, Western Australia, have been a prolific source of pearls. The modern, "artificial" version is sold unadorned, just as it was extracted from the seashell, or made up into necklaces, brooches or rings.

Sheepskin. With sheep outnumbering people by maybe ten to one, it's only logical that sheepskin products are available all over Australia, and usually at good prices. If it isn't too hot to think about such things, look over the sheepskin boots, hats, coats, rugs and novelty items.

Souvenirs, ingenious or hackneyed, indigenous or slyly imported, pop up

44

everywhere you travel, in cities, resorts and along the way at roadside stands. Tourists seem unable to resist miniature kangaroos, koalas and, in Tasmania, almost-lovable Tasmanian devil dolls. Koalas come in every conceivable size and mode: at the Sydney Opera House they sell little koala dolls dressed in ballerinas' tutus. Plastic boomerangs and beer-can holders head the very long list of even less artistic souvenirs, followed by saucy T-shirts.

Tasmanian timber. Huon pine grows for centuries before it gets big enough to interest Tasmania's lumbermen. Eventually this long-lasting, fine-grained, fragrant wood is carved into furniture, bowls, eggcups, candlesticks, even rolling-pins. Or you can take home a sachet of the shavings, suitable for sniffing when you're feeling nostalgic for Tassie.

Toys. Aside from all the usual stuffed animals, have a look at the mythical characters like flying pigs and Catastrophe Cats, hand-made in Australia and sold in the imaginative chain of toy shops called Lost Forests.

Woollen goods. Those sheep again: look for high-quality sweaters and scarves, and tapestries and rugs, too, in traditional or avant-garde patterns. You can also buy hand-spun wool along with pattern books to show you what to do with it.

Prices

To give you an idea of what to expect, here are some average prices in Australian dollars. However, these can only be approximate in view of the problem of inflation. And in a land this big and varied prices differ from state to state and region to region.

Air fares. Sydney–Adelaide–Sydney economy $498, "See Australia" fare $374; Melbourne–Sydney economy $136; Melbourne–Cairns ("See Australia" fare) $321.

Airport transfer. From Sydney airport to city: coach: $4, taxi: $10–12. Melbourne airport to city, coach: $8.50, taxi: $20.

Car hire. Economy (unlimited kilometres) $59 per day plus $12 insurance, $357 per week plus $70 insurance; business class $89 per day, $532 per week (insurance included); luxury class $200–250 per day, $1,000–1,500 per week. Monthly rates are also available.

Cigarettes. Australian $2.50 for 20, $2.80–3.00 for 30; imported similar prices.

Coach tour. Half day $20–35, full day $50–70.

Hairdressers. *Ladies'* haircut $25–30, shampoo and set $15–20. *Men's* cut $15–20.

Hotels. Luxury double $300 to $550 per night; premium $150 to $350; moderate $60 to $110; budget $30 to $50.

Meals and drinks. In a moderate restaurant, lunch $25, dinner $35. Bottle of wine (from bottle shop) $7–20, beer $2, soft drink $0.80–1.20.

Night-life. Nightclub, cover charge or minimum $8–12; concert $35 and up; theatre $25 and up ; cinema $10.50.

Taxis. Sydney, Circular Quay to Kings Cross $8; Melbourne, Flinders St. Station to Victorian Market $6.

Trains. Sydney–Brisbane first-class $111; berth $151, economy $79; Melbourne–Adelaide first class $75, berth $115, economy $53; 14-day economy Austrail pass $415.

Hairdressers

There are unisex hairdressing salons for the sophisticates, or you can stick to more traditional segregated establishments, even old-fashioned, no-nonsense men's barber shops with girlie magazines for clients waiting their turn. Some beauty salons feature manicures, pedicures, facials, make-ups and massage. Tipping is not a preoccupation in Australia, but a gratuity would not be refused.

Laundry and Dry Cleaning

Hotels and motels usually offer same-day laundry and dry-cleaning service for guests, though it tends to be quite expensive. Ask the receptionist, porter or maid. Many hotels and motels also have do-it-yourself clothes washers and dryers on the premises.

Photography

There's so much to focus on that you'll probably run out of film. No problem, though: internationally known brands are sold everywhere in Australia. Quick-processing establishments are found in all the cities.

In the desert and the tropics, keep your camera and film out of the hot sun, and beware of sand, dust and moisture. The best photographers avoid the Outback's midday sun, which can spoil the colours; by coincidence, this policy cuts down on sunstroke.

Many Aborigines do not like having their photos taken—ask before you aim. Some Aboriginal sites, even well-known landmarks, are sensitive subjects for filming, so don't make a scene if you're waved away. Professional photographers are in a more delicate position, as the Aborigines object to the wider dissemination of controversial shots.

Wildlife is a fascinating subject, but it's only prudent to keep your distance when, for example, crocodiles or wild boar appear in the viewfinder. And buffalo can be much more dangerous than they appear.

Electric Current

The standard throughout Australia is 240–250 volt, 50 cycle AC. Three-pronged plugs, in the shape of a bird's footprint, are universal, so you should take an adaptor. Most hotel rooms also have 110-volt outlets for razors and small appliances. Otherwise, you'll need a voltage convertor, but even so, American devices geared to 60-cycle current will act eccentrically.

Water

Yes, you can drink the water from the tap in any Australian town, unless it's specifically marked otherwise. In the Outback, warnings might read "Bore-water" or "Not for drinking".

Weights and Measures

Since the 1960s Australia has adhered to the metric system's kilometres and kilogrammes, litres and metres, and with the Celsius temperature system taking over from Fahrenheit. Old-timers may still reckon distances in miles, but generally the abandonment of British Imperial measures is total.

Communications

Post Office

Australia's 4,500 post offices are sign-posted "Australia Post". Most adhere to a 9-to-5 schedule Monday to Friday, though Sydney's historic General Post Office (GPO) also opens Saturday mornings. In Melbourne the GPO is open from 8.00 a.m. to 6.00 p.m. Monday to Friday with an after-hours counter as well. Many post offices have self-service shops selling stamps including philatelic packs, postcards, envelopes, packing cartons and other supplies. Hotels and souvenir shops also stock stamps. Letter-boxes throughout Australia are red with a horizontal white stripe.

If you don't know exactly where you'll be staying, you can have letters addressed to you c/o Poste Restante or the Post Office Delivery Desk at the General Post Office in a city on your itinerary. You'll have to show identification when you pick up your mail. At the GPO in Sydney the Poste Restante bureau is computerized: type in your name (there are instructions in six languages), and if mail awaits you

*Y*ou can't miss them: *red is the colour of Australian post boxes.*

the machine prints out a ticket; take it to the window, where a human will hand over your letter.

Telephone

Telecom Australia runs more than 8 million telephones, more than 99 per cent of them linked to automatic exchanges. The network is highly sophisticated; from almost any phone, even in the Outback, you can dial anywhere in the country, and the signal is loud and clear. Many hotel rooms have phones from which you can dial cross-country (STD) or internationally

(IDD). Some hotels add a surcharge to your telephone bill.

There are four kinds of coin-operated telephones. Green, gold and blue phones accept 10c, 20c, 50c and $1 coins and may be used for IDD or STD calls as well as local numbers. Red phones are for local calls only; put 30 cents in the slot. Public telephones geared for credit cards are installed at airports and city locations.

Telephone directories give full instructions on dialling and details on emergency and other services. To reach an overseas number, dial 0011, then the country code of the destination, the area code and the local number. (Dialling *to* Australia from overseas the country code is 61.)

Telegrams and Cablegrams

These can be sent from any post office or dictated over the phone from your hotel or motel room. Most post offices have **telex** and **fax** facilities, as do hotels.

Newspapers and Magazines

More than 500 newspapers are published in Australia, from internationally esteemed big city dailies like the *Sydney Morning Herald* and *The Age* of Melbourne to backwoods weeklies. As in the United States, papers have traditionally served local communities or states rather than a nationwide readership. The first national newspaper, Rupert Murdoch's *The Australian*, was founded in 1964. Dozens of periodicals aimed at the immigrant communities are published in Dutch, French, German, Greek, Italian and other languages. In the biggest cities specialist newsstands sell newspapers

*H*ot off the press: a Brisbane news vendor, dressed for the climate, picks up the latest edition.

airlifted from London, Rome, Paris, Hong Kong and Singapore as well as weekly and monthly American and European magazines.

Radio and Television

Government-funded stations of the Australian Broadcasting Commission (ABC) and the Special Broadcasting Service (SBS) compete with a range of commercially run stations. Sydney and Melbourne have five television channels each, which operate from 6 a.m. to midnight or later. The SBS stations are devoted to "multicultural" programmes, which are primarily in foreign languages with English subtitles. The big cities have a profusion of AM and FM radio stations for all tastes. The output of ABC-FM is almost entirely composed of classical music. Short-wave listeners can pick up Radio Australia (the overseas service of the ABC) and other long-range broadcasters such as the Voice of America, BBC World Service and Asian stations.

Religious Services

The majority religion in Australia is Christianity. The biggest denominations are Anglican (Church of England) and Roman Catholic, followed by Uniting Church, Presbyterian and Orthodox. Of the non-Christian faiths, Muslims are the largest group, followed by Jews and Buddhists. To find the church of your choice, check at your hotel desk or look in the telephone directory under *Churches and Synagogues.*

Daily Life

Clothing
Whatever your itinerary, whatever the season, forget your overcoat. But a sweater may come in handy, even in summer when, after a hot day in the sun, the evening breeze can seem downright chilly. A light raincoat will serve near the coast in almost any season. Anywhere you go you'll need comfortable walking shoes. Because of the strong sun, a hat is advisable—particularly in the Outback.

In cities like Melbourne and Sydney, businessmen wear suits and ties except on hot summer days, when they put on walking shorts and long socks. They still suffer neckties but abandon jackets. In less formal circumstances—sightseeing or shopping, for instance—both men and women wear shorts when it's warm. Some restaurants require jacket and tie, and even Outback restaurants and hotels may bar T-shirts and shorts or ripped jeans in the evening.

Courtesies
If you're accustomed to formality at home, you're in for a surprise. In Australia's egalitarian atmosphere, people usually introduce themselves by their first name, even in business relationships. (Don't be shocked if the motel receptionist first-names you, too.) Punctuality is the order of the day in spite of the relaxed atmosphere, and visitors are expected to follow the rules.

Many areas of the country, and not only in the Outback, contain places or things of special meaning to the Aborigines. These "sacred sites" are protected by law. Visitors should show respect for their historical significance.

Hours
Business hours vary slightly from place to place, but not as much as you might expect in a country spreading over three time zones. Here are a few guidelines, subject to local variations:

Banks: 9.30 a.m. to 4.00 p.m. Monday to Thursday, till 5.00 p.m. Fridays. (but some big-city banks open earlier and close later for foreign currency exchange.)

Post office: Mostly 9.00 a.m. to 5.00 p.m. Monday to Friday.

Shopping: 8:30 or 9.00 a.m. to 5.00 or 5.30 p.m. Monday to Friday and from 9.00 to 12.00 noon on Saturday. Each town has one late shopping night per week when stores stay open until 8.00 or 9.00 p.m.

Offices: 9.00 a.m. to 5.00 p.m. Monday to Friday.

Bars/pubs/hotels: Licensing hours vary considerably from state to state and even hotel to hotel, but a typical schedule would be 10.00 a.m. to 10.00 p.m. Monday to Saturday, with some places permitting drinking after noon on Sundays. Nightclubs carry on until 2 a.m. or later.

Museums: 10.00 a.m. to 5.00 p.m. Monday to Saturday, 12.00 noon to 5.00 p.m. Sundays.

Language

Australian, a highly spiced version of the English language, is spoken everywhere in the nation. The vernacular is called *Strine*, which is the way the word "Australian" sounds in an extreme Australian pronunciation. The vocabulary is rich in inventive and amusing words spoken in what the uninitiated may take for a profound Cockney accent piped through the nose. Foreigners who listen carefully usually understand what's said, at least when it's repeated. The regional variations are insignificant.

Australia produces a bumper crop of dictionaries and books, both erudite and jokey, delving into the derivation of local words and the unusual rhyming slang, as well as tongue-in-cheek "Australian self-taught" cassettes and manuals. To tide you over, a few dinkum Aussieisms are given in the table (opposite).

In addition to English a host of foreign languages serve the immigrant communities. Multicultural radio stations broadcast in more than 50 languages. (*See* also RADIO AND TV.)

Non-English speakers with problems can get help from the Telephone Interpreter System (TIS), which can translate on telephone calls to doctors or emergency services. Interpreters on call can handle many languages including French, German, Greek,

*A*n invitation, or command, in Adelaide. Since the liberalization of laws limiting drinking hours, the Australian way of life has become even more relaxed.

Some dinkum Ausseisms!

ace	excellent
back of beyond	the Outback, remote area
beaut	beautiful, very good
billabong	water hole
bush	country area
bushranger	outlaw
dinkum	honest, authentic
dinky-di	the truth, genuine
footy	rugby-style football
fossick	to search, as for precious stones
joey	baby kangaroo
Kiwi	New Zealander
mate	good friend
ocker	a stereotypical Australian
Oz	Australia
paddock	field, often fenced
Pom, Pommy	English person
roo	kangaroo
station	ranch
tinny, or tube	can of beer
tucker	food
ute	utility truck
whinge	to complain

Italian and Spanish. They operate round the clock in the bigger cities, for the price of a local phone call. Some TIS numbers: Sydney 221 1111; Melbourne 416 9999; Adelaide 213 1999; Perth 325 9144; Hobart 34 2599. Operating 8 a.m. to 6 p.m. only: Brisbane 221 5233 and Darwin 82 2111. For Canberra and outside major cities: 008 11 2477 or 008 33 3330.

Meeting People

Australians are eminently approachable and convivial people, so you will be able to strike up a conversation al-most anywhere—at a bus stop, at the beach or in a pub. One way to get close to the people is to stay in bed and breakfast accommodation in family homes. Farmhouse vacations can also be arranged.

Public (Legal) Holidays

January 1	New Year's Day
April 25	Anzac Day
December 25	Christmas
December 26	Boxing Day

Moveable dates: Australia Day (Monday closest to Jan. 26)
Good Friday
Easter Eve
Easter Monday
Queen's Birthday

Other public holidays are celebrated only in certain states or a single region, for example Picnic Day in the Northern Territory in August, and Melbourne Cup Day in the metropolitan area in November. Still other holidays are observed at different times in different states: Labour Day comes any time between March and October, according to where you are.

Smokers

On public transport, in theatres and elevators, as well as in government offices, smoking is prohibited. Some hotels and restaurants have established smoke-free zones.

Smokers can find a big selection of Australian and imported cigarettes on sale everywhere. They come in packs of 20, 25 or 30 cigarettes. Specialist shops also stock a plethora of imported cigars and pipe tobacco. Prices vary from state to state.

Tipping

For most foreigners the Australian view of tipping takes some getting used to. Virtually no one in the service sector of the economy expects to be tipped. Nobody's livelihood depends on tips. A gratuity is optional, a reward for good service but not a requirement.

In hotels frequented by foreigners, porters are accustomed to receiving tips. In good restaurants a tip of 5 to 10 per cent is a just reward for efficient, courteous service. Taxi drivers accept but don't expect tips. In fact, drivers have been known to round *down* the fare to the nearest convenient sum to facilitate change-making. But it won't hurt any feelings if you *do* give an appreciative tip.

Toilets

Australians manage without euphemisms for "toilet", though in a country so rich in slang you won't be surprised to come across some wry

They call toilets *"toilets" in Australia and signpost them. This far-west scene is in Kalgoorlie, WA.*

department. In Sydney, for instance, there is one Lost Property Office for things lost in taxis, and another for property left behind in buses, trains and ferries. Otherwise, try the police.

Complaints

As Australia has no special agency to deal with complaints, your best bet is to work out any problems face to face with the shopkeeper, hotel manager or whoever is involved. If you think you've been overcharged or unfairly dealt with, the personal approach should be the most effective remedy in plain-talking Australia.

Crime and Theft

Although murder remains a sensational rarity in Australia, mostly involving family or friends, lesser crimes are steadily on the increase. As in most countries, it's wise to take precautions against burglary and petty theft. Check your valuables in the hotel's safe deposit box. Lock your room and your car. Be alert for pickpockets, who often look for targets in crowded buses and markets.

Anti-drug laws vary greatly from state to state. Possession of 100 g (3½ oz) of cannabis or even less can mean up to two years in jail.

synonyms. When you find them, the facilities are often distinguished by the letters "M" and "F" for Male and Female. Public conveniences usually adhere to a high standard of cleanliness and comfort, even in the Outback.

Lost Property

If you've lost something, your hotel receptionist can probably tell you where to find the relevant Lost and Found

Police

Each state (and the Northern Territory) operates its own police force, covering both urban and rural areas. The Australian Federal Police, based in Canberra, has jurisdiction over government property, including airports, and deals with interstate problems like drugs and organized crime.

Emergencies

Ambulance—Fire—Police: Dial **000.** The 000 number—no coin required from public telephones—is in service in all cities and most towns. If you're in a remote area, however, look for the emergency numbers inside the front cover of the local telephone directory. In the big cities there are round-the-clock dental emergency services as well as hospital emergency wards.

Festivities

Year in and year out, Australia organizes something like 400 arts festivals, not counting special events as original as the begonia festival in Ballarat, the Bendigo bonsai exhibition and the absurd dry-river regatta in Alice Springs. You might not drop everything for one of these manifestations, but knowing when and where the special events are scheduled might add that extra splash of local colour to your holiday. A few fun ideas, subject to confirmation:

January: *Sydney* Festival, a month of concerts, drama, exhibitions, sports and special events. *Perth* Cup horse racing classic at Royal Ascot Race-

*D*ressed to kill, a participant in an Alice Springs fête smiles through the devilish desert heat.

course. *Hahndorf, South Australia* Schuetzenfest. *Nationwide* Australia Day holiday.

February: *Hobart* Royal Regatta. *Perth* Festival, sporting and cultural events. *Melbourne* Victorian Open golf championships.

March and April: *Ballarat, Victoria* Begonia Festival, flower displays and artistic events. *Melbourne* Moomba, carnival with parades, fireworks, sports events, cultural attractions. *Adelaide* Festival of Arts (even-numbered years), three weeks of opera, ballet, theatre, art and literary events. *Canberra* Festival, pop concerts, fairs, flypasts. *Barossa Valley, South Australia* Vintage Festival, celebrating the wine harvest (odd-numbered years) with German-Australian gaiety. *Sydney*

Royal Easter Show, Sydney Showgrounds, Australia's largest country fair. Sydney Cup Week, a pageant of horse racing.

May: *Alice Springs* Bangtail Muster, rodeo extravaganza. Camel Cup. *Adelaide* Cup horse race and associated festivities (a legal holiday locally). *Hobart* Arts Festival.

June: *Darwin* Beer Can Regatta, in which all the boats are ingeniously constructed of used beer cans. *Perth and beyond* Western Australia Week, commemorating the state's original settlement with cultural and sporting events. *Brisbane* Cup, horse race.

July: *Gold Coast, Queensland* Marathon. *Melbourne* Grand National Steeplechase. *Darwin* Show, agricultural exhibition.

August and September: *Brisbane* Royal National Show, agricultural roundup with animals, fireworks and fun. *Mt. Isa, Queensland* Rodeo, Australia's biggest. *Alice Springs* Henley-on-Todd Regatta, bottomless boats racing hilariously on a waterless riverbed. *Thredbo, New South Wales* Ski championships, Snowy Mountains. *Adelaide* Royal Show, South Australia's agricultural summit meeting. *Melbourne* Royal Show, ten days of bucolic attractions, sports competitions and amusements. *Townsville, Queensland* Pacific Festival, cultural and artistic events with strong Aboriginal participation. *Toowoomba, Queensland* Carnival of Flowers, floral parade and gardening competitions. *Various capital cities* Australian Rules football finals. *Brisbane* Warana festival, floats, bands, concerts.

October: *Perth* Royal Show, state fair with animals, farm equipment and sideshows. *Hobart* Royal Show, Tasmanian agricultural exhibition. *Bowral, New South Wales* Tulip Time, display of spring flowers. *McLaren Vale, South Australia.* Wine Bushing Festival, celebrating vines and wines. *Adelaide* Australian Formula 1 Grand Prix.

November: *Melbourne* Victorian Spring Racing Carnival, culminating in the nation's biggest, highest-stake race, the Melbourne Cup. *Adelaide, Melbourne, Perth* Gold tournaments.

December: *Perth* Australian Derby, horse race. *Sydney to Hobart* Yacht Race and *Tasmanian* Fiesta, carnival and sports competitions.

At a festival in the Barossa Valley, a well-travelled tuba player awaits his cue.

Marvels Galore and a Big Hello on the World's Biggest Island in the Sun

Almost anything the other continents can offer, "little" Australia can equal or better: the great outdoors in all forms, winning cities, beaming sun, a friendly welcome, and limitless things to see and do. Every taste, profound or flighty, is catered for, though, of course there's a shortage of ancient palaces and medieval churches. In Australia the most historic local monument is likely to be a jail.

But, then, a jail (spelled gaol) can be awfully significant in a country of escapists that was first settled by convicts. In the 18th century a ticket to Australia was small consolation for avoiding the gallows; the descendants of the pioneers are grateful that they survived and even prospered.

Throughout its recorded, often distorted, history, Australia has always seemed bizarre to distant observers. In Queen Victoria's heyday, a character in an Oscar Wilde play summed up the foreigner's blurred impression of

A koala's keeper poses *for the camera as the drowsy marsupial hangs on bravely.*

Down Under: "It must be so pretty with all the dear little kangaroos flying about. Agatha has found it on the map."

The preconception hasn't changed much in more than a century. To people in the northern hemisphere, Australia still appears to be the most curious upside-down continent of off-colour trees, grizzled prospectors and absurd if lovable animals. And not only the kangaroos (and sleepy koalas and incredible platypuses) but the people, too, sound a bit frivolous, what with everybody sunbathing, surfing and swilling beer all the time.

Like most clichés, there's something in it. The Australians are fanatics of the outdoor life. They radiate rude health and tanned muscles. If they're

not actually at the beach, they're probably hiking, jogging or playing football, or at least out in the garden barbecueing slabs of beef. In hand: an icy beer to pacify the fiercest thirst. The Australians are not quite the world's most insatiable beer drinkers, but they're working on it.

Prospectors seeking gold or lesser minerals, roam the Outback, where life is hard. Remote cattle farms (stations) are so big that cowboys conduct their roundup by helicopter; one of the ranches is about the size of Belgium. As an environment, the Outback is as inhospitable as a rock. The people of the Outback, are hard as rock, apparently immune to sunstroke and flood, snakebite and crocodile nip. (In the Northern Territory tourists can buy crocodile insurance, mostly for fun; but the warnings are serious.)

In a cloud of dust, a herdsman looks after his charges on a Northern Territory cattle station. The lonely life appeals to the imagination but the huge majority of Aussies live in towns.

Life in the bush may be the stereotype, but camping holidays are as close as the overwhelming majority of citizens ever get to it. The average Australian today is a confirmed city-slicker. About 70 per cent of the population lives in the ten biggest cities. Few Australians have ever seen a koala dozing in a eucalyptus tree or a kangaroo suckling her joey—except at the zoo or wildlife park, like all the other tourists.

The Start of Isolation

In the childhood of the earth, Australia was land-linked to India, Africa and Antarctica and more. It all comprised a supercontinent. The planet's growing pains and continental drift broke up the conglomeration, the oceans intervened, and eternities of isolation ensued. Plants and animals, cut off from the evolutionary mainstream, developed in freakish ways that were to engross generations of scientists and ordinary tourists. On the other side of the coin, some of the most familiar fauna and flora from Europe were eventually imported to Australia, sometimes with dire results.

The only humans sharing the continent with the native animals were nomadic Aboriginal tribes. These first Australians, inventors of the round-trip boomerang, are thought to have arrived from Asia perhaps 40,000 years ago. Everything went smoothly until the 18th century, when British convicts were shipped out to colonize Australia on behalf of King George III. If the Americans hadn't revolted a few years earlier, the North Atlantic would have remained the obvious route to exile; there'd have been no need for dumping the outcasts on such extravagantly distant shores.

At the time the British Empire casually seized their traditional lands, the dark-skinned hunters who met, or more likely avoided, the new arrivals were still in the Stone Age. They may have numbered 300,000. Now the Aboriginal population is about two-thirds that. No easy answers have been found for their problems of adjustment to the white society around them—life expectancy is about 20 years less for Aborigines—but the government keeps trying to right a lengthy list of age-old wrongs.

The fact that the construction of modern Australia was begun by chain gangs of convicted felons rather than firm-jawed idealists was bound to affect the national psyche. Does this quirk of history explain why Australians are defensive about their country, asking foreigners what they think about it, then waiting anxiously for the answer? Does the family tree account for the imaginative, cockneyesque brand of English spoken by Australians of all classes and regions? Is today's social mobility and sense of egalitarianism a reaction to those early days of keepers and convicts, rulers and ruled? Does the macho tradition stem from the scarcity of female companionship in the young colony?

Australia's geographical superlatives are clear-cut. It's the earth's biggest island. More accurately, call it the smallest and least populous (16.5 million) of the continents, but the only one housing a single nation. Australia occupies about as much space as the 48 mainland states of the US, or 24 times the area of the British Isles. Something to think about when you plan your See-All-of-Australia-in-a-Hurry itinerary.

Another claim for the record book: Australia is the flattest continent. Having had plenty of time to be worn down, the ancient terrain hardly ever rises above middle-ranking hilltops. But the nation's summit, Mount Kosciusko (elevation 2,228 m or 7,316 ft) is almost as high as Mexico City. If August is hot where you live, you can zip over to ski in the

59

Australian Alps. Or alternate between the snowdrifts and the trackless desert: come down to earth at salty Lake Eyre, the continent's lowest point, 16 m (39 ft) below sea level.

Australia is the driest continent, the mass of its interior a blotter of desert, a parched rebuff to all but the most dauntless pioneers. Although the Murray River and its tributaries add up to a Mississippi or a Yangtse in length, few other Australian rivers rate much more than a rowing boat. And many of the refreshing blue squiggles on maps are just sand traps for at least part of the year.

The coastline is the least ruffled of all the continents, a circumference of 36,700 km (almost 33,000 miles) devoted to sweeping beaches rather than coves and creeks. Here you can dip a toe, or a surfboard, in legendary seas and oceans, among them the Coral Sea, the Timor Sea, the Indian Ocean and the Southern Ocean.

Australia is a long way from familiar climes: 9,600 km (6,000 miles) from the United States, 17,700 km (11,000 miles) from Britain. Much more distant in cultural terms are Australia's nearest neighbours, Indonesia and Papua New Guinea, only a kangaroo's hop to the north. The Asian connection is becoming ever more important, politically, economically, strategically, and in human terms: a look at the faces on any city street shows the increased flow of immigrants from the Pacific.

But European influences still dominate in spite of the dilution of the original British character of the country. The Australian melting pot now contains a savoury mixture of fish and chips, spaghetti, souvlaki and sauerkraut and portions of Peking duck and Vietnamese spring rolls. Don't be surprised if you hear radio programmes in Arabic or—how exotic can you get?—Welsh.

Sunset among the lilies at Fogg Dam, near Darwin, a favourite haunt of water birds.

A relic of the age of dinosaurs, a crocodile in the wild takes the sun in Kakadu National Park. The crocs can afford to rest easy here as a protected species.

Gums and Wattles

Australia's isolation and climate account for the unfamiliar flora. At almost all latitudes of the continent's sprawl from jungle and mangrove swamp through fertile farmlands to snowy peaks, you'll see hardy perennial trees of two main families. More than 500 types of eucalyptus, mostly grey-green, are native to Australia, and 600 species of flowering acacia are at home. Where the earth is chronically thirsty they look scrubby but brave, while in the nicer neighbourhoods they are as robust as Bondi Beach bathing beauties. Unromantically terse, the Australians call eucalyptus "gum" and acacia "wattle", making them sound rather like wizened bushes with poisonous berries. But by any alias, gum and wattle remain noble, useful, and often lovely. Closer to the ground, wild flowers as vivid as desert pea and kangaroo paw thrive on the morning dew. Even where abundant, they are too precious to pluck.

The indigenous animals are as odd as they are charming. Consider the monotremes, on which Australia has a virtual monopoly. The generic name for these most primitive of all mammals may not ring a bell, but you'll recognize the individual exhibits—the spiny anteater (who keeps in check Australia's 1,500 species of ants) and the platypus, a remarkably cheery looking compromise between a bird, a reptile and a mammal. More familiar are the marsupials, with pouches to solve the babysitting problem. Bounding across the landscape are dozens of varieties of kangaroo, from pocket-sized wallabies to giant red roos big enough to cow any heavyweight boxer. Another marsupial, the adorable koala, eschews violent exercise, spending its days drowsing in a eucalyptus haze.

Birdwatchers can count hundreds of species. Thrillingly colourful birds are as common as sparrows, and lyrical or humorous bird-calls provide every evening's country music. The local stars have names like flowerpecker, honeyeater and kookaburra, but the favourite bird of crossword puzzlers, the emu, can't sing—or fly.

Divers go down under Down Under to admire the sort of fish you see in a collector's tropical tank—but in these seas they're ten times bigger. Gorgeous angel fish and moorish idols glide past the enthralled skin-diver's mask. Big-mouthed sharks and venomous scorpion fish may also turn up, but they are subjects for more serious study.

For enthusiasts of underwater spectacles, the most exciting place in the world is the Great Barrier Reef. This 1,930-km (1,200-mile)-long miracle—a living structure of coral—thrills the imagination in its immensity and in the intricate detail of brightly hued organisms shaped like antlers, flowers,

One's a crowd on a popular stretch of the world's beachiest island; in the distance, the high-rises of the popular resort of Surfer's Paradise.

fans or brains. The most sublime tropical fish congregate there, too.

The Reef, one of Australia's top priority tourist destinations, has become ever more accessible. So has Ayers Rock, with its own airport and hotel complex. Australia's highly developed transport system puts the whole continent within reach: beaches and ski resorts, dynamic cities and Outback ghost towns.

Seeing the Continent

Considering the country's admittedly out-of-the-way location, it's remarkable that tourism has become the industry bringing in the biggest hoard of foreign exchange. More than 2 million foreign tourists a year head for Australia. The most popular tourist corridor slices through the south-east corner, where there's a choice of big cities, beaches and the bush.

Sydney, the brash, brassy city where the history of Australia began, is no more typical of the country than Manhattan is representative of America. But the setting is sensational, and you only have to travel beyond the suburbs to see your first "Caution—Kangaroos" highway sign.

The rival metropolis, the river city of Melbourne, has a Chicago dynamism, grandiose business buildings, and more than its share of parks. Add sophisticated shopping, eating and night-life, and the capricious weather seems less of a drawback.

To avoid political friction, the federal capital was built on neutral ground between Sydney and Melbourne. The result, Canberra, is a forested exercise in town planning, with enough crescents, circles and curving roads to baffle Henry the Navigator.

The other sizeable cities, which double as state capitals, share a clean, relaxed air: gracious, parklike Adelaide and Perth; sunny, subtropical Brisbane; and the most modern of towns, the reborn Darwin. Hobart, the brisk and tidy capital of Tasmania, is a seafarers' haven that everybody enjoys.

Notwithstanding the charm of the cities, most visitors search for the "real" Australia in the Outback, a land of rocky hills, desert or rainforest and adventure. When you imagine the middle of nowhere, back of beyond, the never-never, this is the place. In the Northern Territory—about the size of France, Spain and Italy combined—the population density works out to more than 8 km^2 (3 square miles) of land for each inhabitant.

Most of the total area of Australia is occupied by similarly vacant wilderness. You drive for hours to the next town on the map and discover it's no more than a pub with a petrol pump. No wonder the Aussies are so friendly!

Among the less obvious things tourists come to see are the country's other industries. Visiting a "station" is seeing the Australian myth come to life—livestock extending beyond the horizon, doctors who fly their own planes to their patients' bedsides, suntanned children who ride horseback but have never seen a cinema or supermarket, an escalator or even a flight of stairs.

Some tourists arrange fossicking expeditions—freelance digging for gold or opals. Others go to an isolated vantage point to survey an enormous opencast bauxite mine or descend the shaft into the richly claustrophobic mysteries of a gold mine. (History's biggest nugget emerged in New South Wales in 1872, yielding about 100 kg or 220 lb of pure gold.)

Putting the country's mineral resources into perspective, Australia is the world's No. 1 exporter of coal, the biggest producer of bauxite, and in the top international rank when it comes to mining iron, lead, zinc, uranium and precious stones. Above ground, grazing land predominates, and the sheep outnumber the people by about ten to one. Australia is the world leader in wool production. Its farms also supply

A barefoot bush pilot ties up his seaplane on the beach at Green Island, on the Great Barrier Reef.

many countries with meat, dairy products, wheat, sugar and fruit.

Yet, contrary to its timeless rural image, Australia today is a highly industrialized urban society. Factories turn out everything from ships to chips. The trend, though, is unmistakably towards the service sector—trade, community services and construction. The labour force is highly unionized, and salaries are above the level known in most countries. Prices, too, are high.

Social Notes

Until recent times, Australia was strictly a man's world, where the missus stayed at home scrubbing the floor while the head of the household played football with the gang, talked macho, and drank and drank. The most popular Australian poet, Henry Lawson, explained all this drinking as "a man's

way of crying". More liberal drinking laws have made things less desperate. The gender gulf, too, has narrowed. Liberated women are now seen almost everywhere in the mainstream of society, though some redoubts of awkwardness persist.

For visiting Americans, Australians seem quite English, while British newcomers are reminded of America. The informality and pioneering spirit Down Under do recall the American style, while the social and economic preoccupations—and the attitudes towards food—more often take after the British model. The Australian language may occasionally baffle English-speakers from almost anywhere, but it's admirably ingenious, and as good-humoured as the Aussies themselves.

As for culture, the average Australian might find the word itself rather tedious, maintaining that television and sports are culture enough. But don't you bet on it, mate! Go to any bookstore, or one of the imposing art centres or to any theatre showing a locally produced play or film. All along a varied, challenging front, Australian creativity is thriving.

The federal government pours millions of dollars a year into the arts; so do the states. Check up on the results: the vigorous design of the new museums and opera houses, the high calibre of the performing artists and the enthusiasm of the audiences. For the tourist, Australia is the chance to combine treasures of art with nature's wonders, leaping ballerinas as well as kangaroos. This is the place to soak up some rays, and life and lore and marvels galore. There's more to "the lucky country" than its sunny disposition.

Nothing Personal

Just before you disembark Down Under, the airplane's cabin crew throws a bit of a wet blanket on the big welcome. After warning the passengers to cover their eyes and noses, they come around spraying for bugs.

There's no reason to feel persecuted. Every plane gets the same treatment, because, it is explained, Australia is an island and must protect its animals and plant life from exotic foreign diseases.

The quarantine laws are very stiff (jail terms up to 10 years in some cases) and comprehensive. Among the things you must not bring to Australia without prior authorization: Cats, dogs, birds, eggs, fish, insects, seeds, meat, cheese, fresh fruit and vegetables, live plants ... and the dessert you salvaged from your tray for a midnight snack in Sydney.

History

The written history of Australia, a mere short story by European standards, is as lively as Saturday night in an Outback pub. Mark Twain said it doesn't read like history at all "but like the most beautiful lies ... full of surprises, and adventures, and incongruities, and contradictions, and incredibilities; but they are all true; they all happened".

Early History

But first the *unwritten* history, melting into legend, which goes back many thousands of years, according to scientists; or, alternatively, according to Aboriginal belief, millions of years.

Where did the first inhabitants come from, and when? The Aborigines insist they were here all along, from the birth of the earth. More conservatively,

A bas relief at the National Library, Sydney, shows an early Australian mastering the Stone Age environment.

modern scientists have carbon-dated a human skull found in the New South Wales Outback and pronounced it nearly 40,000 years old; when pressed, some authorities take the story back an additional 40,000 years.

The migration school of thought says the catalyst for the big move was the Ice Age. The Aborigines, according to this version, came to Australia from somewhere in south-east Asia as one of the side-effects of the big freeze. As the bitter cold propelled the cave dwellers of the northern hemisphere toward the sun belt, it set off a chain reaction, forcing more southerly folk to get out of the way of the invaders. Titanic ice-caps accumulated, drastically dropping sea levels and revealing land bridges from island to island, or reducing the distances to be sailed. Thanks to the big dry-out, most of the route from the Asian mainland to Australia would have been walkable, or at least wadeable.

Searching for greener pastures, or more elbow room, or escaping from war or vendetta—or perhaps blown off course on what should have been a routine voyage—the original immigrants arrived Down Under. The first Australians had little problem adapting to the new environment. As Stone Age hunters and food gatherers, they were accustomed to foraging, and the takings in the new continent were good: plenty of fish, berries and roots, and, for a change of diet, why not just spear a kangaroo?

"The Dreamtime" is the all-purpose name for everything that came before. It puts Aboriginal history, traditions and culture under one mythological roof. The Dreamtime's version of Genesis recounts how ancestral heroes created the stars, the earth and all the creatures. The Dreamtime explains why the animals, insects and plants are the way they are, and how humans can live in harmony with nature. To this day, when Aborigines die, they are recycled to the continuum of the Dreamtime.

Every natural object—every tree, rock and river—has its own mystical significance. This is why anthropologists and Aboriginal consultants join the advance party when new construction projects come under consideration in the wilderness: what looks like an innocuous stretch of empty desert may contain sacred sites.

Invaders Ahoy!

For hundreds of centuries the Aborigines had Australia to themselves. Over the last few hundred years, though, the rest of the world closed in.

Like the search for El Dorado, everybody seemed to be looking for *Terra Australis Incognita* or "The Great Land of the South". On and off throughout the 16th century, explorers from Europe kept an eye peeled for the legendary continent and its presumed riches.

The first known landing was by a Dutch captain, Willem Jansz, in 1606. It might be considered a bit of an anticlimax. "There was no good to be done there", was the conclusion as he weighed anchor.

Despite the let-down, the merchant adventurers of the Dutch East India Company, the developers of Java, Ceylon and the Cape of Good Hope, were not to be discouraged. In 1642 the company despatched one of its ace seafarers, Abel Tasman, to track down the elusive treasures of the furthest continent.

On his first expedition, Tasman discovered an island he called Van Diemen's Land, now Tasmania. A couple of years later Tasman was sent back. He covered much of the coast of northern Australia, but still he found no gold, silver or spices. Like Jansz before him, Tasman had nothing good to say about the Aborigines, who impressed him as poor, hungry and generally unattractive brutes. The Dutch gave Australia a grand name, New Holland, but the reports were so unpromising that they surprisingly never bothered to take it a step further and claim the land.

*L**ittle changed since prehistoric times, the Aborigines still look fearsome in this photo taken in the early 20th century.*

Another pessimistic view came from a colourful British traveller, the some-time swashbuckler William Dampier, who had two good looks at the west coast of Australia towards the end of the 17th century. He found no drinking water, no fruit or vegetables, no riches, and "the miserablest people in the world".

And then came Captain Cook, or Lieutenant James Cook, as he then was. In 1770, on a very roundabout trip back to England from Tahiti, the great British navigator landed on the east coast of Australia. Aboard his ship *Endeavour* were two skilled naturalists, Joseph Banks and Daniel Solander. They found so many fascinating specimens that Cook was moved to name the place Botany Bay. (Later, *Endeavour* was holed by coral on a reef off Queensland; thus you could say Captain Cook discovered, the hard way, one of the natural wonders of the world, the Great Barrier Reef.)

Although the Dutch and probably the Spanish and Portuguese had been here before him, Cook claimed all the territory he charted for King George III. He coined the name New South Wales. Returning to London, he issued glowing reports of the Australia he had glimpsed: a vast, sunny, fertile land, inhabited by Aborigines who were "far more happier than we Europeans". The captain's positive thinking about "noble savages" was to be the death of him. A few years later, on the island of Hawaii, he was slain and dismembered by a mob of angry Polynesians.

Pioneers in Chains

In 1779, Joseph Banks, by now the president of the Royal Society, came up with a novel idea. He formally proposed colonizing Australia but instead of the conventional type of settlers, he would send out convicts in the role of pioneers. This plan, he contended, would solve the crisis in Britain's overflowing jails. In those days even amateur lawbreakers like petty larcenists, bigamists and army deserters faced exile.

For most of the 18th century, the British had disposed of troublesome convicts by banishing them to North America. With the American Revolution, this desirable destination had to be dropped from the itineraries. The motherland's prisons couldn't possibly cope, and the supplementary river hulks that were used as floating jails threatened riot and disease.

Sting-Ray Harbour

Captain Cook described the Aborigines he met with considerable warmth, but the truth is that he had to shoot his way ashore on that historic Sunday, 29 April 1770. At the place he first called Sting-Ray Harbour, later Botany Bay, Cook led a small landing party.

"As we approached the shore," his private log reports, "the natives all made off, except two who at first seemed resolved to oppose our landing. We endeavoured to gain their consent to land by throwing them some nails, beads, &c., ashore, but this had not the desired effect; for, as [we] put in to the shore, one of them threw a large stone at us, and as soon as we landed, they threw two darts at us, but [after] the firing of two or three muskets loaded with small shot, they took to the woods, and we saw them no more."

So much for friendly persuasion.

69

The Banks proposal for a colossal British version of Devil's Island seemed far-fetched and expensive, but nobody had a better idea, and in May, 1787, His Majesty's Government began the transportation of criminals to Australia. The programme endured for 80 years. In that time more than 160,000 convicts were shipped out to a new life Down Under.

Captain Arthur Phillip, a retired naval officer, was given command of the first fleet of 11 sailing vessels carrying nearly 1,500 souls, more than half of them convicts, on an eight-month voyage from Portsmouth to New South Wales. Remarkably, every one of the ships finished the trip and the death rate was only around two per cent.

Under the new title of Governor, Captain Phillip came ashore in full ceremonial dress but unarmed. Spear-toting natives milled about like an unwelcoming committee but nothing untoward occurred. A lieutenant on the flagship wrote: "I think it is very easy to conceive the ridiculous figure we must appear to these poor creatures, who were perfectly naked."

Unveiled, too, was the bleak truth about Botany Bay. Captain Cook's rosy claims faded fast when it was discovered there was no shelter from east winds, that much of the alleged meadowland was actually a swamp, and that there wasn't enough fresh water to go around.

Luckily, the next best thing to paradise was waiting just around the corner. Governor Phillip and a reconnaissance party sailed 19 km (12 miles) up the coast and discovered what Fleet Surgeon John White called "the finest and most extensive harbour in the universe". It could, he reckoned, provide "safe anchorage for all the navies of Europe". It was also strikingly beautiful. We call it Sydney Harbour.

The fleet reassembled at Sydney Cove on 26 January 1788 (the date is recalled every year as the Australian national holiday), and the British flag was raised over the brand-new colony. A few Aborigines put on a noisy Aliens-Go-Home demonstration, but empire-builders never let local opinion discourage them.

Although Captain Phillip decreed coexistence, his underlings were hostile or at least insensitive to the native population. Colonists trampled sacred Aboriginal sites and stole Aboriginal food and property. The natives retaliated with force and the colonists replied in kind. Violent incidents went on for years.

For the record, the Aboriginal population before colonization is estimated to have been 300,000. By the early 20th century it had fallen to five figures. But in recent years the Aboriginal census results topped 225,000.

The Ordeal Begins

Real life fell dangerously short of London's great expectations for New South Wales. The soil of Sydney was unpromising, and even if the convicts had wanted to pitch in, the summer was too hot. In any event, most of the outcasts were city-bred and couldn't tell the difference between a hoe and a sickle. Livestock died or disappeared. Hunger crept into ambush. (Even the city-slickers weren't much good for the development of the colony; many convicts were ill after the voyage, or too

old for heavy physical work, and almost all were untrained in any useful trade.)

For nearly two years, delays in London and shipwrecks *en route* frustrated relief shipments. As food supplies dwindled, rations were cut. Prisoners caught stealing food were flogged. Finally, to set an example, the governor ordered a food-looter executed.

In June 1790, to all-round jubilation, the supply ship *Lady Juliana* reached Sydney harbour, and the long fast ended. As agriculture finally began to blossom, thousands of new prisoners were shipped out to Australia. And even voluntary settlers chose Down Under as the land of the future.

When Governor Phillip retired, the colony's top army officer, Major Francis Grose, took over. His army subordinates fared very well under the new regime, which encouraged free enterprise. The officers soon found profitable sidelines, usually at the expense of the British taxpayers. The army's

*A*ctors impersonating Redcoats take a break in a pub at Old Sydney Town; the reality of early colonial life was much harsher.

monopoly on the sale of rum made quick fortunes; under some tipsy economic law, rum began to replace money as Australia's medium of exchange. Even prisoners were paid in alcohol for their extra-curricular jobs. Many hangovers ensued.

Reports of the army's racketeering prompted London to send out a well-known disciplinarian to shake up the colony. He was Captain William Bligh, who had been the target of the notorious mutiny on HMS *Bounty* seven years earlier. Bligh meant to put fear into the hearts of backsliding officers, but his temper was beyond control. His New South Wales victims nicknamed the new governor Caligula and plotted treason.

As the colony was toasting its 20th anniversary on 26 January 1808, a group of insurgent officers deposed Captain Bligh. They held him prisoner for months. The Rum Rebellion, as the mutiny was dubbed, led to a radical reorganization and reshuffle in personnel. But members of the inevitable court martial seemed to understand how Bligh's personality and methods had galled his subordinates.

The Mutiny Man

Revisionist historians admit that Captain Bligh might not have won any popularity contests, but they credit him with more than his quota of courage. Some highlights from a life of action:

• He sailed around the world with Captain Cook in 1772–74.

• He served in naval battles in 1781 and 1782.

• In 1789 he showed superhuman survival instincts when the *Bounty* mutineers set him adrift in the Pacific. With fortitude, luck and exceptional navigating skill, he lived through a voyage of 5,790 km (3,600 miles) in an open boat.

• A year after his ordeal, he commanded HMS *Providence* on another voyage of exploration to the Society Islands.

• He was back in combat in 1797, against the Dutch at the Battle of Camperdown; later in the year he helped suppress a naval mutiny in Ireland.

• He took part in the naval bombardment of Copenhagen in 1801.

After the Rum Rebellion, routine promotions rounded out Bligh's career. In 1814, he reached the rank of vice admiral. He died three years later, ashore in England. In spite of all his achievements, the 20th century remembers Admiral Bligh as the cold, ruthless captain, one of Hollywood's perfect villains.

The mutineers were given more than a rap on the knuckles but less than they might have expected.

Opening a Continent

Under Governor Lachlan Macquarie, New South Wales overcame the stigma of a penal colony and became a land of opportunity. The idealistic army officer from Scotland—who exposed the cruelty of conditions on some of the prison transport ships—built schools, a hospital, a courthouse, and roads to link them.

To inspire exiles to go straight and win emancipation, Macquarie appointed an ex-convict as Justice of the Peace, and he invited others to dinner, to the horror of the local élite. One of the criminals the governor pardoned, Francis Greenway, became the colony's prolific official architect.

Some ex-convicts fared so well under Macquarie's progressive policies that he was accused of pampering the criminal class. London prescribed tougher punishment, along with the total separation of prisoners from the rest of the population. All this led to long-lasting conflict between reformed criminals and their children on one side and a privileged class of voluntary immigrants on the other. Nowadays, the shoe is on the other foot: descendants of First Fleet prisoners often express the same kind of pride as those rare Americans of *Mayflower* ancestry.

For Governor Macquarie and his immediate successors the biggest problem was the most obvious: the colony's seaside location, confined by mountains. There wasn't enough land to provide food for the expanding population. The Blue Mountains, which

Schoolchildren learn about their heritage at one of the first of Governor Macquarie's buildings, the Hyde Park Barracks for convicts.

assistance from convicts and the Aborigines—opened territories that were more distant but no less promising. Land was either confiscated or bought from the indigenous tribesmen: for some 40,000 ha (100,000 acres) of what is now Melbourne the entrepreneurs gave the Aborigines a wagonload of clothing and blankets plus 30 knives, 12 tomahawks, 10 mirrors, 12 pairs of scissors and 50 pounds of flour. It turned out to be a keen bargain, but a generous innovation: the landowners received compensation.

By the middle of the 19th century, thousands of settlers had poured into Australia, and all of the present state capitals were on the map.

Road Works

Some of the explorers who dared venture into the continent's interior in the 19th century are commemorated on today's road maps. Surviving hardships from snakes to sunstroke, they *walked* the route you drive. A who's who: Hume Highway, Sydney to Melbourne, honours Hamilton Hume, who explored much of southern Australia. He also discovered the Murray River.

Eyre Highway, across the Nullarbor Plain: John Edward Eyre, discoverer of Lake Eyre; last survivor of a band of explorers killed by Aborigines in the desert.

Sturt Highway, from southern New South Wales to Adelaide: Charles Sturt, secretary to Governor Darling; discovered the Darling (no coincidence) River and trekked as far as the Simpson Desert.

Stuart Highway, between Adelaide and Darwin: in 1860 John MacDougall Stuart reached the geographical bull's-eye of Australia, near Alice Springs, and later attained the northern tip of the continent.

---

boxed in Sydney Cove, seemed a hopeless barrier. Every attempt to break through the labyrinth of steep valleys failed. Then in 1813, an unconventional idea struck the explorers Gregory Blaxland, William Wentworth and William Lawson: they would try the high road, crossing the peaks rather than the vales. And it worked. On the far side of the Blue Mountains they discovered a land of plenty, endless plains that would support a great new society.

Other explorers—mostly surveyors, army men and eager colonists, with

Age of Gold

A rancher named Edward Hargraves was understandably overwrought when he declared: "This is a memorable day in the history of New South Wales. I shall be a baronet. You will be knighted, and my old horse will be stuffed, put in a glass case, and sent to the British Museum."

The scene was near Bathurst, some 200 km (130 miles) west of Sydney, the date 1851. Hargraves' audience consisted of one speechless fellow traveller, his guide. The occasion was the discovery of gold in Australia. Hargraves named the place Ophir, after the site of

Nowadays non-claustrophobic tourists can take the plunge into a gold mine that once boomed in Kalgoorlie.

a phenomenal gold strike in the days of King Solomon.

Within months of the Ophir bonanza, prospectors from Melbourne struck gold at Ballarat. The news that two colonies—New South Wales and Victoria—were booming triggered an invasion of adventurers from Europe and America. Among them were Australians who had tried to get rich in California's '49er stampede. By 1860 Australia's population had reached one million. Thirty-three years later the celebration—madness, really—spread from coast to coast as gold was discovered in Kalgoorlie, Western Australia.

Life in the gold-fields was rugged, aggravated by lack of water, the climate, the flies and the tax collectors. Whether big winners or, more likely, small losers, all the diggers had to pay the same licence fee. Enforcement and fines were needlessly strict. Justice, the miners felt, was tilted against them. They burned their licences and demonstrated for voting rights and other reforms. In the subsequent siege of the Eureka Stockade at Ballarat in 1854, troops were ordered to attack the demonstrators. There was heavy loss of life. The licence fee was abandoned.

Another riot, in 1861, pitted the white prospectors against Chinese miners, who were resented for their foreignness, for working too hard and spending too little. At Lambing Flat, New South Wales, thousands of whites whipped and clubbed a community of Chinese. Police, troops and finally the courts dealt leniently with the aggressors. It was the worst of several race riots. With the tensions of the gold rush, the notion of the yellow peril was embedded in Australia's national consciousness.

Transportation of convicts finally ended in 1868, when London had to admit that the threat of exile to golden Australia was no deterrent to crime.

In Australia itself, crime was always something of a problem. Nobody really expected every last sinner to reform as soon as he arrived. Some wily characters, often escaped convicts, became bushrangers, the local version of highwaymen. They occasionally attracted sympathy from Outback folk because they tended to rob the rich and flout authority. As the crimes grew more ambitious or outrageous, the fame of the bushrangers captured the Australian imagination. Among the big names in creative thuggery: Matthew Brady, Martin Cash, Ben Hall, but above all Ned Kelly, a cattle rustler who became a national legend.

The New Century

With the blessing of Queen Victoria, the colonies of Australia formed a new nation, the Commonwealth of Australia, on New Year's Day, 1901. This federation retained the Queen as head of state, and bowed as well to the parliament and privy council in London.

Loyalty to the British Empire was tested twice, extravagantly, in the world wars. The Allied defeat at Gallipoli in 1915 was the first and the most memorable single disaster for the gallant "diggers". By the end of World War I, more than 200,000 Australians—two-thirds of the entire expeditionary force—had been killed or wounded. The death rate was the highest in the empire.

The Worst War

Although the battles were fought on the other side of the world, Australia suffered far more in World War I than in any other conflict.

Patriotism was never more fervent. A day before Britain's declaration of war on Germany in August 1914, Australia offered the motherland an expeditionary force. Less than three months later, Australian and New Zealand troops sailed to combat. On 25 April 1915, the Anzacs landed at Gallipoli, a key to the Dardanelles. Doomed by bungled planning and keen defences, the operation killed about 8,000 Australians and wounded another 20,000. Later, the survivors were deployed in the trenches of France, where casualties were even heavier but less dramatic.

However, it wasn't all one-sided. In retaliation against the enemy, the Nomenclature Act of 1917 changed the name of the Australian town of Kaiserstuhl to Mount Kitchener, Hahnsdorf to Ambleside, and Germantown Hill to Vimy Ridge.

The combat came closer in World War II, when Japanese planes bombed Darwin 64 times, enemy submarines penetrated Sydney harbour, and invasion was perceived as a very real threat. Australians were reassured when American General Douglas MacArthur, chased from the Philippines, established his headquarters here to organize the counter-attack. Nearly a million Australians went to war but casualties were far lower than in World War I. Poignantly, nearly one in three Australians held prisoner by the Japanese died in captivity.

Postwar Australia was transformed. Psychologically involved with Asia at last, feeling vulnerable, Australia grew

dependent on the United States rather than Britain. ANZUS, a defensive alliance of Australia, New Zealand and the United States, was founded in 1951.

Sharing the anticommunist stance of the US, Australia sent land, air and sea forces—40 per cent of them conscripts—to fight alongside the Americans in Vietnam. The involvement lasted from 1965 until 1972. Mirroring the American experience, it was a painful era of bitter divisions on the home front.

The tilt towards Asia and America showed up, as well, in the trade balance. Before World War II, Britain accounted for 42 per cent of Australia's overseas trade. In recent times, the entire European Community is down to second or third place in the commercial charts, behind the US or Japan or both.

A Cosmopolitan Country

Another obvious change in orientation is the racial and national background of Australians. Before World War II, 98 per cent of the population was British born or of British descent.

Every 25 April, Australian patriots commemorate the disastrous Anzac landing at Gallipoli in World War I.

After the war, throngs of Greeks, Yugoslavs, Italians and northern Europeans settled in Australia; more than 10 per cent of immigrants were refugees or displaced persons. The fortress walls of the "White Australia" immigration policy, enacted in 1901 to maintain racial purity, stood firm for well over half a century. But now the Asian presence, swelled by more than 100,000 boat people and other southeast Asian refugees, has begun to reflect the strength of trade ties with Australia's neighbours.

Policy towards the Aborigines softened as well. As recently as 1960,

Cranes on the Perth skyline: the 1980s property boom added daring new buildings, but in most cities too many offices remained unsold and unoccupied.

Australia's first settlers were finally granted citizenship and social service benefits. While the Aborigines struggled for land rights, the government intensified efforts to overcome their disadvantages in health, wealth and education, with few visible results. Aborigines mainly now live in cities.

In the usual cut and thrust of politics, prime ministers of right and left came and went, but two of them departed dramatically. In 1967 Harold Holt vanished while swimming off the coast of Victoria. In 1975, in a profound constitutional crisis, Gough Whitlam was deposed by the governor-general, Sir John Kerr.

In the 1980s and into the '90s, international and domestic economic difficulties darkened the abiding Australian dream of boundless prosperity, and unfinished and unoccupied skyscrapers troubled the cityscapes. Tightened belts had been out of fashion since hunger gnawed at the First Fleet, but the government turned to unpopular austerity measures to ride out the crisis. With more than two centuries of pioneering spirit behind them, the new Australians have placed their bets on natural resources like sunshine and friendly charm, aiming for a snowballing success in the area of international tourism.

Facts and Figures

Geography: area 7,682,300 km² (2,966,250 square miles), about the size of the continental United States, between the Pacific and Indian Oceans. Nearest neighbours: Indonesia, Papua New Guinea, Solomons, Fiji and New Zealand. Highest point: Mount Kosciusko, 2,228 m (7,316 ft); lowest: Lake Eyre, 16 m (39 ft) below sea level.

Population: about 16.5 million, mostly settled in cities along the coastal plains. One person in four is either an immigrant or the child of an immigrant. Less than 2 per cent of the population is Aboriginal, of whom two-thirds live in cities or towns.

Capital: Canberra (population 280,000).

Major Cities: Sydney (3.4 million), Melbourne (2.9 million), Brisbane (1.2 million), Adelaide (993,000), Perth (1 million).

Government: Democratic federal constitutional monarchy: Queen Elizabeth II is formally Queen of Australia, represented by a governor-general. Federal government is headed by the prime minister, who is leader of the elected parliamentary majority. Other levels of government: state governments and legislatures, and municipal administrations. There are six states plus two mainland territories—the Australian Capital Territory (ACT) and the Northern Territory, which has been self-governing since 1978. Voting in federal elections is compulsory for everyone except the Aborigines, who can choose whether or not to register. If they register, they are obliged to vote.

Economy: strongest in agriculture and mining, Australia is a leading exporter of beef, lamb, wool, wheat, gold, bauxite, nickel, coal, iron ore. Inflation, unemployment and the balance of trade give cause for concern.

Religion: more than three-quarters of Australians who claim a religion are Christians, mostly Anglicans and Roman Catholics. There are also significant Islamic, Jewish and Buddhist communities.

Language: English with colourful antipodal embroidery.

Historical Landmarks

Dreamtime

40,000 BC   Aboriginal people, Stone Age migrants from Asia, inhabit the Australian continent, developing traditions of a society that survives by hunting, fishing and gathering food.

Discoveries

c. AD 1600   European explorers sight *Terra Australis Incognita* but are unimpressed.

1606   Willem Jansz makes first known landing.

1642   Dutch navigator Abel Tasman discovers and names Van Diemen's Land (Tasmania) and Statenland (New Zealand).

Settlement

1770   Captain Cook explores east coast of Australia, names it New South Wales and claims it for King George III.

1788   First Fleet establishes British penal colony at Sydney Cove.

1793   Free settlers begin to arrive. Estimated Aboriginal population of 300,000 forced to make way for colonists.

1808   Rum Rebellion overthrows the governor, Captain William Bligh.

1813   Explorers Blaxland, Wentworth and Lawson cross the Blue Mountains.

1823   John Oxley discovers Brisbane River; 2 years later Brisbane is founded.

1828   In the first census, 36,000 free settlers and convicts are counted.

Age of Gold

1851   Edward Hargraves discovers gold near Bathurst in New South Wales; 6 months later, gold is found at Ballarat.

1854   Conflicts between miners and Ballarat authorities touch off Eureka riot.

1860   Population reaches 1 million.

1861   Anti-Chinese riots in gold-fields.

1868   British government ends transportation of convicts to Australia.

1899   Australian troops sent to South Africa to fight in the Boer War.

New Century

1901   Commonwealth of Australia proclaimed on New Year's Day.

1908   Canberra chosen as site for a new federal capital.

1911   Canberra designed by American architect Burley Griffin; building begins.

1914–18   Australia joins Allies in World War I, suffering very heavy losses in Gallipoli and in France.

1917   Transcontinental railway opened.

1920   First airline service begins.

1927   Seat of government is moved from Melbourne to Canberra.

1942–45   In World War II Japanese bomb Darwin and other coastal towns, threaten invasion. Australian forces count 35,000 dead.

Nuclear Era

1953   British atomic weapons tested in the South Australian desert.

1960   Australia grants citizenship to Aborigines; 2 years later they get vote.

1965   Australian troops, including conscripts, sent to fight in Vietnam War.

1972   "White Australia" immigration policy abandoned.

1988   Bicentennial celebrations with counter-demonstrations by Aborigines; Queen Elizabeth II opens new Parliament House in Canberra.

1990   Airline deregulation: new competition stimulates tourism.

1991   Economy hits worst level since the Great Depression.

Just the Essentials

Our choice of the really best places to go throughout Australia is, inevitably, subjective, but it may help you decide on an itinerary. In view of the vast distances, chances are you'll stick to two or three of these little packages of ideas, but they can be combined and re-combined to fit your priorities, the season, and the time and money at your disposal.

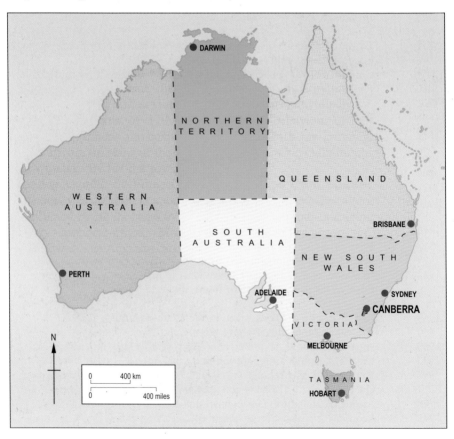

Sydney
The harbour: a dream setting
The Bridge: still in business and
  looking good
The Opera House: a touch of class
The Rocks: history and distractions
Darling Harbour: mostly for fun

Farther Afield in NSW
Blue Mountains: forests, cliffs and
  caves
Hunter Valley: wine among rolling
  hills
Snowy Mountains: wild flowers or
  skiing
Lightning Ridge: black opal
  bonanza
Broken Hill: prospectors and artists

Canberra
Lake Burley Griffin: artificial but
  lovely
Botanic Gardens: 6,000 Aussie
  species
War Memorial: 100,000 memories
National Gallery: from prehistoric
  to modern art
Parliament House: low-rise grandeur

Queensland
Brisbane: skyscrapers and swagger
Gold Coast: surfers in funland
Sunshine Coast: beachy relaxation
Great Barrier Reef: miraculous
  playground
Tropical Queensland: canefields
  and rainforest

Northern Territory
Darwin: disaster-proof optimism
Kakadu National Park: crocodiles
  and the Louvre of Aboriginal art
Katherine Gorge: torrents and
  whirlpools
Alice Springs: pioneers and dream-
  ers
Ayers Rock: sacred and inspiring

Western Australia
Perth: handsome riverside "city of
  lights"
Fremantle: yachts and freighters,
  quaintly
Wave Rock: a surfer's dream in
  stone
The Pinnacles: pillars in the desert
South-west WA: forests, flowers
  and beaches
Kalgoorlie: gold-rush memories

South Australia
Adelaide: culture and the good life
Port Adelaide: one big maritime
  museum
Barossa Valley: cozy villages and
  vineyards
Kangaroo Island: koalas, emus, too
Coober Pedy: opals at world's end

Melbourne
Yarra River: reflecting skyscrapers
Victorian Arts Centre: culture un-
  der a spire
Collins Street: shopping in style
Royal Botanic Gardens: 13,000
  varieties
Toorak: suburban elegance

Farther Afield in Victoria:
Dandenong Ranges: forests to
  vineyards
Phillip Island: mini-penguins on
  parade
Ballarat: rich in gold-rush relics
South-west coast: not just the
  breathtaking views

Tasmania
Hobart: harbour of history and
  charm
Port Arthur: pioneering cruelty
  revisited
Launceston: rose bushes and cannon balls
Mount Field National Park:
  wilderness that's accessible

Going Places with Something Special in Mind

Most excursions, aiming for the lowest common denominator, offer a flash of exotic scenery, a dash of history and a rash of statistics and superlatives. Real people, though, have their own interests, which don't necessarily fit the pattern. The things they want to see may not be better or more logical, just different. To supplement or supplant the standard itineraries around Australia, you might prefer pursuing your own themes—nostalgia or art or a hobby. The individual twists are infinite, from plantations to platypuses, from shipwrecks to sheepshearing. Here, scattered around the continent, are some themes and variations, to prompt your own planning.

Awesome Rocks

Long before the Sydney district of The Rocks was named, Australia's geological convulsions had thrown up some fantastic rock formations of world renown. Here's a check-list of the most evocative, from north to south:

1 THE OLGAS (NT)
Like a scattering of sleeping elephants, taller than Ayers Rock.

*A*ustralia's beaches are just one of many attractions that you can discover.

2 AYERS ROCK (NT)
This is the paragon of symbolic, sacred rocks.

3 THE PINNACLES (WA)
A myriad of limestone pillars jutting from the desert.

4 WAVE ROCK (WA)
A freak formation recalling a surfer's dream.

5 THREE SISTERS (NSW)
Legends inevitably surround the Blue Mountains landmark.

6 HANGING ROCK (VIC.)
The spooky rock that inspired a memorable Australian film.

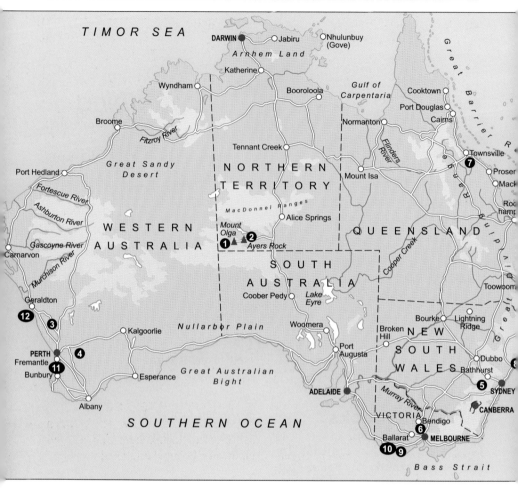

*A*ustralia's best rock formations (1–6) and places with a shipwreck history (7–12).

Shipwrecks

Mainland Australia's coastline of 33,535 km (20,825 miles) is not all beaches. The reefs, rocks and cliffs have always attracted shipwrecks. Most evidence has been recycled by the raging waves, but here and there relics of inopportune landfalls are visible.

7 TOWNSVILLE (QLD)
Divers take day-trips to the wreck of the *Yongala*, a passenger liner inhabited by fish since 1911.

8 NEWCASTLE (NSW)
The barque *Adolphe*, which perished here in 1904, is partly visible in the Stockton breakwater.

9 WARRNAMBOOL (VIC.)
Flagstaff Hill museum displays the Loch Arde Peacock and other testimonies to disasters.

84

10 PORT FAIRY (VIC.)
A "shipwreck walk" shows tourists the last resting places of doomed ships.

11 FREMANTLE (WA)
Shipwrecks ashore in the Maritime Museum, starring the *Batavia*, lost in 1629.

12 GERALDTON (WA)
Relics of old Dutch wrecks in the local Maritime Museum.

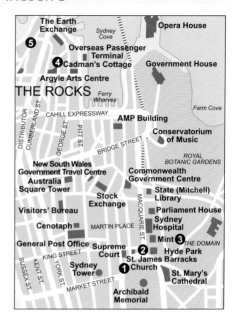

Some colonial landmarks in Sydney.

Colonial Sydney

Governor Lachlan Macquarie (1762–1824) was the administrator who transformed New South Wales from a prison camp to a colony on the way to self-rule. Remarkable for his humanity and energy, he built roads and buildings that were worthy of posterity. A few Macquarie-era landmarks still standing in Sydney:

1 ST JAMES'S CHURCH
The convict-architect Francis Greenway, pardoned by Macquarie, planned this gracefully steepled Georgian church, Sydney's first.

2 HYDE PARK BARRACKS
A stately three-storey dormitory, also by Greenway, designed to keep the convicts off the streets.

3 MINT MUSEUM
One wing of what was originally (1816) Macquarie's "Rum Hospital".

4 THE ROCKS
Cadman's Cottage (1816) is called the oldest house in Australia.

5 HERO OF WATERLOO
A working pub since 1815, when sailors who drank here had a good chance of being shanghaied.

Darwin Wildlife

Animal oddities crop up all around Australia, from the gregarious dolphins of Monkey Mia (WA) to the platypuses of Eungella National Park (QLD) Here are a few living curiosities to look forward to in and near Darwin:

DARWIN: AQUASCENE
Feeding the fish as you've never fed them before—knee-deep in the hungry maelstrom!

DARWIN: INDO-PACIFIC MARINE
Aquatic wonders, including living coral under glass.

EAST OF DARWIN
In the bush: "magnetic anthills"—termite mounds taller than humans.

REPTILE WORLD
Snakes, lizards and other lovelies.

RIVER QUEEN
Boat trip to visit jumping crocodiles.

CROCODILE FARM
On the Stuart Highway, more than 7,000 crocs to glare at you.

TERRITORY WILDLIFE PARK
Rabbit-eared bandicoots, dingoes, birds and fish.

NSW Fossicking

This distinctively Australian word means searching for something, but more specifically scratching about in likely terrain for gold or precious stones. Not surprisingly, most of the likely sites of mineral bonanzas are far from civilization. Here are some New South Wales fossicking spots where tourists are catered for:

1 WHITE CLIFFS
The tourist office arranges opal fossicking expeditions; some visitors decide to stay.

2 LIGHTNING RIDGE
Areas abandoned by the professionals have been assigned to tourists eager to fossick for black opal.

3 GLEN INNES
Sapphire, emerald, topaz: the tourist office has licences and maps for budding prospectors to go out and try their luck.

4 OPHIR
Gold was discovered here in 1851; fossickers hope some is left over.

Gaols

Considering that Australia began as a penal colony, it's not surprising that some of the country's most interesting historic monuments are jails. Here are some sturdy 19th-century relics you can see in the oldest state, New South Wales:

5 GRAFTON
An escaped convict may have been the town's first settler, but the jail came much later, in 1893.

6 SOUTH WEST ROCKS
Constructed 1886 as a clifftop rehabilitation centre, the institution held German internees during World War I.

7 MAITLAND
This Hunter Valley town has an 1889 jail, constructed by convicts.

8 BERRIMA
In 1839 convicts built their own jail in this charming Georgian village.

9 HAY
Since the 1970s the old jail, which housed everybody from mental cases to POWs, has been a museum.

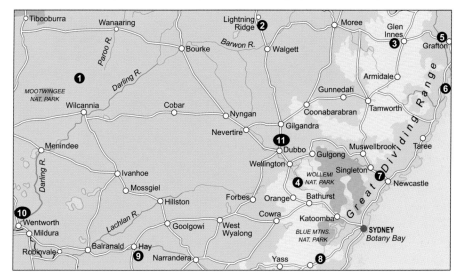

10 WENTWORTH
More than a million bricks were used in construction of the jail (1879).

11 DUBBO
Gallows and all, the old jail has been a museum since the 1960s.

More Top Gaols
Tasmania, the original prison island, is clearly the place for specialists in historic gaols, but in cities all over the mainland you can visit some impressive penal monuments.

1 DARWIN
Fanny Bay Gaol: founded 1883, scene of a double-header hanging in 1952.

2 ALICE SPRINGS
Old Stuart Town Gaol: oldest building in town, dated 1907.

3 MELBOURNE
Old Melbourne Gaol: built 1841, its gallows served more than 100 prisoners, including Ned Kelly.

Where to go fossicking (1–4) and to see those old 19th-century gaols (5–11) in New South Wales.

4 ADELAIDE
Adelaide Gaol: begun 1841, closed 1988; 45 hangings.

5 YORK (WA)
Attached to the court-house; prisoners' graffiti preserved.

6 FREMANTLE (WA)
Round House: built 1831, mostly for lesser criminals.

7 PERTH
Built 1856, now part of the Museum of Western Australia complex.

8 DERBY (WA)
Prison Tree: transient prisoners were accommodated in a huge hollow-trunked boab tree.

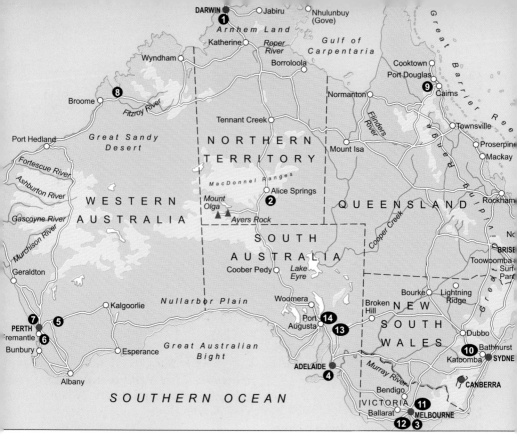

Vintage Trains

Railway enthusiasts who long for the wail of a steam whistle and the chug of a straining locomotive can find nostalgia well served in Australia. All aboard the vintage trains!

9 KURANDA (QLD)
The narrow-gauge line from Cairns to Kuranda, finished in 1891, forges through gorges and rainforest for 34 km (21 miles) of thrills. Daily.

10 LITHGOW (NSW)
Just for tourists, the 1868 Zigzag line runs on weekends and during school holidays.

11 BELGRAVE (VIC.)
A highlight of the Dandenong Ranges,

*S*ome more gaols (1–8) throughout Australia and where to catch a steam train (9–14).

"Puffing Billy" started narrow-gauge passenger operations in 1900. Operates daily.

12 QUEENSCLIFF (VIC.)
The Bellarine Peninsula Railway operates its old steam trains to Drysdale on Sundays, public holidays and during school holiday season.

13 PETERBOROUGH (SA)
The narrow-gauge line to Orroroo and Eurelia runs seasonally, but you can visit the Steamtown railway museum anytime.

14 QUORN (SA)
The Pichi Richi Railway, on a tourist schedule, follows a rugged part of the original Ghan's route—43 km (27 miles) round trip.

Historical Brisbane

Chain gangs built Brisbane, the penal colony designed for convicts too tough for New South Wales. Few of the early buildings are left, but in the shadow of the skyscrapers you can still find historic stones.

1 OLD WINDMILL
It failed to work on wind power, so offenders were exercised on treadmills to grind the grain.

2 ALL SAINTS CHURCH
Dating from the 1860s, this Anglican church is noted for its stained-glass windows.

3 ST JOHN'S CATHEDRAL
Gothic style for a 20th-century cathedral, still unfinished; the bells are older than the church.

4 ST STEPHEN'S CATHEDRAL
The Catholics called on the same architect who designed All Saints.

5 QUEENSLAND CLUB
Verandahed classic from the 1880s in splendid gardens.

6 PARLIAMENT HOUSE
Stately French Renaissance-style building in which the Queensland parliament first met in 1868.

7 OLD COMMISSARIAT STORES
Convicts built the first two floors; free men raised the roof 85 years later.

Captain Cook

In 1770 Captain James Cook (a lieutenant at the time) set foot on the east coast of Australia. He liked what he found, named it New South Wales and claimed it for his king. Traces of the great explorer can still be discovered.

1 MELBOURNE
Captain Cook's Cottage, reconstituted in Fitzroy Gardens.

2 SYDNEY: BOTANY BAY
The discovery site: museum and monuments and markers.

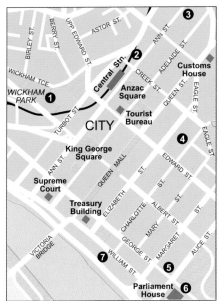

A selection of Brisbane's more historic sights.

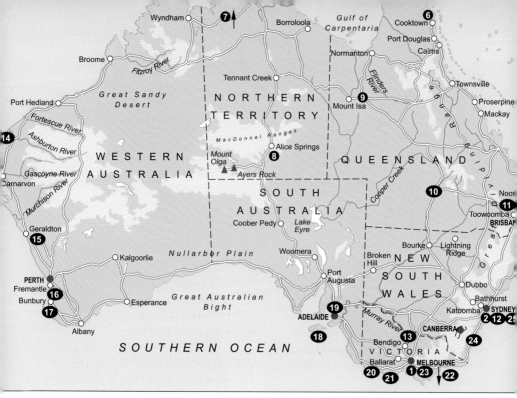

Air Pioneers

A *selection of tributes to Captain Cook (1–6), the great air pioneers (7–13) and some other seafarers (14–26).*

The great distances between pockets of civilization have always given aviation a vital role in Australian life. From bush pilots to cross-country commuters, everyone enjoys the legacy of the daring, far-seeing pioneers. Museums and monuments pay tribute.

3 CAPE BYRON (NSW)
Cook named it after the poet's grandfather; view from Cook Lookout.

4 TWEED HEADS (NSW)
Stupendous Cook monument-cum-lighthouse at Point Danger (well named by Cook) on Queensland border.

5 CALOUNDRA (QLD)
Replica of Cook's ship, *Endeavour* at Seafarers Wharf.

6 COOKTOWN (QLD)
The James Cook Historical Museum shows how the *Endeavour* was beached here, and the aftermath.

7 DARWIN
Aviation Museum, on the edge of the airport: vintage planes and engines plus a B-52 bomber.

8 ALICE SPRINGS (NT)
Aviation Museum on site of the town's first airport: famous wrecks and relics of the pioneers.

9 CLONCURRY (QLD)
Memorial on the site of the first base (1928) of Royal Flying Doctor Service.

10 CHARLEVILLE (QLD)
A plaque at the airport commemorates the first Qantas flight, which took off from here in 1922.

11 BRISBANE
Southern Cross, in which Charles Kingsford Smith flew across the Pacific in 1928, stands in its own hangar of honour at the Brisbane airport.

12 SYDNEY
Heroic vintage planes hang from the ceiling in the Powerhouse Museum.

13 WANGARATTA (VIC.)
At Airworld, see flimsy pioneer airplanes, or sign up for a sightseeing flight in an original Tiger Moth.

Old Salts

You don't have to be a seafarer to see the drama in a lonely lighthouse, or to find fascination in old ships. Australia's coasts are well supplied with such monuments and maritime museums. A sampler:

14 VLAMING HEAD (WA)
North of Exmouth, a sturdy lighthouse (built in 1912) marks the tip of North West Cape.

15 GERALDTON (WA)
Maritime museum with relics of ancient wrecks, and the unsuccessful prototoype of a minisubmarine for fishermen.

16 FREMANTLE (WA)
Beautifully reconstituted wreck of the *Batavia* and other ocean lore.

17 BUNBURY (WA)
A black-and-white-checked lighthouse blinks a warning to ships 27 km (17 miles) away.

18 KANGAROO ISLAND (SA)
Cape Willoughby light dates from 1852, Cape Borda from 1858.

19 PORT ADELAIDE (SA)
You can climb the spiral stairway of the 1869 lighthouse. Below, exhibits of the South Australia Maritime Museum sprawl over three sites.

20 WARRNAMBOOL (VIC.)
At Flagstaff Hill, an 1853 lighthouse and a maritime museum reflecting 19th-century courage and despair.

21 CAPE OTWAY (VIC.)
An 1848 lighthouse atop a 100-m (more than 320-ft) cliff; nearby, a cemetery with a view—for lighthouse-keepers and shipwreck victims.

22 HOBART (TAS.)
Tasmania's maritime museum, in historic Secheron House, features photos and relics.

23 MELBOURNE
A square-rigger from the late 19th century sets the tone for a maritime museum.

24 JERVIS BAY (ACT)
The remains of the 19th-century Cape St George lighthouse, built in the wrong place. Navy guns finished it off.

25 SYDNEY
At Darling Harbour, the Australian National Maritime Museum covers all

aspects of exploration, trade, war and fun on the high seas.

26 BRISBANE

Queensland Maritime Museum displays models and relics, with a few floating exhibits outside the door.

The Kelly Saga

Ned Kelly, outlaw and folk hero, made an indelible mark on the Australian consciousness. The paramount bushranger operated near the border of Victoria and New South Wales. Some souvenirs:

1 JERILDERIE (NSW)

Kelly held the whole town hostage in 1879; details in the Telegraph Office Museum.

2 BEECHWORTH (VIC.)

The courthouse where Kelly stood trial, and the gaol where he was kept twice.

3 GLENROWAN (VIC.)

The Ned Kelly Memorial Museum

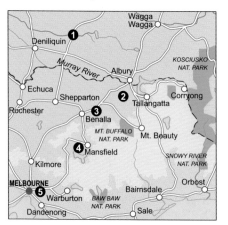

documents the local lad who won eternal fame at a heavy cost in lives. He took this town hostage, too.

4 MANSFIELD (VIC.)

A marble monument commemorates three slain mounted policemen among Kelly's victims.

5 MELBOURNE

Old Melbourne Gaol was Kelly's last stop; see the gallows.

Mining Tours

The Outback provides the minerals that keep the Australian economy ticking over. To see the complexity of it all, you can stop by one of these huge installations for a conducted tour if you're in the neighbourhood.

1 MT. ISA (QLD)

Silver, copper, lead and zinc are produced here; underground and surface tours.

2 NEWMAN (WA)

Iron ore in mind-boggling volume is shipped by rail from here to Port Headland; the company offers tours of the site.

3 OLYMPIC DAM (SA)

The management offers visitors a two-hour surface tour of this sprawling source of copper, uranium, gold and silver.

*T*he Ned Kelly connection in south-east Australia.

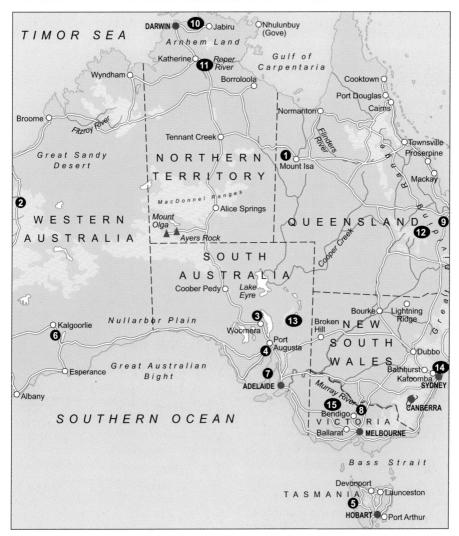

*P*laces offering a mining tour *(1–9)* and where to see those wonderful examples of Aboriginal art *(10–15).*

4 WHYALLA (SA)
In "Steel City", there are tours of the BHP steelworks and of the iron mining operations.

5 QUEENSTOWN (TAS.)
Gold gave way to copper, still profitable at the Mt. Lyell mine, with tours at least once a day.

Defunct Mines

6 KALGOORLIE (WA)
Retired miners guide visitors through the exhausted labyrinths of the fabulous Hinault Gold Mine.

7 MOONTA (SA)
A tourist train surveys what was the country's richest copper mine.

8 BENDIGO (VIC.)
Surface or underground tours of the old Central Deborah gold mine.

9 MT. MORGAN (QLD)
Tours look over this whopping crater, source of a historic bonanza of gold, silver, copper, etc.

Aboriginal Sites

Museums all around the country deal with Aboriginal art, but there's no substitute for seeing it on the spot, on the walls of caves or cliffs. Primitive or surprisingly sophisticated, ritual paintings and engravings are on view, relatively accessibly, in national parks. A few suggestions:

10 KAKADU (NT)
Bonanza of rock art, ancient and modern, at hundreds of locations; park rangers lead art appreciation tours.

11 KATHERINE GORGE (NT)
Boat excursions point out paintings of animals high above flood level.

12 CARNARVON (QLD)
Hikers can see great galleries of Aboriginal wall carvings and paintings.

13 FLINDERS RANGES (SA)
Several sites of rock paintings (but avoid summer heat).

14 KU-RING-GAI CHASE (NSW)
Just a short hop from Sydney, a site which has hundreds of rock carvings easily reached.

15 GRAMPIANS (VIC.)
Dozens of sites, of which several are signposted and easily accessible.

Kitschorama

Only a masochistic sociologist would plan an itinerary covering outstanding examples of dubious taste. But Kitsch is part of the Australian scenery, and culture. Here are a few of the excesses to look out for.

NAMBOUR (QLD)
The Big Pineapple, gigantic fibreglass trademark of a plantation-cum-tourist centre.

COFFS HARBOUR (NSW)
The Big Banana, fronting for a plantation, is big enough to walk through.

GOULBURN (NSW)
Inside the Big Merino, a sheep as tall as a three-storey house, you can study the art of sheepshearing.

MEREDITH (VIC.)
What's claimed to be the world's largest egg draws attention to the Happy Hens, a tourist complex.

BERRI (SA)
Inside the Big Orange are regional exhibits.

GUMACHERA (SA)
The Big Rocking Horse, with three observation platforms, has a toy shop below.

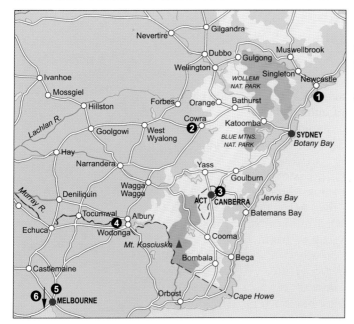

Sites in the south-east with World War II connections.

KINGSTON SE (SA)
The Big Lobster, grossly magnified with claws and all, houses restaurants and a souvenir shop.

War in the South-East

In World War II, Darwin, Broome and other northerly targets were bombed and a Japanese invasion seemed probable. There are relics and monuments all over the threatened areas. Less predictably, the traces of war reach as far as the south-east.

1 NEWCASTLE (NSW)
Fort Scratchley: see the only naval guns to have fired in anger—at a Japanese submarine, which promptly withdrew.

2 COWRA (NSW)
A monument marks the site of a prison camp for Japanese POWs, scene of a disastrous mass escape attempt; a Japanese war cemetery is nearby.

3 CANBERRA
Names of all the war dead inscribed in the War Memorial; symbolic Australian-American Memorial, hailing the wartime alliance.

4 WANGARATTA (VIC.)
Airworld: a collection of vintage planes, including a Hudson bomber still in airworthy condition.

5 MELBOURNE
Shrine of Remembrance includes World War II section.

6 PORTSEA (VIC.)
The first salvo of the war is said to have been fired here, across the bows of an unidentified ship; the target, unfortunately, was Australian.

Animal Oddities

You wouldn't travel the 385 km (240 miles) from Sydney to Gundagai just to see the statue of a dog, but it's right on your way to Wagga Wagga anyway. A small herd of animal curiosities, inanimate, that you might stumble on:

GUNDAGAI (NSW)
A stubborn, uncouth dog who sabotaged his master "five miles from Gundagai" is celebrated in bush ballads and in sculpture east of town.

CORRIGIN (WA)
Five km (3 miles) west of town, a cemetery for sheepdogs: herdsmen remember faithful friends with loving inscriptions.

TANTANOOLA (SA)
In 1899 a farmer shot an Assyrian wolfhound thinking it was a tiger. The bizarre predator, stuffed, is on view in the Tantanoola Tiger Hotel.

MELBOURNE
Also under glass: Phar Lap, Australia's greatest racehorse, in the National Museum.

Wine Routes

Every Australian state—even the Northern Territory—makes wine, and several states have enough vineyards in a single area to make wine-tasting expeditions feasible. In Europe each region has its own species of grapes and specialities, whereas Australian regions do a bit of everything. Serious connoisseurs should consult the tourist boards for much more complete information. But here are some starters.

Barossa Valley (SA)
Perhaps 10 per cent of the nation's wine comes from this delightfully scenic area. The big wineries offer tours, the small ones cellar-door tastings.

GAWLER
Once called "Athens of the North" for its stately buildings.

LYNDOCH
Small, hospitable family wineries surround the town.

TANUNDA
A traditional German town noted for good food and wine.

NURIOOTPA
Biggest Barossa town (pop. nearly 3,000), home of giant Penfolds and Kaiser Stuhl wineries.

ANGASTON
Historic town, home of wineries dating from mid-19th century.

Hunter Valley (NSW)
Rolling hills within day-trip distance of Sydney provide the setting for intensive wine production—everything from whites and reds to bubblies and brandies.

CESSNOCK
Coal mining and wine-making are the foundation for Cessnock's success. The local tourist board issues a most useful wine-lover's guide.

POKOLBIN
Centre of some 20 wineries—small family affairs as well as producers owned by international conglomerates. Some have tourist-friendly tasting facilities.

ROTHBURY
Cellar-door sales at a couple of family-owned wineries.

ALLANDALE
A chance to visit a couple more of the small, family-owned wineries.

Swan Valley (WA)
They've been making wine here for 150 years or more. This close to Perth, a wine-tasting expedition is essentially a suburban survey. There are boat excursions up the Swan River, or you can drive. Between drinks, drop in at the museums and wildlife parks.

SOUTH GUILDFORD
Founded 1829, Olive Farm is a historic monument that works; tours can be arranged.

CAVERSHAM
Several family-owned wineries; the big Sandalford establishment was founded 1840.

WEST SWAN
Little River Wines produces reds, whites, ports, etc.

HENLEY BROOK
Evans & Tate is the big name here.

MILLENDON
Several family-owned cellars; Lamont has a restaurant on the premises.

HERNE HILL
Several more family-run establishments.

MIDDLE SWAN
Houghton Wines, founded 1836, in a beautiful setting, has tours.

History for Kids

All over Australia are tempting attractions for children, often involving animals or water—giant water slides and koala parks, for instance. There are also some re-creations of history to stimulate young minds.

WAUCHOPE (NSW)
Timbertown is a fascinating reconstructed sawmill complex from the 1880s.

GOSFORD (NSW)
Old Sydney Town: street theatre in a reconstituted colonial Sydney.

CANBERRA
Bywong Town: a gold-mining village revived.

BALLARAT (VIC.)
Sovereign Hill: re-creation of a gold rush township, horses and all.

SWAN HILL (VIC.)
Pioneer Settlement: a Murray River town as it looked in the heyday of paddle-steamers.

ARMADALE (WA)
Pioneer World: here you will find a re-creation of colonial shops, workshops; gold panning, too.

Memorable Pubs

It took decades before Australian beer evolved from the tepid English model into the icy refresher so much appreciated today. Some of the old pubs, historic monuments by now, are still dispensing rivers of hospitality.

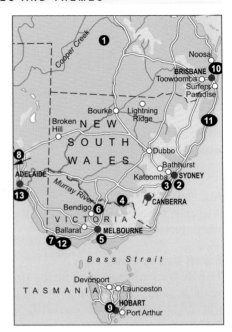

1 BIRDSVILLE (QLD)
Hundreds of kilometres from anywhere, the Birdsville Hotel, built in 1885, is no mirage.

2 SYDNEY
Lord Nelson Hotel has been in business since 1842; the Hero of Waterloo is slightly newer.

3 BERRIMA (NSW)
Dated 1834, the Surveyor-General is rich in atmosphere.

4 ALBURY (NSW)
Cheating, but fun: the Ettamogah Pub is a reconstitution of a mad fictional pub.

5 MELBOURNE
A notorious nude painting has enlivened Young & Jackson's pub since 1880.

6 BENDIGO (VIC.)
The Shamrock, restored from Victorian boom times.

7 PORT FAIRY (VIC.)
The Caledonian has been operating since 1844.

8 PORT LINCOLN (SA)
First pub on the Eyre peninsula, the Caledonian (1844).

Some of Australia's old pubs (1–9) and lookout points for whales (10–13).

9 NEW NORFOLK (TAS.)
The Bush Inn (1825) claims to be the oldest licensed hotel in the country.

Watching Whales

Humpback whales spend the summer feeding in the Antarctic, returning to warmer Australian waters in winter for calving. The migration routes come close to shore in some regions, offering yet another sightseeing opportunity, in season. Among lookout points:

10 HERVEY BAY (QLD)
Between August and October excursion boats are despatched on whale-watching expeditions.

11 CAPE BYRON (NSW)
In June and July whale-spotters convene here to count the migrating humpbacks.

12 WARRNAMBOOL (VIC.)
A lookout spot on Logan Beach provides pictures and diagrams to aid whale-watching

13 VICTOR HARBOR (SA)
Initially a whaling station, Victor has become a favourite resort for whales and whale-watchers.

Melbourne Gardens

Colour Melbourne green—the parks and gardens, and trams that match. The city has some sumptuous breathing spaces. Take a break.

1 FLAGSTAFF GARDENS
Lookouts here used to signal the arrival of a ship.

Relax in some of Melbourne's gardens.

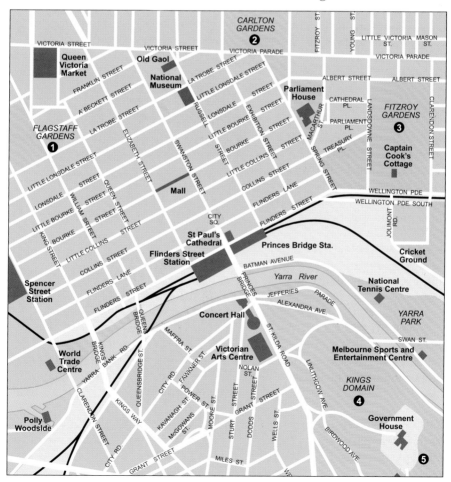

2 CARLTON GARDENS
Memories of the Great Exhibition of 1880, held here.

3 FITZROY GARDENS
Trees from northern and southern hemispheres shade Melbourne's first park, begun in 1857.

4 KINGS DOMAIN
Acres of lawns surround Melbourne's first government house, also Shrine of Remembrance and other monuments.

5 ROYAL BOTANIC GARDENS
Lovely landscaping accentuates the beauty of thousands of species on show.

Caves

Spelunkers can choose from a varied honeycomb of caves and caverns around Australia. For non-experts, some of the better-known caves are open for tours—a safe yet exciting underground experience.

1 CUTTA CUTTA CAVES (NT)
Along the Stuart Highway, these tourable caves are inhabited by some rare bats.

2 JENOLAN CAVES (NSW)
Discovered in 1838 and more popular than ever; the tours cover only a small proportion of the hundreds of linked caves.

3 NARACOORTE CAVES (SA)
In this cave, park rangers escort visitors among nicely lit stalactites and stalagmites.

4 TANTANOOLA CAVES (SA)
Near the home of the fabled Tantanoola Tiger, explore caves half a million years old.

5 HASTINGS (TAS.)
Daily tours of three beautiful limestone caves, a few kilometres inland from the port of Hastings.

Waterfalls

On a hot day nothing refreshes the senses like the sight and sound of cool water plunging from a clifftop. A disclaimer: some waterfalls are seasonal, so today's Niagara may be tomorrow's trickle. Some of the cascades to admire in north and east Australia:

6 WANGI FALLS (NT)
South of Darwin, a lovely swimming hole at the bottom of the chute.

7 JIM JIM FALLS (NT)
Some Kakadu tours take in the spectacle of the multi-stage descent of Jim Jim.

8 ROBIN FALLS (NT)
Just off the old Stuart Highway south of Adelaide River; unimpressive in the dry season.

9 EDITH FALLS (NT)
On the way to Katherine, Edith's cascade winds up in a refreshing swimming spot.

10 MILAA MILAA FALLS (QLD)
Probably the nicest of a group of waterfalls in this rainforest area; good swimming.

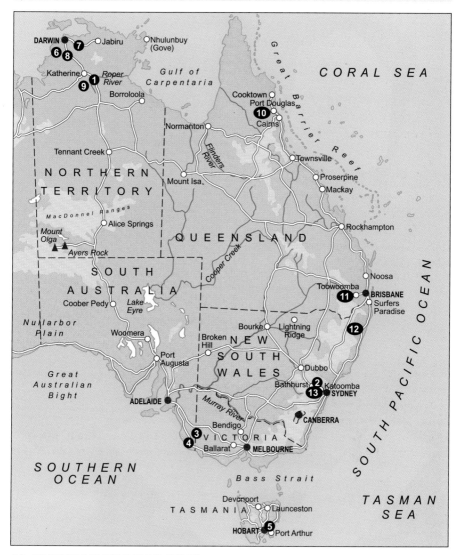

11 QUEEN MARY FALLS (QLD)
In the cool foothills of the Great Dividing Range; you can walk to top and bottom of these falls.

12 WOLLOMOMBI FALLS (NSW)
On the New England plateau, east of Armidale, mountain water crashes down toward the sea; possibly the country's tallest waterfall.

Caves open to the non-expert (1–5) and where to see those plunging falls (6–13).

13 FITZROY FALLS (NSW)
An accessible highlight of Morton National Park; picnic area nearby.

From the Nation's First City to the Back of Beyond

Australia's most populous state occupies only about one-tenth of the continent's area, but it packs in everything from dairyland and vineyards to desert and craggy mountains. In an area six times the size of England live 5½ million people: cowboys and coalminers, sailors and scientists, trendy media manipulators and some of the world's most relaxed beachcombers.

New South Wales covers a lot of latitude and altitude, from the country's tallest peak to convincingly desolate desert. But wherever the land is fit for cultivation, anything grows: bananas, cotton and sugarcane in the north, apples, cherries and wheat in the south.

For all its attractions, New South Wales just can't help but be dominated by its metropolis, Sydney, which is Australia's biggest, oldest and liveliest city. After all, that's where most of the

*P*ort arms! An actor revives the spirit of 1788, when keepers and convicts founded a new nation at Sydney Cove.

state's population lives. Sydneysiders wouldn't trade it for anyplace in the world.

Sydney

First there was the harbour. Ever since 1788, when the initial convoy of convicts arrived to construct a new nation, the harbour has always stolen the show. It is so stunning that people alongside are inspired to achievement and *joie de vivre.*

Most of the world's great cities have a landmark that serves as an instantly recognizable symbol. Sydney has two such emblems, and both built on the harbour: the perfect arch of the Harbour Bridge and the billowing roofs of

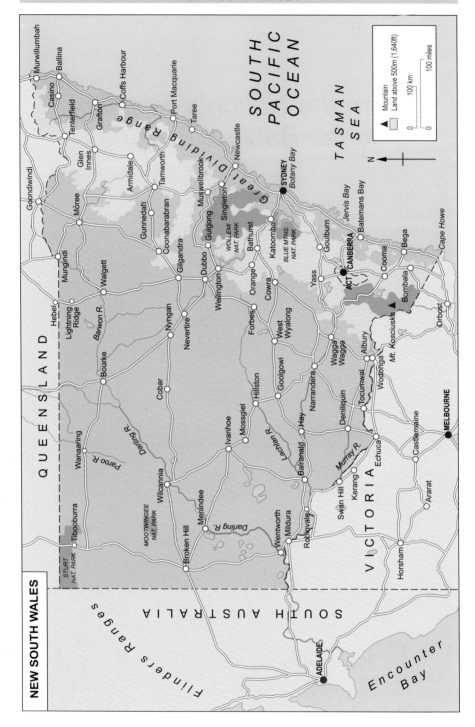

NEW SOUTH WALES

*M*ap *of the main towns, cities and roads in New South Wales.*

the Opera House. That's what happens when engineers and architects embellish a haven coveted by artists as well as admirals.

Brawny and brazen, Sydney is a sophisticated financial, communications and manufacturing centre. After hours—and Sydneysiders live for the after hours—there is every imaginable cosmopolitan delight. (Things have become so international that you can order a bagel and brie with your cappuccino; souvlaki and terriyaki seem no more exotic here than hot dogs; the

*L*ike Hong Kong, *Sydney is a delightful place to discover from the deck of a harbour ferryboat.*

graffiti you see in a public convenience may be scrawled in Chinese.) The city's 3¹/₂ million inhabitants, who tend to be friendly and witty, have good reason for self-satisfaction, for the city has everything anyone could ask for, tangible or inspirational. It's a sunny coincidence that more than 30 beaches famous for surfing and scenery are only minutes away.

City Sights
Tireless travellers often debate the virtues of the world's most dramatic harbours: Hong Kong, Rio de Janeiro, San Francisco ... Sydney is always on the list, but it's up to you to decide whether it's the most beautiful of all. To start your evaluation, gaze out from the top of Sydney's tallest building or take a helicopter tour. See the clear blue tentacles of water stretching from the South Pacific into the heart of the city. Schools of sailing boats, their multicoloured spinnakers puffed with pride, vaunt the harbour's perfection in the reflection of the

skyscrapers, the classic bridge and the exhilarating opera house.

*T*own plan of Sydney.

It's a pity Captain Cook never even noticed the glorious setting of **Port Jackson** (the official name for Sydney harbour). The great explorer sailed right past it on his way home from Botany Bay.

Most sightseeing tours—by land or sea—leave from **Circular Quay**, short for *Semi*-Circular Quay, as it was named in olden times; in reality it's rather rectangular. Cruise ships, sightseeing launches and water taxis alike tie up here, but most of the action involves workaday ferryboats and high-speed JetCats. Part of the excitement is the convergence of leisurely tourists gawking at the sights and harried commuters who cross the harbour rarely glancing above the top of their newspapers at the splendour of it all. Adding to the nonstop hum of human

A modern sculpture saluting the pioneers stands among restored early 19th-century houses in The Rocks.

interest are street musicians, artists and hawkers. At the far end of the quay, almost under the bridge, a fanatically discreet hotel hunkers down in low-slung luxury; its name (Hyatt, if you ask) is invisible from the tourist side of the building, and on the entrance it's written so inconspicuously that you're almost in the lobby before you see the sign.

Whether you survey Australia's busiest harbour from the deck of a luxury liner, a sightseeing boat or a humble ferry, don't miss the invigorating sea-level angle on the city's skyline.

The Rocks

To start at the beginning, stroll through the calculatedly charming streets of the Rocks, where the Australian equivalent of the *Mayflower* is remembered with pride, whether one's ancestors were crewmen, guards or involuntary passengers. Here the founding fathers—convicts charged with anything from murder to

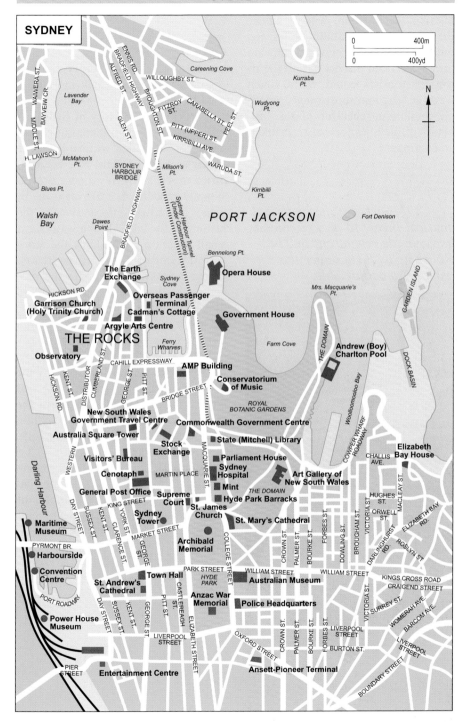

SYDNEY

0 ——————— 400m
0 ——————— 400yd

N

WAIWERA ST.
BAYVIEW CR.
MIDDLE ST.
Lavender Bay
ENNIS RD.
BRADFIELD HIGHWAY
ALFRED ST.
BROUGHTON ST.
GLEN ST.
WILLOUGHBY ST.
Careening Cove
FITZROY ST.
CARABELLA ST.
PITT (UPPER) ST.
KIRRIBILLI AVE.
PEEL ST.
Kurraba Pt.
Wudyong Pt.
H. LAWSON
McMahon's Pt.
SYDNEY HARBOUR BRIDGE
Milson's Pt.
WARUDA ST.
Blues Pt.
Kirribilli Pt.

Walsh Bay
Dawes Point
BRADFIELD HIGHWAY
Sydney Harbour Tunnel (Under Construction)

PORT JACKSON

Fort Denison

Bennelong Pt.

The Earth Exchange
Sydney Cove
Opera House

Mrs. Macquarie's Pt.

HICKSON RD.
Overseas Passenger Terminal
Garrison Church (Holy Trinity Church)
Cadman's Cottage
Government House

Argyle Arts Centre

THE ROCKS
Ferry Wharves
Observatory
HICKSON RD.
KENT ST.
DISTRIBUTOR
CUMBERLAND ST.
GEORGE ST.
PITT ST.
CAHILL EXPRESSWAY
AMP Building
Conservatorium of Music
BRIDGE STREET
GARDEN ISLAND
Farm Cove
THE DOMAIN
Andrew (Boy) Charlton Pool
DOCK BASIN
Woolloomooloo Bay
COWPER WHARF ROADWAY

ROYAL BOTANIC GARDENS

New South Wales Government Travel Centre
Commonwealth Government Centre
Australia Square Tower
WESTERN
Stock Exchange
MACQUARIE ST.
State (Mitchell) Library
Visitors' Bureau
Parliament House
Sydney Hospital
Elizabeth Bay House
CHALLIS AVE.
Cenotaph
MARTIN PLACE
Mint
Art Gallery of New South Wales
VICTORIA ST.
HUGHES ST.
MACLEAY ST.
ELIZABETH BAY RD.
General Post Office
KING STREET
Supreme Court
THE DOMAIN
Hyde Park Barracks
ORWELL ST.
Darling Harbour
DAY STREET
SUSSEX ST.
KENT ST.
YORK ST.
CLARENCE ST.
Sydney Tower
MARKET STREET
St. James Church
St. Mary's Cathedral
FORBES ST.
DOWLING ST.
BROUGHAM ST.
DARLINGHURST RD.
ROSLYN ST.
● **Maritime Museum**
PYRMONT BR.
Archibald Memorial
COLLEGE STREET
CROWN ST.
PALMER ST.
BOURKE ST.
● **Harbourside**
● **Convention Centre**
PORT ROAD
St. Andrew's Cathedral
DAY STREET
SUSSEX ST.
KENT ST.
PITT ST.
GEORGE ST.
Town Hall
PARK STREET
HYDE PARK
Australian Museum
WILLIAM STREET
WILLIAM STREET
KINGS CROSS ROAD
CRAIGEND STREET
SURREY ST.
WOMERAH AVE.
BARCOM AVE.
Anzac War Memorial
CASTLEREAGH ST.
Police Headquarters
● **Power House Museum**
LIVERPOOL STREET
ELIZABETH STREET
OXFORD STREET
CROWN ST.
PALMER ST.
BOURKE ST.
FORBES ST.
LIVERPOOL STREET
BURTON ST.
LIVERPOOL STREET
PIER STREET
Entertainment Centre
Ansett-Pioneer Terminal
BOUNDARY STREET

thieving—came ashore in 1788 to build the colony of New South Wales. Recently restored and revivified, this historic waterfront district has all the resources tourists could want: lovely views at long and short range, moody old buildings, cheerful plazas, and plenty of facilities for eaters, drinkers and shoppers.

Carrying the historical nautical theme to an extreme, a harbourside restaurant in The Rocks holds forth under the masts of a sailing ship.

Wander at will or first pick up local leaflets and maps at **The Rocks Visitors Centre**, 104 George Street. This building, too, has a bit of history, but less than a century of it; built in 1907, it used to be the Coroner's Court.

Next door, **The Story of Sydney** is one of those "multi-dimensional experiences" designed to introduce the visitor to the local scene. Not just a sit-down movie show, it's a very professionally produced extravaganza of videos and special effects covering the history of the city. On the way out, a small museum rounds out the story with documents and artefacts as well as reminders of the wildlife the pioneers found, starting with a stuffed dingo emitting recorded howls.

On the opposite side of the Visitors Centre, **Cadman's Cottage** is Sydney's oldest (1816) surviving house—a simple stone cottage long occupied by the government's boatsmen. A pardoned convict named John Cadman was the original coxswain. The house includes a small collection of old anchors, sails, oars and the like.

Campbell's Storehouse, farther along the cove, is a venerable warehouse converted into an attractive complex of shops, restaurants and a wine bar for connoisseurs. Another commercial highlight in a former warehouse, **Argyle Arts Centre** now houses restaurants, arts-and-crafts shops and galleries.

Winning Museums

A popular museum in The Rocks, **The Earth Exchange**, at 18 Hickson Road, enhances a geological exhibition with ecological messages. Expertly aimed at keeping children interested, it provides "hands-on" devices and fun interludes, and many exhibits are placed at adult knee-level. Definitely *not* a "hands-on" part of the museum is the big, dramatically lit display of precious stones from all over Australia and the world. Ironically, the Jubilee Nugget, said to be $1^1/2$ million dollars worth of raw gold, must be the ugliest item in the show; it's shaped like a huge human brain. The biggest crowds are attracted to an earthquake simulation, although it's hardly more violent than a ferryboat nudging the pier. In reality, Australia has rarely experienced big quakes, being, in seismic terms, an underprivileged country.

Like The Earth Exchange, the **Museum of Contemporary Art** gives new life to an old building—the former state Maritime Services Board headquarters, an Art Deco classic overlooking Circular Quay West. The museum's benefactor, an Australian-born artist named John Power, died in obscurity in 1943. About a thousand of his paintings, influenced by Cubism and Surrealism, make up the core of the collection, while another 3,000 or so come from artists as celebrated as Roy Lichtenstein, Robert Indiana, Gilbert and George, and Cindy Sherman. Also on show are some contemporary works by Aboriginal artists.

More History

In Playfair Street, off George Street, a Westpac Bank branch will not only change foreign currency for you; upstairs is a small, free **museum** documenting the history of banking since the foundation of its predecessor, the Bank of New South Wales, in 1817, from the "holey dollars" punched out

in the early colonial days to today's "plastic money".

Argyle Cut, a shady underpass, indicates why the first generation of convicts named this district The Rocks. To excavate this route, work parties in chains were ordered to chop through solid rock with pickaxes. It took years. The topless tunnel was later widened by mechanical means. In Sydney's boisterous 19th century, this was the likeliest place in town to be mugged.

High above The Rocks, **Observatory Hill** is a choice spot to observe the heavens, or the heavenly prospect of Sydney harbour. The hill has been the site of a fort, a signal station and an astronomical observatory. Since the middle of the 19th century, at precisely 1.00 p.m. every day, a ball has been dropped from a mast here so ship's captains can set their chronometers. In navigation, as in so many things, timing is essential.

Clumps of terrace houses on the **Millers Point** side of the peninsula are preserved as architectural monuments. So are a couple of the oldest **pubs** in Australia, redolent of history as well as beer. If you really need an excuse, the Hero of Waterloo in Lower Fort Street and the Lord Nelson Hotel near Argyle Place are worth visiting for scholarly purposes. For history without the beer, see the **Garrison Church**, officially Holy Trinity Anglican Church, which dates from the early 1840s. As the unofficial name indicates, it was the church for members of the garrison regiment, the men who commanded the convict colony.

Back on the waterfront, **Pier One** is an old multi-storey shipping terminal now done up as a big tourist-tilted

More than 60 years old and still looking good, the Sydney Harbour Bridge carries eight lanes of cars. The new Harbour Tunnel is designed to reduce traffic jams.

shopping and leisure centre. From the grassy hillside of **Dawes Point Park**, studded with old cannon, you can survey the harbour's froth of ferries, Jet-Cats and sailing boats. On a warm day you'll appreciate the shade of the trees and the bridgework directly above. This is not just any old bridge. With its drive-through stone pillars and geometrically impeccable steel arch, the **Sydney Harbour Bridge** strides confidently across the harbour, linking the city and the north, adding to the fascination of an already splendid scene.

Graphically nicknamed "The Coathanger", the bridge was officially opened on 19 March 1932. In more than the obvious way it was a day to remember. As the premier of New South Wales prepared to wield his ceremonial scissors, a figure on horseback, dressed in an old British army uniform, galloped up and slashed the symbolic ribbon with a sabre. The intruder, Francis de Groot, leader of a fanatical right-wing organization, was bundled off the bridge and later fined for offensive behavior and damaging government property (the ribbon). In a dreary anticlimax, the ribbon was retied and then snipped with official pomp. Before the day was over, about 300,000 people really made it official: they hiked across the bridge.

For viewing the bridge, the harbour and the skyline, an unusual vantage point is the top of one of the bridge's massive pylons. The **lookout** is in the south-east tower, and the stairway—200 steps, if you're up to it—can be reached via Cumberland Street, The Rocks. It's best to confirm opening hours: phone 247 3408.

Bridging the Harbour

It took nine years to build the Harbour Bridge, one of the foremost engineering achievements of the era. During the Great Depression, Sydneysiders called the bridge the Iron Lung, for it kept many people "breathing"—in economic terms. The old Coathanger remains a steady source of employment, for instance for tollkeepers and daredevil painters and maintenance men. Repainting the entire bridge is a 10-year job, and then it's time to start again.

For the record, the bridge's single arch is 503 m (1,650 ft) across, and carries eight lanes of cars, two railway tracks, plus lanes for pedestrians and cyclists. The arch was built first, and then the roadway was hung beneath it. The steel in the arch alone weighs 39,000 tonnes. The top of the arch is as high above the harbour as a 40-storey building. Every year about 40 million vehicles use the landmark; at the rush hour it may feel as if all 40 million are simultaneously stalled on the approach roads.

City Centre

Skyscrapers are ever more common-place in central Sydney, but at last report the **Sydney Tower** at Centrepoint still held the title: the city's highest vantage point, 305 m (1,000 ft) above the street, not to mention being the highest building in the southern hemisphere. It's open every day of the year except Christmas. In only 40 seconds you whoosh straight up to the observation decks (and the revolving restaurants travellers can hardly avoid at such altitudes). Amateur photographers get that glazed look as they peer hungrily through the tinted windows to unlimited horizons. Thoughtfully, the

T owering views: higher than all the other skyscapers in Sydney, Centrepoint, at left, is more than just an observation post and revolving restaurants; it stands atop a shopping centre.

management also installed some *un-tinted* glass so that cameras can capture authentic colours. On a flawless day you can see all the way to Terrigal and Wollongong, or far out to sea or to the Blue Mountains. Closer in, there's a new perspective on the glory of the harbour and the precarious coexistence of Sydney's skyscrapers, superhighways, parks and historic buildings.

Most Australian cities and towns now have pedestrian malls, normally the heart of the downtown shopping district, lined with department stores and fashionable boutiques. Sydney's centre has a different sort of mall: **Martin Place** is a wide, car-less street of trees, sculpture and fountains, less commercial than relaxing. It's just for strolling, meeting friends, enjoying a takeaway lunch, and breathing some non-air-conditioned air. At midday free shows are staged in a small amphitheatre in the middle of the mall, anything from rock to chamber music. Martin Place is the spot where Sydney's official Christmas tree is erected in the heat of December.

While you're here you can mail your postcards authoritatively from the imposing Victorian Renaissance building of the **General Post Office**. During World War II the GPO's landmark clock tower was dismantled—not because the correct time was a military secret, but for fear Japanese bombers might zero in on the tower. It wasn't put back again until more than 20 years later.

From the same era as the GPO, but even grander, the **Queen Victoria Building** occupies an entire block on George Street, Sydney's main street (and the oldest street in the country). In the

Every neo-Classical theme is mobilized to enhance the grandeur of Sydney's Town Hall, more than a century old.

beginning it was a vast municipal market and commercial centre, including a hotel and a concert hall and topped by 21 domes. But business turned bad and in the bleak 1930s the city government converted it for offices and a library. In the 1980s a Malaysian company took over what had become an eyesore. In exchange for a 99-year lease the company restored the building's fine stonework and interior details and created an appealing all-weather shopping centre. The QVB, as it is called, houses close to 200 boutiques, cafés and restaurants in an atmosphere of calculated Victorian-era charm.

Next door, Sydney's **Town Hall** enlivens a site that used to be a cemetery. Compared to the skyscrapers elsewhere in the area, this overblown Victorian building seems to be kneeling. Home of the city council, it is also used for exhibitions and concerts—the 8,500-pipe organ is a landmark in itself.

Darling Harbour

Take the monorail from the central district to the all-purpose leisure centre at Darling Harbour. The elevated track covers a 3.6-km (2.2-mile) loop of six stations. Although it's gravely overcrowded at times, for instance at rush hour on rainy days, the monorail

Since 1988, tourism in Sydney has tilted towards the perky new Darling Harbour development.

is mostly for fun. (*Serious* transport systems usually go in two directions, but this one travels only counter-clockwise.) It may not be terribly practical, and many consider those ubiquitous pillars a blot on the cityscape, but the monorail does serve as a vehicle for some good sightseeing. And it's an introduction to the futuristic developments at and around Darling Harbour. On the other hand, you can walk it. Or if you have a car to worry about, Darling Harbour is equipped with 6,000 parking spaces.

Every Australian town built something new in honour of the Bicentennial observance of 1988, and Sydney's contribution was the nation's biggest ever urban redevelopment programme. The evolution of Darling Harbour from a derelict seaside embarrassment to a powerful pole of attraction for tourists and the locals alike was

accomplished in only four years. Government and private funds were poured into the 54-ha (113-acre) building site to create a cheerful new world devoted to recreation and shopping.

The shopping "opportunities" in the Harbourside marketplace range from gemstones and fancy fashions to the silliest souvenirs; you can never predict what the next shop will offer. On every side there are food outlets, dishing out fast food by the billions of calories; and health faddists are not ignored.

The **Australian National Maritime Museum**, on the harbour next to the market, occupies a big, glass-walled building that looks as if the architect was inspired by the sails of the Sydney Opera House while designing the last word in airport terminals. The exhibits are divided into several themes: early explorers and what they found; the saga of the pioneers; the navy then and now; and how the seas serve the needs of commerce and recreation. Just outside are floating exhibits as varied as a century-old racing cutter, a battleship-grey destroyer named HMAS *Vampire* and a fragile Vietnamese fishing boat that brought refugees to Australian shores in 1977.

Superaquarium

Across the historic **Pyrmont Bridge**, a drawbridge 30 years older than the Harbour Bridge, is what the management calls the world's most spectacular aquarium. To test the claim, or quibble over it, you can walk across the bridge or take a boat. You won't run out of things to see and do in the **Sydney Aquarium** for a couple of fascinating hours. You can start with the crocodiles, whose baleful immobility

seems to challenge the crowds to hang around until one of them stirs. There are northern and southern Australian river fish and a cross-section of brilliantly coloured fish borrowed from the Barrier Reef; you can learn their names before your snorkelling excursion to Queensland. For children, a "touch pool" provides the ultimate "hands-on" experience—sea urchins, shore crab, abalone, anemone and other living creatures to be fondled under the supervision of a friendly, knowledgeable guard. Microaquariums are equipped with remote-controlled video cameras that youngsters of the high-tech generation enjoy manipulating to zoom in on tiny exhibits. But the most stirring experience is under sea level, where the visitors are propelled through acrylic tunnels surrounded by sharks, graceful rayfish and other big game of the deep; gawking at the wonders here is the next best thing to getting wet. Two oceanariums, devoted to deep-sea and Sydney harbour fish, contain a total of 2.75 million litres. (600,000 gallons) of water. The astonishing sound effects were recorded live.

At the inner end of Cockle Bay, the Darling Harbour **Convention Centre**, Australia's biggest, can convene 3,500 delegates at a time, or feed more than 2,000 banqueters. Next door, the **Exhibition Centre** is designed on the suspension bridge principle, with cables attached to masts holding up the roofs. The glass walls look out on **Tumbalong Park** and adjoining open spaces, predictably more than just a pleasant place to take the sun. There are brilliantly original fountains, some almost guaranteed to incite children to get

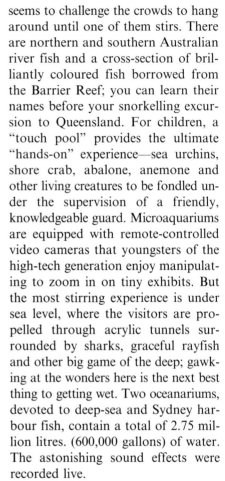

delightedly wet. Also free are swings, slides, mazes and geometrical challenges, all a couple of generations ahead of conventional playgrounds.

Show Biz and Contemplation

The **Sydney Entertainment Centre**, a border post between Darling Harbour and Chinatown, predates the big harbourside development. It was designed to be used for sports events, concerts and almost any other public event. A full house here amounts to 12,500 spectators.

Next door, the **Pier Street Pumphouse**, a historic building, once supplied hydraulic pressure to operate lifts and the weighty doors of bank vaults. Restored, it serves the tourist imperative as a tavern and boutique brewery.

Darling Harbour's **Chinese Garden**, which is officially called the Garden of Friendship, was a co-production of the governments of New South Wales and Guangdong Province (whose capital is Guangzhou, better known as Canton). The garden is packed with plants and trees as appealing as apricot and azalea, jasmine and weeping willow, in fact so many treats for the senses that the site seems bigger than its 1 ha (about 2^1/2 acres). The paths, pavilions, ponds and rock formations, too, are designed to spur meditation. In the tea house they serve 10 varieties of Chinese tea, plus foreign teas and soft drinks—even apple strudel. With these minor exceptions the atmosphere is divinely authentic, like the entire, meticulously planned and tended garden.

 The good news about the estimable **Powerhouse Museum**, just beyond the monorail track at the south-west

corner of Darling Harbour, starts at the entrance: admission is free. Architecturally and otherwise the establishment fascinates, adding postmodern touches to memories of the Industrial Revolution. Called Australia's largest museum complex, this was indeed a powerhouse, generating electricity for the trams that used to ply Sydney's streets. The premises are big enough to house thousands of exhibits, from an ancient steam locomotive to a Catalina flying boat, which hangs from one of the ceilings. Essentially a science-and-industry museum with a sociocultural slant, the Powerhouse is generously supplied with "interactive" attractions to keep the children awake; some of them, like pumping an exercise bike, involve so much exertion the toddlers might need a nap. There are also relics of space exploration, including space suits and samples of dehydrated food used by astronauts and cosmonauts. You can eat better at the museum's café or its outdoor food kiosk.

On a warm day in central Sydney, the fountain in Hyde Park provides passersby with a refreshing oasis.

Parks and History

Skyscrapers shade the streets of central Sydney, but trees, grass and flowers are never far away. For sightseers, there's a happy mixture within easy walking distance: the parks are as historic as the buildings around them.

Although **Hyde Park** is only a fraction of the size of its namesake in London, it provides the same sort of green relief. The land was cleared in the beginning of the 19th century as a recreational area, with a racetrack as its first big attraction. Hyde Park was also the site of boxing matches; gloves came later. And the new colony's first cricket pitch was here. The most formal

feature of these semi-formal gardens, the **Anzac War Memorial** commemorates the World War I fighters in monumental Art Deco style.

Sightseers who collect old churches should mark three targets on the edge of Hyde Park. To the north, the early colonial **St James' Church** in Queens Square was the work of the convict architect, Francis Greenway. Actually, it was supposed to be a courthouse but the plan changed for economy reasons when it was half built. Across College Street on the east, **St Mary's Cathedral** stands on the prominent site of the colony's first Catholic church. Its Gothic-style spires were designed in the second half of the 19th century. From the same era, the **Great Synagogue** faces the park across Elizabeth Street. Jews have lived in Sydney since the arrival of the first shipment of prisoners.

The **Australian Museum**, on College Street, provides a one-stop survey of natural history, from fossils and dinosaurs to current ecological cares. The stuffed birds—and bees, flies and spiders—are the sort of things children are dragged to museums to be shown. But you can learn a lot about Australian fauna here. Another highlight is the section on the art, culture and recent history of the Aborigines. While you're there, browse through the Aboriginal arts and crafts on sale in the big Museum Shop. For what it's worth, a tourist brochure issued by Sydney's Natural Gas Company says the Australian Museum "is recognized as one of the top five museums in the world!" The enthusiastic punctuation comes with the claim.

Children are well catered for in the restored **Hyde Park Barracks**, between the park and the Botanic Gardens. Designed by the prolific Francis Greenway as the first respectable flop-house for convicts, it is now a museum of social history. On the top floor of the barracks, one large room is a reconstruction of the dormitory life of the prisoners. The present keepers don't seem to mind when youngsters overcome their shyness and start testing the hammocks.

The Mint, next door, has exhibits on money, stamps, flags and other acute angles on Australian history. Here you can see the "Holey Dollars"—Spanish coins recycled to ease a desperate shortage of cash in New South Wales. The new colony used the equivalent of both the doughnut and the hole: the centres were punched out and used as 15-pence coins, while the outer rings that remained became hollow five-shilling coins, worth four times as much.

Continuing north along Macquarie Street (named for himself by the memorable if immodest governor), **Sydney Hospital** superseded the notorious Rum Hospital of early colonial days. The name refers to the sideline of the firm that built it, compensated by a fat contract as importers of rum. The verandahed **State Parliament House,** adjoining, has resounded to political debate, mostly sober, since the days when the colony's population was under 40,000. The elegant houses on the opposite side of the street, which are among the city's most desirable, contain a high proportion of doctors' and lawyers'offices.

The $10 Man

Can you think of any other country in the world that would put the portrait of a convict on its $10 bills? And a forger, at that.

He was Francis Greenway, a bankrupt architect in England, convicted of forging a clause in a building contract. In 1812 this crime carried the death penalty, but he was lucky: his sentence was commuted to 14 years of exile in Australia. The dynamic Governor Lachlan Macquarie "discovered" Greenway, the only competent builder in town, appointed him government architect and pardoned him. Greenway designed everything from churches to a lighthouse. His projects grew ever grander, to the delight of the governor. But the rulers in London finally complained that extravagance had no place in a penal colony. Greenway was fired in 1822, but his monuments are all around you in the city he built. If colonial Sydney had been ready for an opera house, Greenway would have designed it.

More than a Park

The **State Library**, bordering the in formal park called the Domain, is the ultimate trove of documents on early explorations, the First Fleet and other historical themes. Classical columns announce the main portal, but around the side a nifty 1988 addition boosts the institution's size and spirits.

For more than a century, **The Domain** has contained the Sydney version of London's Hyde Park Corner, where anyone can climb aboard a soapbox and make a speech; Sunday is the day of the orators and hecklers. Seven days a week art lovers come to the Domain to explore the **Art Gallery of New South Wales.** It consists of an old and newer building attached like ill-matched Siamese twins, plus a brilliant modern (1988) extension that adds glass and light and broadens perspectives with views of east Sydney and part of the harbour. The gallery provides a crash course in more than a century of traditional and modern Australian art. First rate, too, is an Asian collection going back 3,000 years, and an enviable hoard of the sculptures and masks of South Pacific islanders. The concise review of Australian Aboriginal art—wood sculptures and paintings on bark and canvas—covers a lot of ground, artistically and ethnologically.

Sydney's **Royal Botanic Gardens** began as a different sort of garden: this is where the early settlers first tried to grow vegetables. The First Fleet had picked up plants and seeds on the way to Australia, but nobody in the new colony seemed to have a green thumb. Only a few steps from the busy skyscraper world of downtown

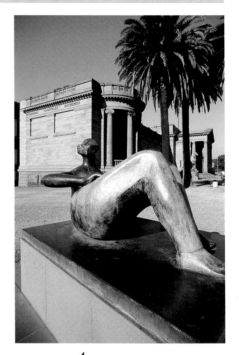

A figure by Henry Moore stands out against the sobriety of the original wing of Sydney's Fine Art Gallery of New South Wales.

Sydney, you can relax in the shade of Moreton Bay fig trees, palms or mighty mahoganies, or enter a glass pyramid full of orchids and other tropical beauties. Birds of many species inhabit the trees, inspect the lawns and take advantage of the fountains; the snack bar just inside the Macquarie Street entrance is haunted by a gaggle of ibises, hanging around like so many panhandlers.

The gardens curve up around Farm Cove to a peninsula with the quaint name of **Mrs Macquarie's Point**. The lady thus immortalized, the wife of the go-ahead governor, used to admire the view from here; nowadays it's better than ever.

Sydney Opera House

Australia's symbol, a one-in-a-million building covered in a million tiles, does the impossible: it embellishes the perfect harbour. In a country with a notoriously casual lifestyle, the Sydney Opera House, startlingly, conveys a real sense of occasion. The building has brought glory to the city, the country, and the controversial architect who left in a huff at an early stage of construction.

Harbour tourists snap extreme close-ups of Australia's best known monument, the Sydney Opera House.

Until the opera house idea caught on, the promontory was wasted on a fancy, turreted depot for tramcars. At the end of the line, Bennelong Point was hardly a site for sore eyes. In the 1950s the government of New South Wales decided to build a performing arts centre on the spot. A Danish architect, Jørn Utzon, won an international competition to design it. His novel plan included problems of spherical geometry so tricky that he actually chopped up a wooden sphere to prove it could be done.

The inspiring shell of the complex had virtually been completed when Utzon walked out; the interior, which was in dispute, became the work of a committee. Even so, from the tip of its highest roof, (67 m (221 feet) above sea level) to the Drama Theatre's orchestra pit (more than a fathom *below* sea

level) this place has grace, taste and class.

The name "Sydney Opera House" is as renowned as it is inaccurate. The actual opera theatre is only one of the centre's five halls, and not the biggest. (Incidentally, if you're "fashionably late" for the opera, there's no admission until the first break, probably the end of the first act—and that goes for VIPs as well as tourists.) It's well worth taking one of the guided tours around the premises.

Under the Sails

To bring it all down to earth, those ingenious billowing roofs, which have inspired more metaphors than the love of a long-winded poet, weigh 160,965 tonnes. Covering the roofs, 1,056,000 ceramic tiles wash themselves when it rains; they were made in Sweden. There are 6,223 sq m (66,985 sq ft) of glass, made in France. The biggest of the five theatres seats 2,690 people.

At the outset, the opera house had a budget of $7 million. By the time it was finished 19 years later, the price had zoomed to more than $100 million. The problem was solved in a thoroughly Australian way: to make up the difference, culture-lovers bought special lottery tickets that more than paid the bill.

Kings Cross

In Queen Victoria's day, Kings Cross was called Queens Cross. If Victoria came to visit now, she would not be amused. Just east of the niftily named district of Woolloomooloo, loose-moraled Kings Cross is Sydney's answer to Paris's Pigalle or London's Soho. By night it's electric, sleazy and fun, crawling with hedonists of many persuasions. Everything is for sale in The Cross. Doormen representing the fleshpots importune almost all the passers-by, and so, less pushily, do hordes of streetwalkers. On the margins, fortune-tellers, artisans, drug vendors and eccentrics round out a rich cast of characters.

But the gaudy night-life district has more to offer than mere sin. There are reputable hotels and shops, a very original fountain commemorating the World War II battle of El Alamein, and some good ethnic restaurants.

A five-minute walk from Kings Cross Station, **Elizabeth Bay House** is a stately home built in 1835, now restored and open for inspection (but never on Mondays). It was supposed to recall the lines of a Grecian villa. Beyond the classically inspired porch, the centre of architectural interest is an ingenious elliptical staircase, suitable for the most dramatic entrance. The upper floor offers a gorgeous view of the eastern reaches of the harbour.

If you have time for one more inner suburb, make it **Paddington**, south-east of Kings Cross. Its trademark is the intricate wrought ironwork, known as Sydney Lace, on the balconies of 19th-century terraced houses. This frilly feature, and the rather bohemian atmosphere, reminds some travellers of New Orleans. After decades of dilapidation, the district has come up in the world as a fashionable, rather arty place to live. "Paddo", as the locals like to call it, is full of far-out ethnic restaurants, antique shops, art galleries and trendy boutiques.

The **Victoria Barracks**, along Paddington's Oxford Street, is a formidable example of mid-19th-century military architecture. Convicts

If you don't mind the traffic jams, Sydney Harbour is the best and most colourful place to be at regatta time.

built it, far from what was then the centre of Sydney, to house a regiment of British soldiers and their families. At 10.00 a.m. every Tuesday (except in December and January) a formal changing of the guard ceremony, marching band and all, is held at the barracks. Afterwards, visitors can tour the establishment. It's all free.

Around Sydney Harbour

The best way to get to know the ins and outs of Sydney Harbour is aboard your own boat, or, if your yacht is tied up elsewhere, you can hire one for the occasion. Or you can get closer to the people, joining the cheery throng aboard one of the many sightseeing cruises departing Circular Quay; the commentary is usually enlightening and amusing. Even a couple of ferry rides will broaden your horizons, though you may miss hidden beaches,

islets, mansions old and new, and a couple of unsung bridges.

Fort Denison occupies a small harbour island graphically known as "Pinchgut". A lonesome pine is the only obvious sign of life, though there are inconspicuous shrubs and gardens. In the colony's early days, it served as a prison island. Considering that all of Australia was a prison island, it must have been pretty bad. Indeed, troublesome convicts banished to the rock endured a bread-and-water diet; the meagre rations seem to account for Pinchgut's nickname. In the middle of the 19th century the island was fortified to guard Sydney from the far-fetched threat of a Russian attack. But the only attack on Fort Denison came in World War II when a stray shell from an American warship nicked the top of Old Pinchgut's martello tower.

A 12-minute ferry ride from Circular Quay, **Taronga Zoo** is where most foreign tourists have their first meeting with kangaroos and koalas. You can't beat the setting. Over the heads of the giraffes you can look across the harbour to the skyscrapers of Sydney. Taronga Zoo claims a particularly

Surfing wasn't actually invented in Sydney, but the pastime soon became a prime local obsession.

chirpy collection of 1,500 Australian birds of about 200 species. As for the indigenous animals, they're all on view, including night creatures illuminated in artificial moonlight. See the incredible-but-true platypus swimming in his big fishbowl. The koalas are rallied for a photo opportunity from 1.00 to 2.00 p.m.; around 3.00 p.m., they re-awaken at mealtime. The feeding schedule for all the animals is posted and the keepers give knowledgeable talks while distributing food. In addition to Australian fauna, lovable or slithery, the zoo has everything from elephants to chimpanzees. The signs say, "Please do not feed the animals. Love and respect are all they need."

Shark Island, popular with picnickers, is no more prone to fishy perils than any other place in the harbour; its shape, though, may have reminded early mapmakers of a shark. Until anti-shark nets were installed at Sydney beaches in the 1930s, Australia could boast the world's highest incidence of shark attacks.

A stately home with its own beach, **Vaucluse House** adds its mock-Gothic turrets and crenellations to the skyline. The mansion began more humbly as the home of a colourful ex-convict, Sir Henry Brown Hayes, who had been the sheriff of Cork before being banished to Australia for the abduction of his bride. In the 1830s the new owner, William Charles Wentworth, expanded the place into a 15-room homestead, now run by the state's Historic Houses Trust. Wentworth, whose mother was a convict, won distinction for himself as a statesman and explorer.

At Last: the Beaches

Farther afield, both north and south of Sydney, are miles of inviting beaches. **Manly** got its name, we're told, because the first governor of the colony thought the Aborigines sunning themselves on the beach looked manly. The cheerful resort of Manly offers a tale of two beaches—the open-ocean beach popular with surfers, the harbourside crescent fit for children. Linking the beaches, the lively Corso is a Mediterranean sort of promenade lined with restaurants, fast-food emporia, ice-cream stands and souvenir stores. And there are tables for picnickers. To defend local modesty, daylight bathing was forbidden in Manly until 1903. For decades the resort has used the slogan, "Seven miles from Sydney—and a thousand miles from care."

The Manly **Oceanarium**, upgraded in 1988 from the former Marineland, claims to have Australia's largest collection of marine life. Among the highlights are the high-jumping fur seals, whose feeding sessions please the crowds. Supplementing the conventional viewing tanks, the so-called Tunnel of Life offers a thrilling perspective on undersea life: a moving walkway traverses an acrylic tunnel surrounded by freely swimming sharks, rays and friends.

At North Head, south of Manly, the **Old Quarantine Station** is an Australian version of New York's Ellis Island, where new immigrants waited for clearance. Here the passengers of ships suspected of harbouring disease underwent fumigation and a long wait to see who was healthy enough to be admitted. Some arrivals had so much time to wait that they carved formal inscriptions in stone—or at least graffiti—commemorating the name of their ship, the date and other data. The Quarantine Station operated for more than a century and a half before it was belatedly abandoned in the 1980s, then restored as a tourist attraction.

Back to the beach scene, and **Bondi**, pronounced *bond-eye*, is the closest ocean beach to central Sydney, a

A devotee of Bondi Beach finds his place in the sun near sea-level.

The Jolly Swagman, Continued

When you telephone the Australian Tourist Commission in Sydney and they put you on hold, a familiar, lilting tune comes on the line. The song is known in the far corners of the world, and like a kangaroo or a koala it is as instantly identifiable as Australian. It's the next best thing to a national theme song, even though the lyrics are a mite undignified.

Notwithstanding some dispute about the facts, the words to *Waltzing Matilda* are widely believed to have been written in 1895 by Andrew Barton "Banjo" Paterson, who was not the country bumpkin you might assume from the subject and style. A law graduate of the University of Sydney, he worked as a solicitor, then served as a foreign correspondent covering the Boxer Rebellion in China and the Boer War in South Africa. He published several books of poetry, generally bush ballads.

However cheerful the music, the plot of the *Matilda* story can be depressing at first glance: a roving character who hijacks a sheep, then dives into a waterhole to drown rather than be captured for his crime. But Aussies consider it an emotional tribute to the rebellious character of their pioneer forefathers.

Once a jolly swagman[1] camped by a billabong,[2]
Under the shade of a coolibah-tree[3]
And he sang as he watched and waited till his billy[4] boiled,
"Who'll come a-waltzing Maltida[5] with me?"

Chorus
"Waltzing Matilda, Waltzing Matilda,
Who'll come a-waltzing Matilda with me?"
And he sang as he watched and waited till his billy boiled,
"Who'll come a-waltzing Matilda with me?"

Down came a jumbuck[6] to drink at the billabong.
Up jumped the swagman and grabbed him with glee,
And he sang as he shoved that jumbuck in his tuckerbag,[7]
"You'll come a-waltzing Matilda with me."

Up rode a squatter[8] mounted on his thoroughbred,
Down came the troopers,[9] one, two three,
"Where's that jolly jumbuck you've got in your tuckerbag?
You'll come a-waltzing Matilda with me."

Up jumped the swagman and jumped into the billabong,
"You'll never take me alive," said he.
And his ghost may be heard as you pass by that billabong:
"You'll come a-waltzing Matilda with me!"
(Verse reprinted by courtesy of Angus & Robertson, Ltd., publisher.)

[1] a wanderer in the Outback	[2] waterhole in a river system	[3] a eucalyptus species
[4] can for brewing tea	[5] over-the-shoulder blanket roll	[6] sheep
[7] food bundle	[8] landowner	[9] lawmen

distinction assuring it a full house on summer weekends. The varied cast of characters on the sand includes ancient sunworshippers, bathing beauties, fanatical surfers and a statistically improbable crowd of New Zealanders. If a warning bell clangs, it's not the end of the shift for the lifeguards; it signifies a shark alert. The Life Saving Club here, founded in 1906, was one of the first in the country. Armed with rope reels or rescue boards and boats, the lifesavers in colourful bathing caps are a reassuring part of Australia's seaside scenery.

First Landing

Most tourists who see **Botany Bay** at all see it from the window of an airliner descending on final approach to Kingsford Smith airport at Mascot. Captain Cook's landing place, where the colony of New South Wales was almost founded, is bypassed by excursion coaches and beyond the range of public buses and trains. It's about 30 km (19 miles) by car from the central business district to Kurnell, where the National Parks Service runs a museum celebrating the 1770 visit of Cook and his eager botanists.

The scene today, looking across the bay to the oil tanks and the distant skyscrapers is a far cry, as they say, from what the explorer found. Lining a path in the park beyond the museum, monuments and markers point out details such as the stream from which the *Endeavour* took fresh water and the burial place of the first European to die in Australia. The park is alive with Australian magpies and flashy lorikeets, just the sort of exhibits that the pioneering bird-watcher

Joseph Banks would have loved to catalogue.

On the opposite (north-east) shore of Botany Bay, the **La Pérouse Museum** salutes a French explorer who visited the bay in 1788, immediately after the arrival of the First Fleet. In fact, Captain Phillip and his men were the last to see Jean François de Galaup, the Count of La Pérouse, alive. Thirty-eight years later, the remains of his research ships, *L'Astrolabe* and *La Boussole,* were found in the Solomon Islands. Radar, sonar and satellite navigation came a lot later.

Excursions from Sydney

Tour companies schedule excursions from Sydney in all directions but easterly; only the South Pacific Ocean blocks their enterprise. The most popular northern destination is the Hunter Valley, a picturesque wine-growing and grazing region. To the south lie stunning seascapes, heart-warming countryside and historic towns; they even run gruelling day-trips to Canberra and back. Westward the big attractions are the inspiring Blue Mountains and Jenolan Caves. Whether you sign up for a coach tour or use public transport or drive yourself, they are all worthwhile outings, subject only to restrictions of time and money. Some highlights to help you choose.

Westward Ho!

Driving through the inner city suburbs of Sydney is hardly designed to inspire the traveller. Some streets are as rundown and cheerless as London's East

Gentlemen Farmers

James Ruse claimed to have been the first man ashore when the First Fleet landed. He seemed to be the only convict with farming experience in the Old Country, and the colony was desperate for food. So the governor granted him a 16-ha (40-acre) spread in Parramatta, which was called *Experiment Farm*. Ruse provided the hungry colony's first wheat crop.

A farmer of quite a different style, John Macarthur, arrived as a young officer with the Second Fleet. He named his 40 ha (100-acre) Parramatta estate *Elizabeth Farm*, after his wife. Their house, now "the oldest existing house in Australia", was a very well-designed three-room cottage. Much expanded over the years, it's quite stately today, with lovely gardens. Like *Experiment Farm Cottage* and several other historic sites in Parramatta, it's open for visits.

John Macarthur made history of another sort when he led, from a prison cell, the Rum Rebellion that overthrew Captain Bligh in 1808. The wily Macarthur managed to escape prosecution when imperial power was restored.

End ever offered, a total contrast to the glitter of the business district or the landscaping and architecture of the "better" suburbs.

Sydney's suburbs sprawl relentlessly. Population statistics show the centre of gravity of the metropolitan area has reached the historic town of **Parramatta**, about 25 km (15 miles) west of the central business district. The first governor of New South Wales, Captain Arthur Phillip, founded Parramatta in 1788, only months after the First Fleet arrived at Sydney Cove. He

*H*ighlight of the Blue Mountains, the Three Sisters rock formation inspired an Aboriginal legend.

came by boat, along the Parramatta River, in search of agricultural land. The first harvest, of wheat, barley and maize, was welcomed just over a year

126

later. Parramatta (originally named Rose Hill) claims many other "firsts" in Australian history: first marketplace, tannery, woollen mill, vineyard, observatory, and a final achievement—the first legal brewery. The town became an important farming and, eventually, industrial centre, and it is now a city in its own right, with a 21-storey building, but speckled with historical monuments.

Blue Mountains

Botanists, geologists, ornithologists and just plain tourists rave about the Blue Mountains, the spectacular range that hems in metropolitan Sydney. Rugged enough to have cramped the young colony of New South Wales into a corner of the continent, the mountains of the Great Dividing Range weren't really insurmountable. Only the valleys—deep gorges like a

Grand Canyon filled with giant euca-lyptus forests—were impassable. Or so it seemed until it was discovered, much later, that Aborigines had inhabited the valleys for thousands of years.

Upon reflection, the solution to the problem seems obvious: take the high road. In 1813 a party of explorers—Blaxland, Lawson and Wentworth—finally conquered the obstacle by cross-ing the summits.

What a thrill the first over-the-top travellers must have felt when they spied the western plains beyond the "impenetrable" Blue Mountains. The blueness, incidentally, is explained by the refraction of light through the haze of eucalyptus oil evaporating from the billions of leaves.

Today's Sidneysiders choose the Blue Mountains as an easy-to-reach (only 65 km or 40 miles) escape from the summer heat, a chance to inhale the cool, fragrant air and listen to the birds. The region's tourist centre, the 19th-century town of **Katoomba**, looks out on a famous rock formation, the **Three Sisters**. This is the kind of sculptured outcrop that is bound to be shrouded in legend. The three sisters were turned into stone by their witch-doctor father, to save them from the jaws of the dreaded "bunyip" whom they accidentally awakened. The father changed himself into a lyrebird and hid in a little cave, but lost his magic bone in the process. He is still looking for it today, and while the three sisters watch and wait on their mountain ledge, you can hear the call of Tyawan the lyre-bird echoing through the valley.

Everywhere there are memorable bushwalks along clifftops or valley floor, and basalt and sandstone cliffs to please the most discerning moun-tain-climber. Exciting perspectives on all this are offered from the Scenic Railway, claiming to be the world's steepest railway line, with an incline ratio of more than one in two, and the Scenic Skyway, an aerial cable-car dangling high above the valley.

For more than a century, spelunkers and ordinary tourists have admired the stalactites, stalagmites and special ef-fects of **Jenolan Caves**, at the end of a long, steep drive down the mountains from Katoomba. It's said the caves were discovered, in 1838, by a lawman tracking down a fugitive. Guided tours through the spooky but often awesome limestone caverns last about an hour and a half. There are several different tours to choose from, according to the degree of exertion you're up to. The atmosphere is cool in summer, warm in winter, and always drippily damp.

Beyond the Mountains
The Great Western Highway leads be-yond the Great Dividing Range into the Central West region of New South Wales. It's a striking introduction to the land opened in the early 19th cen-tury by highly motivated pioneers, in-cluding the enthusiastic convicts who built the road in exchange for pardons.

The industrial and coal-mining city of **Lithgow**, 140 km (87 miles) west of Sydney, is hardly a glamorous way to start, but railway buffs will want to stay a while. The Lithgow Valley Zigzag Railway, tortuously linking mountain and valley, was one of the wonders of Victorian-era engineering. Tunnel-building progress made it re-dundant in 1910, but the original route was so remarkable, and the views so glorious, that part of the itinerary has been revived for vintage steam fans.

Australia's oldest inland city, **Bathurst**, was founded in 1815 by Governor Macquarie himself. A relic of the era, Old Government House, dates from 1821. There are other historic buildings, none more splendid than the Victorian Renaissance courthouse in a gardened setting facing Kings Parade. The tourist office and a historical museum occupy the east wing. If Bathurst is known beyond the state, it's because of the Mount Panorama motor-racing circuit, the venue for the James Hardie 1000 race, held every October. You won't be in Bathurst long without hearing about the city's favourite son, Ben Chifley (1885–1951), a railway engine-driver who went on to trade union activism, politics and, from 1945–49, the job of Prime Minister of Australia. Pilgrims come to visit the humble family home in Busby Street, South Bathurst.

Mudgee, only seven years younger than Bathurst, is the centre of an agricultural region with riches ranging from cattle to wheat to wine. There are about 20 wineries in the area, most of them still family-owned and hospitable. Honey is another valuable "crop" in these green valleys, suggesting more tastings for the discerning palate. The bees also pitch in to help produce honey wine, or mead.

Gulgong once called itself the Athens of the West, but that was in the gold rush days when the footlights were up at the Prince of Wales Opera House. The local Pioneer Museum reflects most aspects of frontier life with invaluable artefacts. Around the town, 170 buildings are classified as historically significant. This is where the bush poet Henry Lawson grew up; he and Gulgong were immortalized on the back of the Australian $10 note.

Dubbo is the sort of place where the Old Gaol, meticulously restored, is a prime tourist attraction, gallows and all. Just out of town, the Western Plains Zoo, Australia's first open-range zoo, is a cageless convention of koalas, dingoes and emus, plus more exotic (to Australians) animals like giraffes, zebras and monkeys. There are a couple of thousand creatures in all, including endangered species. Although the zoo is open all day, the cool of the early morning is the best time to visit—before the animals snuggle into shady escapes from the heat.

Hunter Valley

The famous wines of the Hunter Valley go back to the early days of Australian history. The young colony's first vines, planted in Sydney, had come a cropper because of the soil, the climate and the salt air, so the experiment was transferred to the rolling hills of the Hunter Valley. By the middle of the 19th century the region was producing hundreds of thousands of bottles of wine per year. Nowadays Australia accounts for about 1 per cent of all the world's wine. That might not sound like much, but it's more than enough to keep the country in good spirits; the overspill is exported.

In the Hunter Valley, still one of the nation's main wine regions, they take what they do, from rieslings to madeiras, very seriously. The scenery of gentle hills is attractive, the more so when the vines are arrayed on a slope with mountains as the backdrop.

The wine district's main town, **Cessnock**, 195 km (120 miles) north of Sydney, is surrounded by about 30 wineries. Many of these establishments are open for wine tastings, which can be jammed on Sundays and holidays. To discourage the flightier sort of visitors, who tend to bolt down the samples in undiscerning haste, most of the wineries now charge an entry fee. But you're under no obligation to buy a bottle of the local speciality or any of the other souvenirs on sale. If the wine-tastings go to your head and you're not being driven home—by a coach driver or your own chauffeur—it's reassuring to know that Cessnock has a broad selection of hotels and motels.

Beyond the grapes, the region is an industrial stronghold. The Hunter's biggest city, the seaport of **Newcastle**, is a coalmining and shipbuilding centre recently emphasizing tourism and high-tech industries. It's strong on parks and beaches, including a super surfing beach. In the port, the sprawling Queen's Wharf tourist development has replaced a drab warehouse zone. On a promontory overlooking the harbour, naval guns still testify to a historic incident of World War II: Fort Scratchley was the only battery in Australia to have fired in anger. The target was an attacking Japanese submarine, which quickly fled. If you're in a cultural mood, check out the modern Newcastle Regional Art Gallery, home of some admirable Australian paintings.

South of Newcastle, and an extension of its "aquatic playground" theme, is Australia's largest saltwater lake. **Lake Macquarie** is popular with weekend fishermen and sailors who like a good yacht race without having to risk their lives in the Pacific. In fact, regattas have been held here regularly for more than a century. Because of the intricate ins and outs of its shoreline, Lake Macquarie's perimeter is four times that of Sydney Harbour.

Hawkesbury River

According to some enthusiasts, the Hawkesbury River, north-west of Sydney, is the most beautiful river in the whole country. If not, it's certainly in the running. Boatsmen rave about its sparkling waters and ever-changing vistas—coves and bays and steep wooded banks. One unusual way of experiencing the river is aboard the mail boat, which maintains the backwoods postal lifeline. It departs Monday to Friday mornings and again on Wednesday and Friday afternoons from the port of Brooklyn.

Wisemans Ferry has been a port since 1817, when an enterprising former convict named Solomon Wiseman opened an inn there and started ferrying cattle and people across the river. **Dharug National Park**, on the far shore, is a mostly unspoiled place for bushwalks and camping. There are ancient Aboriginal sites, and by way of more recent history you can walk part of the Old Great North Road, built by chain gangs in the 1820s.

North of the Hawkesbury, at Gosford, history buffs can surround themselves with the atmosphere of the original penal colony, reconstructed at **Old Sydney Town**. Something startling is usually going on: budding actors in period costumes duel, march, fire musket and cannon, and generally keep busy to amuse and inform visitors. A

Wagon trails converge in a theme park devoted to history, Old Sydney Town.

blacksmith, a potter and a candlestick-maker work at their traditional crafts, and a "magistrate" shows the way summary justice used to be dealt.

On the way to Old Sydney Town, the Pacific Highway cuts through **Ku-ring-gai Chase National Park**. This compact area of unspoiled forests, cliffs and heathland is home base for numerous species of animals and 160 varieties of native birds. But you have to find them for yourself; it's not a zoo. By way of man-made attractions, the Aborigines who lived in this area long before the foundation of New South Wales left hundreds of rock carvings—pictures of animals and supernatural beings. The information

centre in the park has maps pinpointing the location of the most interesting carvings. From the information centre a 15-minute orientation walk has been laid out; it's so easy you could do it with a baby buggy or a wheelchair. Along the path, kangaroos linger like so many artists' models holding their poses.

Southern Highlands

The Hume Highway, heading south from Parramatta, is named after the explorer Hamilton Hume, who discovered the Murray River in 1824. The road links Sydney and Melbourne, so you can be sure of heavy traffic, including impatient truck-trailer rigs, almost any time of the day. The good news, though, is the scenery as the highway traverses the Southern Highlands—lush grazing land interrupted by towns and villages right out of the history books.

131

*F*lowers by the basketful adorn the Georgian-era gentility in the Southern Highlands. The region is rich in history and scenery

Victorian-age history comes first, at the "gateway to the Southern Highlands", **Mittagong**. In the middle of the 19th century this was an iron-smelting town, but the industry fizzled before the turn of the century. Among the tourist attractions, you can lose yourself in a king-sized maze or commune with flocks of lepidopterous delights in a butterfly house. Just 5 km (3 miles) south, **Bowral** is a nicely gardened small town with an annual tulip festival. It used to be a favourite resort for Sydney's upper crust.

The Hume Highway slices through charming **Berrima**, a Georgian gem so precious that all of it is listed as a national monument. The town can vaunt many a monument, not least the Surveyor General Inn, established 1834, advertised as Australia's oldest continuously licensed inn. Another landmark is the Berrima Gaol, from the same era; in the beginning of the 20th century it was reserved for habitual criminals, but after big renovations it became a rehabilitation centre. On a higher plane, two fine churches from the mid-19th century overlook the stately Common: Holy Trinity for the Anglicans and St Xavier's for the Catholics.

Bundanoon was a honeymoon haven for Sydneysiders a couple of generations before the discovery of cheap flights to Bali. The town sits on the edge of **Morton National Park**, noted for its gorges and gullies, and suitable for either peaceful strolls or rigorous bushwalks. A moving highlight is **Fitzroy Falls**, cascading 82 m (269 ft) from a sandstone cliff.

Wildlife Outings

Within day-trip distance of Sydney, many private parks cater to visitors who'd like to get to know the native animals. Some are on the excursion-coach itineraries. A sampler of wildlife parks and the like, in alphabetical order, follows.

Australian Reptile Park, near Gosford. Lovely alligators, crocodiles, pythons and cobras are waiting to greet you. If you're not keen on fondling a lizard or watching the handler milking a venomous snake you can concentrate on more cuddly exhibits, like koalas and kangaroos.

Australian Wildlife Park, one hour's drive west of central Sydney, has kangaroos as tame as your cat, but friendlier. If the koalas are unenthusiastic about posing for pictures with the clients, it may be because they are nocturnal creatures and would rather be asleep.

Featherdale Wildlife Park, one hour west of Sydney. A big shop stocked with souvenirs relevant to Australian wildlife awaits at the end of a visit to the kangaroos and kookaburras, penguins and pelicans. The koalas come out of their stupor between 10.00 a.m. and 11.30 a.m. and from 2.30 to 3.30 p.m. daily. The flock of native birds is called Australia's biggest privately owned collection.

Forest of Tranquillity, near Gosford. Just a natural rainforest and bird sanctuary, an hour's drive north of Sydney, with special attractions for children (such as a wallaby named Wally). There's a big picnic area. Closed Mondays and Tuesdays except during holidays.

Koala Park Sanctuary, at West Pennant Hills, between Parramatta and Hornsby. Founded 1930. The adorable koalas do little but eat and sleep, yawn and sigh and scratch themselves, like so many furry, roly-poly little old men trying to recover from a hangover. Kangaroos galore wait to be petted. And brilliant native birds hang out in roomy aviaries.

Tobruk Merino Sheep Station, near Wisemans Ferry, is billed as a working sheep station less than 90 minutes from the heart of Sydney. Personable experts explain all aspects of raising sheep, rounding them up, shearing them, sorting the wool and packing it for export. Tourists get to try their hand, often hilariously, at shearing. The sheep don't exactly enjoy it but they tend to protest more mildly than a dog being bathed.

Waratah Park, "35 minutes from downtown Sydney" on the edge of Ku-ring-gai Chase National Park. Koalas available for petting, and gregarious kangaroos, too. The emus are less predictable. Waratah Park was the location for a television series called "Skippy the Bush Kangaroo".

In the wildlife parks tourists make friends with tame kangaroos. In the wild the truth is that the farmers would rather be rid of them.

Farther Afield

North Coast

The farther north you go in New South Wales the more the subtropical climate mellows the holiday atmosphere. Year after year surfers and sunbathers come back to the North Coast of New South Wales, alias the Holiday Coast. Behind the resorts and fishing villages, a rich agricultural region leads up to the magnificent Great Dividing Range.

Port Macquarie, a resort centre halfway up the coast from Sydney to the Queensland frontier, considers that its climate is the best anywhere. Strange, then, that it was originally chosen, in 1820, as a penal colony within the penal colony—a place to send troublesome convicts from the southerly areas. Its inaccessibility was the catch, but that little problem was soon solved, and free settlers swarmed in. Find out more about early colonial life in the Hastings District Historical Museum, in an 1830s commercial building. In addition to beaches and all manner of water sports, the area is rich in commercial tourist attractions like koala parks, dolphin shows and children's amusements.

A prominent tourist attraction inland from Port Macquarie, **Timbertown** is a reconstitution of a 19th-century village and its logging operation.

Catch the Kitsch

Lovers of traditional art and architecture may cringe, but the style known as *Kitsch* reaches some sort of apogee in Australia.

In German, *kitsch* means rubbish. The English language borrowed the word and applied it to vulgar or tawdry art or literature descending to the lowest common denominator of popular taste. In Australia fruit seems to inspire the kitschmasters to create huge symbols: the Coffs Harbour Big Banana, Queensland's Big Pineapple, South Australia's Big Orange. Animals, too, such as the Big Merino at Goulburn, NSW—a sheep as big as a three-storey house.

Is it all in grossly bad taste, or just good, clean fun? The children, in any case, love it.

Covering 35 ha (86 acres), it brings back to life many aspects of the old lumber industry, from the clang of the village smithy to the din of a steam-powered sawmill.

Timber is still a serious endeavour northward around **Nambucca Heads**, a relaxed ocean-and-estuary resort, with everything from surfing to canoeing.

Vastly bigger and livelier, **Coffs Harbour** has beaches beyond beaches; fishing boats and pleasure craft occupy the harbour. Just north of town, you can't miss one of the Australia's pioneer efforts in kitsch gigantism, the Big Banana, a walk-through tribute to a local delicacy. Banana splits, banana cakes and every other variation are sold on the garish premises, now expanded into a horticultural theme park.

Another estuary town, **Ballina,** has an important 19th-century lighthouse and relics of a remarkable expedition. In 1973 three balsa rafts built according to the ancient methods of South American Indians drifted from Ecuador across the Pacific and landed here. An exhibition on Las Balsas Expedition is in the tourist office. Among other spots of touristic interest are an opal and gem museum and a wildlife sanctuary.

The coast road north from Ballina to **Byron Bay** is a real thriller. A brave lighthouse blinks the news that Cape Byron is the continent's easternmost point. The wonderful setting, which is a hang-gliding favourite, and the supply of perfect, underpopulated beaches, attracts artists, surfers and other eccentrics. Presumably for other reasons, it attracts humpback whales, as well; they can be spotted off the cape every winter.

South Coast

The other fellow's grass is always greener, and while Sydneysiders tend to go north for their holidays, people from Victoria arrive to fill in the vacuum along the south coast of New South Wales. There are no complaints about the weather, the beaches, the villages or the scenery.

Highway 1 southward from Sydney is strictly businesslike, but if you choose the coast road, you're in for some invigorating scenery. At the aptly named **Sublime Point**, "415.41 m above sea level", according to the sign, you'll have as grandiose an ocean view as you're likely to see anywhere in the South Pacific. The same scenery can be admired from a different perspective, a few hundred metres south at **Bulli Lookout**, where you can also look straight down on to the thick forest backing the seafront.

From here, too, you can see the smokestacks of **Wollongong**, the state's third largest city. Nearby beaches and a pleasant fishing port soften the industrial profile. Wollongong also has a prize-winning pedestrian mall with 400 shops.

Beyond the seabird-infested salt lake called **Lake Illawarra**, a popular recreation area, a famous natural phenomenon is the **blowhole** at **Kiama**. When the ocean is of a mind, the explosion of sea water is a sight—and sound—to remember. It's so impressive they provide floodlights.

Beyond the commercial fishing port and tourist centre of Ulladulla, beautiful, oyster-rich **Batemans Bay** was named by Captain Cook in 1770. At the foot of the Clyde Mountain Ranges, it's the closest seaside resort to

---

Canberra-by-the-Sea

Gerrymandering has assured landlocked Canberra a toe-hold on the South Pacific. Jervis Bay, a New South Wales peninsula south of Nowra, was annexed to the Australian Capital Territory early in the 20th century on the off chance that the future Canberra might need a seaport. It didn't. The enclave today includes an uncommon combination of facilities: the Royal Australian Naval College, a missile range, inviting dunes and beaches and a nature reserve.

See the wreck of the Cape St George lighthouse. This 19th-century beacon was built in the wrong place, invisible to northbound ships. Worse, the construction itself was considered a hazard to navigation. The navy took aim and reduced it to a historic ruin.

Canberra, so the amateur fishermen in the next boat may well be diplomats or government functionaries.

Big-game fishermen know **Narooma**, from which the boats head for the area of Montague Island, where marlin, kingfish and yellowfin tuna await. The island is a penguin and seal sanctuary.

Another lure for serious fishermen is **Bermagui**. Zane Grey, the American writer of cowboy stories, brought fame to the place when he visited in the 1930s and reported on the marlin he caught. Good game fishing and opportunities for water sports of all kinds extend down the Sapphire Coast, so dubbed for the colour of the sea hereabouts.

The most southerly port in New South Wales, **Eden**, commands spectacular Twofold Bay; someone has calculated that this is the world's third deepest natural harbour. Notwithstanding its virtues, Eden is named after a 19th-century British statesman, not Adam and Eve's garden.

Snowy Mountains

If you've come to Australia in search of snow, go no further than the southeastern corner of New South Wales.

Skiing in the Snowy Mountains is usually restricted to July, August and September, but even in the summer a few drifts of snow remain to frame the wild flowers of the Australian Alps. The top of this world is Mount Kosciusko, 2,228 m (7,316 ft) high, named after an 18th-century Polish patriot by a 19th-century Polish explorer. This is the source of three important rivers, the Murray, the Murrumbidgee and Snowy.

Kosciusko National Park is about 6,300 km² (2,450 miles²) of the kind of wilderness you won't see anywhere else: buttercups, bluebells, eucalyptus and snow, all in the same panorama. All that is missing is a pine tree, or any of the other familiar conifers of the northern hemisphere. Cars must be fitted with snow chains from 1 June to 10 October, but even in summer, when the bushwalks are delightful, the weather can change for the worse, so you should carry a warm, waterproof jacket. Downhill and cross-country skiers can choose from several more or less sophisticated resorts. The best known, **Thredbo** (with the steepest slopes) and **Perisher Valley**, have plenty of accommodation, ski-lifts, and après-ski possibilities.

The Outback

Although New South Wales is the most populous and productive state (in both manufacturing and farming), it extends to infinities of real Australian Outback ... bushland and cattle stations that seem far more than a thousand miles from commuterland.

Lightning Ridge, in the back of beyond near the Queensland border, enjoys one of the most evocative Outback names. Fortune-hunters know it well as the only dependable source of the precious black opal. Within a couple of miles of the town are several tourist-inclined opal mines, well signposted, where you can learn all about opals, and buy some if you wish. Anywhere else in the bleak landscape, proceed with discretion—so you don't fall in a hole, and so you can't be suspected of trying to pillage somebody's stake.

Bourke is a small town whose very name signifies the loneliness of the Outback, where dusty tracks are the only link between distant hamlets. "Back of Bourke" is an Australian expression for *really* far-out Outback. Bourke looks a lot bigger on the map than on the ground. It might be best to stay away in midsummer, when the

At Jervis Bay, a worried rock formation separates beachcombers from the ocean (previous page).

In the Outback the terrain can be anything from menacing desert to grazing land fit for a wild horse (right).

temperature has been known to top 50°C (122°F). But any other time, it's worth soaking up the atmosphere in this old river-port outpost.

Broken Hill (population more than 25,000) is about as far west as you can go in New South Wales, almost on the border of South Australia. The town is legendary for its mineral wealth—millions of tons of silver, lead and zinc ore are extracted every year. The Broken Hill Proprietary Company, which started here in 1885, grew to become Australia's biggest industrial enterprise. Tourists can visit the mines, which are either underground or on the top, and there are mining museums and exhibitions of minerals and relics from the pioneering days. The neatly laid out town, its streets named after minerals—Iodide, Kaolin, Talc—is something of an artistic centre, as well,

Offshore NSW

In the South Pacific, 483 km (300 miles) east of Port Macquarie, Lord Howe Island is called the world's most southerly coral isle. This makes for splendid snorkelling and scuba-diving ... or you can go out to the sea gardens in a glass-bottomed boat. On land there are fascinating plants and birds, most remarkably the local woodhen, which can't fly. Like Ireland, the island is snakeless. Better yet, it's almost carless. Forests, beaches, mountains and all, Lord Howe Island only amounts to a speck in the ocean—1,305 ha (3,225 acres)—so bicycles and motorbikes are ideal for getting around.

You can fly out from Sydney to a sleepy lagoon in a couple of hours. Tourist accommodation is limited—by design—in this World Heritage outpost.

with acclaimed Outback painters on show in a gaggle of local galleries. At Broken Hill airport you can visit the Royal Flying Doctor Service for a briefing on emergency health care back of beyond.

A ghost town, **Silverton**, 25 km (15 miles) west of Broken Hill, looks almost too good to be true. But it's an authentic restoration of the original mining town (one-time population 3,000), with the obligatory gaol as a key historical monument, along with a couple of Victorian-era churches and a former brothel. Dozens of films have been shot here, including *A Town Like Alice*, *Mad Max 2* and *Razorback*. Cool off inside the Wild-West-style pub and consider what a great place Silverton would be to film a beer commercial. (The admen have already thought of it!)

Where Sheep had Grazed, a Model Capital Bloomed

When it came to picking an Australian national capital, the bickering and bargaining of politics had a happy ending. Out of conflict emerged a green and pleasant compromise. Insulated from the pressures of the big cities, in rolling grazing country far from the poles of political power, the young Commonwealth raised its flag in Canberra.

As the new nation was proclaimed at the turn of the 20th century, the perennial power struggle between Sydney and Melbourne reached an awkward deadlock. Each of the cities offset its rival's claim to be the national capital. So they carved out a site in the bush 320 km (200 miles) south-west of Sydney (about twice as far from Melbourne). Soon it began to sprout clean white official buildings, followed by millions of trees and shrubs. As compromises go, it was a big winner.

To design a model capital from scratch, the way Washington, DC, or St Petersburg, Russia, were laid out, Australia opened an international competition. The prize went to an American architect, Walter Burley Griffin. He did, indeed, have a grand design, but it took longer than anyone imagined to transfer his plan from the drawing board to reality, owing to the distractions of two world wars, the depression, and a great deal of wrangling. Burley Griffin, a Chicagoan of the Frank Lloyd Wright school, put the emphasis on coherent connections

Reflecting on a lesson in optics in the sculpture garden of the Australian National Gallery in Canberra.

143

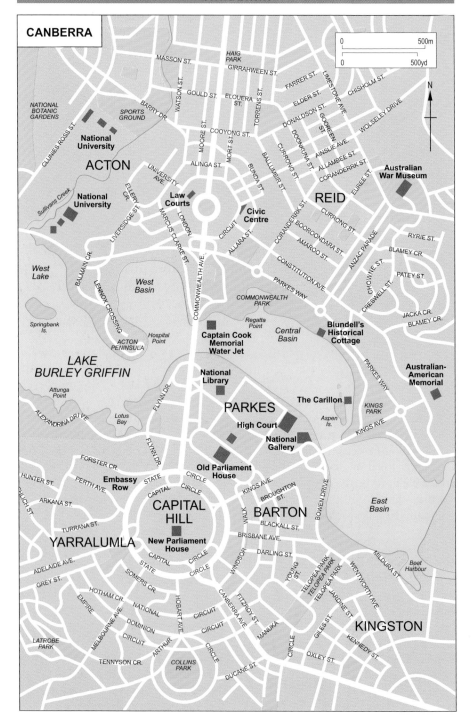

CANBERRA

0   500m
0   500yd

N

NATIONAL BOTANIC GARDENS

SPORTS GROUND

National University

HAIG PARK

MASSON ST.

GIRRAHWEEN ST.

GOULD ST.

ELOUERA ST.

FARRER ST.

ELDER ST.

LIMESTONE AVE.

CHISHOLM ST.

DONALDSON ST.

GOOREEN ST.

WOLSELEY DRIVE

COOYONG ST.

DOONKUNA ST.

AINSLIE AVE.

ACTON

ALINGA ST.

ALLAMBEE ST.

CORANDERRK ST.

Australian War Museum

National University

Law Courts

Civic Centre

REID

CURRONG ST.

RYRIE ST.

BLAMEY CR.

West Lake

West Basin

CONSTITUTION AVE.

PARKES WAY

COMMONWEALTH PARK

PATEY ST.

Springbank Is.

ACTON PENINSULA

Hospital Point

Regatta Point

Captain Cook Memorial Water Jet

Central Basin

Blundell's Historical Cottage

JACKA CR.

BLAMEY CR.

LAKE BURLEY GRIFFIN

National Library

Australian-American Memorial

Attunga Point

The Carillon

KINGS PARK

ALEXANDRINA DRIVE

Lotus Bay

PARKES

High Court

Aspen Is.

KINGS AVE.

National Gallery

FORSTER CR.

Old Parliament House

Embassy Row

STATE CIRCLE

HUNTER ST.

PERTH AVE.

CAPITAL

KINGS AVE.

BROUGHTON ST.

East Basin

ARKANA ST.

CAPITAL HILL

BARTON

BLACKALL ST.

TURRANA ST.

BRISBANE AVE.

YARRALUMLA

New Parliament House

DARLING ST.

Boat Harbour

ADELAIDE AVE.

GREY ST.

HOTHAM CR.

NATIONAL

YOUNG ST.

TELOPEA PARK

WENTWORTH AVE.

MILDURA ST.

DOMINION

CIRCUIT

FITZROY ST.

CANBERRA AVE.

JARDINE ST.

KINGSTON

LATROBE PARK

TENNYSON CR.

COLLINS PARK

MANUKA

GILES ST.

KENNEDY ST.

OXLEY ST.

DUCANE ST.

144

Forget Utopia

Canberra's name, which is said to be derived from "meeting place" in an Aboriginal tongue, was officially chosen in 1913 from among an outpouring of suggestions. Some idealists proposed names as uplifting as Utopia or Shakespeare. Others devised classical inventions like Auralia and Austropolis. The most unusual nomination was a wild coinage designed to satisfy the ambitions of every state capital that lost out in the running for federal power: Sydmeladperbrisho. After that mouthful, the sort of idea committees devise, the name Canberra came as a relief.

*T*own plan of Canberra (opposite).

*N*ew to the busking business, a couple of folk musicians brighten the mood.

between the settings and the buildings, between landscape and cityscape. Burley Griffin died in 1937, years before diplomats and officials started to get the feeling—or more likely orders—that Canberra was a place to settle down as well as work.

At the heart of the Australian Capital Territory, Canberra has a population of 280,000. The local economy is inclined to education and research, and profits much from tourism, yet Canberra is essentially a company town; the local industry is government. The ministries are here, and the parliament with its politicians, lobbyists and hangers-on, and the foreign embassies to add their exotic contribution. In spite of this considerable enterprise, Australia's only sizeable inland city is uncrowded and relaxed. So much green open space has been preserved, and so much inspired landscaping has gone on, that it looks as if they've hardly begun to exploit the place.

City Sights

Seeing Canberra from a hot-air balloon is a good idea. There are several other ways to see the capital, but not on foot; pedestrians are out of luck in the great expanses of this city of parks. As on any map of Australia, the distances are vaster than you think. So it's a good idea to sign up for a bus tour; they come in half-day and all-day versions. Or take the Explorer bus, which stops at all the main sights. You buy an all-day ticket, then hop on and off at will. Or you can drive yourself around town, following itineraries mapped out in a free sightseeing pamphlet. Motorists arriving from either Sydney or Melbourne can pick this up, along with leaflets, maps and advice, on the way into Canberra at the Visitor Information Centre, Northbourne Avenue, Dickson. In the middle of town the Canberra Visitor Centre can be found in the Jolimont Centre, Northbourne Avenue.

An effective starting place for a do-it-yourself tour of Canberra is **Regatta Point**, overlooking the lake that Burley Griffin cleverly surrounded with a city. The **Canberra Planning Exhibition** here uses three-dimensional mock-ups and audiovisual techniques to sum up the capital from its beginnings into the future. It's a painless orientation course.

Lake Burley Griffin, about 35 km (22 miles) around, is generously named after the town planner who realized the value of water for recreation as well as scenic beauty. You can tour the ins and outs of this man-made lake on sightseeing cruise boats. Or look into the fishing, sailing and windsurfing.

Whooshing up from the lake, a giant **water jet** honours the explorer Captain Cook for several hours each day. The **Carillon**, another monument rising from Lake Burley Griffin (actually from a small island), was a gift from the British government. The music of its 53 bells, the biggest weighing six tons, can comfortably be heard within a radius of 300 m (985 ft). Apart from concert recitals, it tells the time every 15 minutes, taking its tune from London's Big Ben.

North of the Lake

Canberra is older and greener than Brasília, and harder to navigate than an earlier "artificial" capital, Washington, DC, which has less than 10 per cent of the area of the ACT. To get the big picture, consider the view from the **Telecom Tower** atop Black Mountain. Millions of sightseers have paid to ascend the 195-m (640-ft) tower for the 360° perspective. What with Canberra's pollution-free atmosphere, it's usually worth the investment, even at night, when the capital's public buildings are illuminated. Enclosed and open-air viewing platforms circle the structure towards the top. The designers couldn't resist adding a revolving restaurant, open day and night for panorama-loving gourmets.

On the eastern slopes of Black Mountain, the **National Botanic Gardens** are entirely devoted to Australian flora—the most comprehensive collection anywhere, with more than 6,000 species of native plants. In spite of Canberra's mostly mild, dry climate, rainforest specimens flourish under

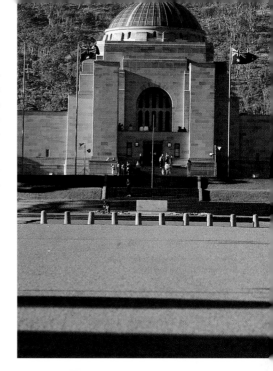

intensive care. Walter Burley Griffin was so fascinated by the native trees and plants that he put this place in his original plan. Nature trails are marked among the 40 ha (nearly 100 acres) of forests and gardens.

The only part of the capital designed with pedestrians in mind is the area around the **Civic Centre**. The original business and shopping district opened in 1927—ancient history by Canberra's standards—with symmetrical white-colonnaded buildings in a mock-Spanish style. Nearby are modern shopping malls, the Canberra Theatre Centre, and a historic merry-go-round.

Distinguished Domes

One of Canberra's best known landmarks, the **Australian Academy of Science**, is for looking and photographing but not for visiting. Architecturally, it's an interesting study in curves. The low-slung copper-plated dome rests on graceful arches standing in a circular moat. Some say it looks like a flying saucer at rest.

A more conventional dome covers the vast **Australian War Memorial**, a sandstone shrine climaxing a ceremonial avenue called **Anzac Parade**. There are war memorials all over Australia, but this is the definitive one, which draws around a million visitors a year. It's hard to avoid being swept up in the mood of the place as you walk past walls inscribed with the names of more than 100,000 Australian war dead. But beyond the heroic statues and mosaic murals, the memorial is a museum, with displays of uniforms through the years, battle maps, and plenty of hardware, from rifles to a real World War II Lancaster bomber.

*I*mperial memories at the War Memorial. Republicans press for the removal of the mini-Union Jack from the Australian flag.

Closer to the lake, one final military monument: the **Australian-American Memorial**, a slim aluminium shaft supporting a stylized eagle with its wings upheld in a V-for-victory mode. It was paid for by public contributions to acknowledge US participation in the defence of Australia in World War II.

South of the Lake

The mostly windowless walls of the **Australian National Gallery** were designed to enclose "a museum of

147

international significance", as official policy decreed. The enterprise has succeeded on several levels, showing off artists as varied as Monet and Matisse, Pollack and de Kooning, and an honour roll of Australian masters. Another indication of the range of interests: displays of art from Pacific island peoples, black Africa, and pre-Columbian America. A high point is the collection of Australian Aboriginal art: dreamily intricate human and animal forms on bark, evolving into today's version in polymer paint on chipboard, dots and whorls and cross-hatching looking at first glance like arbitrary abstractions.

Nothing stodgy about the modern architecture of the High Court, a dramatic sight on the lakeside in Canberra.

The gallery's glistening garden of sculpture can only be seen from outside the building, according to plan, lest the patrons within be distracted.

The **High Court**, linked to the National Gallery by a footbridge, is a bold, boxy building with an immense expanse of glass on its façade. This last stop for legal appeals bears no resemblance to the Victorian halls of justice elsewhere in the country. But it is no less impressive for its unconventional looks. The building's gigantic public hall is sometimes used for exhibitions and concerts.

Also on the lakefront, 44 slender marble columns and expanses of stained-glass windows mark the **National Library**, which houses more than 2,000,000 books—but not for browsing. This institution serves scholars and other libraries, not the drop-in reader. But you needn't feel totally excluded, for there are guided tours and exhibitions.

Embassy Row

The diplomatic quarter, branching out well beyond the leafy suburb of Yarralumla, is a showcase of architectural vanities and charms, well worth a tour by car or sightseeing bus. In the early days of Canberra, diplomats dreaded the prospect of being transferred to the wilds, and most countries dragged their feet about moving until Prime Minister Menzies got tough in the 1950s. The United States was the first nation to open a legation in the new capital. Today's US Embassy, on a hill, is a fine replica of an 18th-century American mansion. Many other countries also decided to erect buildings typical of their cultures on Embassy Row, such as the Thai embassy with its sweeping roofs and the Indonesian compound adorned with statues of legendary figures. The Japanese embassy has a tea house in its formal garden.

Canberra's long-standing temporary Parliament House became the seat of government in 1927. Considering its provisional nature, it had a high degree of low-slung, understated dignity. A new, permanent **Parliament House** to replace it was dedicated by Queen Elizabeth II in the bicentennial year of 1988. You can't miss it: the novel four-legged flagpole stretches 81 m (265 ft) above the roof. Although it aims to avoid visible monumental excess, snuggling into the terrain of Capital Hill, the structure has been called the largest building in the southern hemisphere. The combination of unusual design and exploding building costs made the new complex, on the site originally selected by Burley Griffin, a billion-dollar *cause célèbre*. Taxpayers noted the lavish offices, bars, swimming pool and sauna. But the politicians were prudent enough to include plenty of facilities for the public—galleries for witnessing the debates, exhibitions, a cafeteria and a post office.

Still on the subject of money, they're minting it in the south-western district called Deakin, and you can watch. The **Royal Australian Mint** has a visitors' gallery overlooking the production line where the nation's coins are punched out. The factory also "moonlights" to produce the coins of several other countries. The Mint's own museum contains coins and medals of special value. If you're more attracted to hundred-dollar notes, you've come to the wrong fortress: Australia's paper money is printed in Melbourne.

Out of Town

Animal-lovers have a choice of places to go to meet kangaroos, echidnas, wombats and whatnot. The **Mugga Lane Zoo** is only a few miles southeast of the city centre, in Red Hill. The bird population includes parrots, kookaburras (the largest kingfishers), cockatoos and earth-bound emus. Rounding out the children's department is a complement of animals to fondle.

Rehwinkel's Animal Park, about 25 km (15 miles) north of the city, is actually across the border in New South Wales. In a roomy bushland setting, free-roaming kangaroos are available to be petted. The bird department features black swans and peacocks.

Gerrymandering has given the landlocked Capital Territory a foothold on the Pacific at Jervis Bay.

The **Tidbinbilla Nature Reserve**, 40 km (25 miles) south-west of Canberra, is a much bigger affair—thousands of acres of bushland where the native flora and fauna flourish. Kangaroo fans can feed the bounders in a reserve within the reserve. The walking trails are graded from easy to exhausting.

Next to this unspoiled wilderness, the **Tidbinbilla Deep Space Tracking Station** takes advantage of its isolation, training its immense antennae on the most intriguing novelties of the cosmos. The Australian Department of Science operates the station on behalf of the US space agency, NASA. Exhibitions on space exploration are open to the public.

Along the Barton Highway north of Canberra, the **Opal and Gemstone Museum** is built around what's called the world's largest presentation of Australian opals. Also on show are Aboriginal artefacts. There are demonstrations of cutting and polishing precious stones, but it's not all academic: they're for sale, too.

Across the road, **Cockington Green** is one of those miniature villages that capture the imagination of children. At one-twelfth actual size, the houses and gardens of an "olde world" British village are meticulously transformed to fairy-tale dimensions. Fun, but not exactly dinky-di Australian.

Wildlife Down Under: The ABCs

A is for **Antichinus**, a mousy little marsupial rarely seen because of its camouflage and habit of hiding out in the daytime. Chances are an antichinus never knew its father. It seems the mating season is so intense that all the adult males die of their exertions.

The **Bandicoot** is a distant relative of the kangaroo. A nocturnal prowler with big eyes the better to see in the dark, the bandicoot has long ears and a very long snout. Having a sensational sense of smell helps with the hunting.

Crocodiles come in estuarine and freshwater versions. It's wise to avoid

And P is for Parrots, of which lorikeets are one of about 60 species found in Austrlia.

either one, but the "salty", which may grow as long as a telephone pole, is the noted man-killer. Tending to sunbathe half-submerged in the swamp, a croc can fail to catch your attention until it's too late.

Dingoes, which are supposed to be descended from wolves, have a lot in common with dogs except for their bushier tails and the fact that they don't know how to bark. They have a bad reputation in Australia because, alone or in pairs, they ambush sheep and calves.

Dugongs, also known as sea cows, were once thought to be mermaids, though it wouldn't be easy to fall in love with one of the lumbering, small-eyed, bull-necked creatures. They are mammals inhabiting warm coastal waters, where they thrive on seaweed. Like whales, they are very good at holding their breath.

Echidna is a less formal name than *Tachyglossus aculeatus,* but the little monotreme (egg-laying mammal) is more familiarly known as the Spiny Anteater. The spiny part (think of a porcupine in need of a haircut) is a good defence. The offence is in the long snout, containing a sticky tongue that zaps the hapless ants.

The **Emu**, something of a dodo, is a bird that can't fly. However, this ostrich-like behemoth can run at 50 kmh (30 mph) or more. The male emu is an admirable father: while the young mother is off gallivanting, he guards the eggs and then looks after the chicks until they can face life.

The **Fairy Penguin,** smallest and cutest of all penguins, thrives in the cold southern sea, insulated by waterproof feathers. No bigger than a seagull, it swims fast and effortlessly many miles from home in search of desirable fish. It comes ashore lurching like a drunken sailor, for it swims better than it walks.

Flying Foxes, or fruit bats, are rather more likeable than the kind of bats in nightmares, but not much handsomer. Terrifyingly large colonies of these flying mammals gather in trees, where they sleep head down. If it gets chilly they wrap up in their enormous "wings".

Geckoes may look like mini-dragons but they are harmless lizards that help to control the mosquito population. Australia has dozens of species, the biggest growing nearly a foot long. In a life-and-death confrontation a gecko can escape from a predator by surrendering its tail, which will eventually grow back.

Hopping mice, which propel themselves rather like minuscule kangaroos, live in the desert. Their oversized ears are like cooling towers; they also beat the heat by spending the day deep underground. They are wonderful survivors (mice may have arrived in Australia 5,000,000 years ago).

The **Ibis**, a long-legged, long-necked, curve-billed wading bird, is found in warm Australian scenery such as marshland. It is related to the heron and stork, and to the sacred ibis revered by the ancient Egyptians.

It is also related to the **Jabiru**, the common name for Australia's own stork, the impressive *Xenorhynchus asiaticus.* You might see one in Queensland or the Northern Territory.

Kangaroos come in all sizes, from the red—often taller than a man—to the musk kangaroo, no taller than a year-old child. The joey, born in an embryonic stage, moves into the mother's pouch for about six months of nursing. With their deer-like faces and congenial personalities, these marsupials are big favourites, but not with Australian farmers, whose grain they appropriate.

Koalas, the cuddliest creatures in Australia, require vast quantities of a high-fibre diet of eucalyptus leaves. When they are not eating (no drinking; they get moisture from the leaves) these funny-faced marsupials are usually sleeping in the trees. Like the kangaroo, the koala produces an unfinished baby that matures in the pouch, rear-facing in this case.

The **Laughing Kookaburra** is a kind of kingfisher with a call that's more maniacal than musical. The sound of kookaburras chattering may awaken you almost anywhere in Australia. The bird is prettier than its voice.

Marsupial Moles are denizens of the desert, living in the cool tunnels they dig in the sand. Thus you will probably never see one in the wild. Nor will a marsupial mole ever see you, because it is blind, and deaf, which doesn't hinder its hunt for food—insects.

Numbats look rather like striped squirrels, and they can hop, too. But being beautiful and agile isn't enough in our tough world. Numbats, classified as carnivorous marsupials, are all but toothless, slurping ants and termites the way anteaters do. Since they live in underbrush they are vulnerable to bushfires.

Junior peeks out of the pouch of a common grey Kangaroo, poised on her powerful hind legs and tail.

Ornithorhynchus anatinus is much better known as the **Platypus**, a creature so bizarre that the first reports were dismissed as a hoax. This amphibious Australian exclusive combines characteristics of mammal, reptile and bird. In all, the platypus, a monotreme, looks as unlikely as a winged pig. The male would make an awkward house-pet, due to the poisonous spurs on its hind legs.

Possums, vegetarian marsupials, come in many sizes with varied talents. Some can hang by their tails, some can even fly, or at least glide. They have bulging black eyes, which are useful when foraging on the night shift; in the daytime they mostly sleep, in nests, in tree-branches, or even under a house.

The Eastern **Quoll**, once familiar in eastern Australia, is now found only in Tasmania. Even there it's not exactly popular, for this is a marsupial with a taste for fresh meat, such as somebody's chickens.

Rats, too, have an image problem. In Australia, as elsewhere, they are all too common. There are country rats and city rats, tree-dwelling rats and water rats. The latter may have something approaching webbed feet to enhance mobility.

Skinks, not to be confused with skunks, are lizards with legs so short they look a bit like miniature green slithering dachshunds. A striking member of the skink family is the blue-tongued lizard.

Kookaburras are members of the Kingfisher family. Laughing Kookaburras have a mad, chattering call.

Tasmanian Devils, in spite of their ferocious appearance, are really quite shy, mild of manner and clean. Pink-eared and mousy-faced with flamboyant whiskers, the devil (origin of the name uncertain) is a meat-eating marsupial the size of a small dog.

The **Tasmanian Tiger,** the biggest-ever carnivorous marsupial, is thought to be extinct, or nearly so. The last one in a zoo died decades ago, but sightings are sometimes reported from the Tasmanian wilderness.

Urchin, Sea. The most important point is this: don't step on one of these underwater porcupines while wading into the ocean. Those prickly spines are dangerous. Other echinoderm varieties include the starfish.

Whales are too cosmopolitan to be classed as Australian animals, but they're often seen in the neighbourhood. Humpback whales commute between Australia and the Antarctic. Less charming are the killer whales, who are also around.

Wombats have a lot in common with koalas but they eat all kinds of grasses, herbs and roots and they do their sleeping underground—in elaborate burrows, which they constantly expand and improve. They are about the size of piglets with the muscles of, well, tunnel-builders.

Yellow-Bellied Sea Snakes are the most common sea snakes inhabiting the warmer waters of Australia. Ashore there are 100 or more species of dangerous snakes. The long-fanged Taipan is the most terrible of all; in a supreme example of overkill, it's said to pack enough venom to kill a couple of hundred sheep. But it's shy enough to want to get out of your way. Theoretically.

Zebras, zebus and other really exotic animals don't live here, but they can be inspected in many of Australia's fine zoos.

The Big, Bold, Beautiful State with an Offshore Wonderland

The Sunshine State, the Holiday State, Amazing Queensland—let the admen fight over the slogans. They're on the right track, though, for nature has blessed this relaxed and relaxing state with a unique assortment of delights, fulfilling the vacation dreams of backpackers and billionaires, and almost everybody else.

Twice the size of Texas, sun-soaked Queensland is big and varied enough so you can choose among flashy tourist resorts, Outback mining towns or a modern metropolis; the terrain runs from rainforest to desert to apple orchard. The most amazing attraction of all is Queensland's offshore wonderland—the longest coral reef in the world, the Great Barrier Reef.

Queensland is one of those typical Australian success stories. It was founded in 1824 as a colony for incorrigible convicts, the "worst kind of felons", for whom not even the rigours of New South Wales were a deterrent. To quarantine criminality, free settlers were banned from an 80-km (50-mile) radius. But adventurers, missionaries and hopeful immigrants couldn't be held back for long, and only 18 years after Governor Thomas Brisbane established the penal colony, Queensland was emancipated. The lure of the pasturelands began to look tame in 1867 when the state joined the great Australian gold rush with a find of its own. Prosperity for all seemed just around the corner.

Mining still contributes generously to Queensland's economy. Above ground, the land is kind to cattle and

A picnic at sea enlivens an overcast day in the Whitsunday Islands.

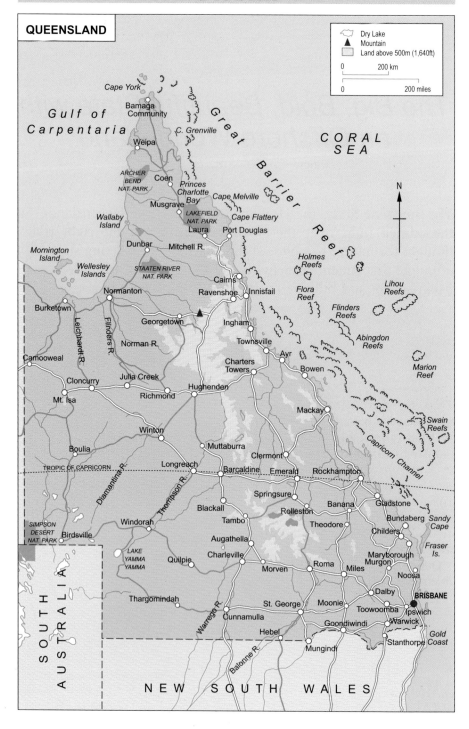

QUEENSLAND

Dry Lake
▲ Mountain
Land above 500m (1,640ft)

0   200 km

0   200 miles

Cape York

Gulf of
Carpentaria

Bamaga
Community

C. Grenville

Weipa

Great Barrier Reef

CORAL
SEA

ARCHER
BEND
NAT. PARK

Coen
Princes
Charlotte
Bay   Cape Melville
Musgrave

Wallaby
Island

LAKEFIELD
NAT. PARK   Cape Flattery

Laura   Port Douglas

Mornington
Island

Dunbar   Mitchell R.

Holmes
Reefs

Lihou
Reefs

Wellesley
Islands

STAATEN RIVER
NAT. PARK

Cairns

Flora
Reef

Normanton   Ravenshoe Innisfail

Flinders
Reefs

Burketown

Georgetown   Ingham

Abingdon
Reefs

Leichhardt R.

Flinders R.

Norman R.

Townsville

Camooweal

Charters
Towers

Ayr

Bowen

Marion
Reef

Cloncurry

Julia Creek

Hughenden

Mt. Isa   Richmond

Mackay

Swain
Reefs

Winton

Capricorn Channel

Boulia

Muttaburra

Clermont

TROPIC OF CAPRICORN

Longreach   Barcaldine Emerald Rockhampton

Diamantina R.

Thompson R.

Springsure

Blackall

Rolleston

Banana

Gladstone

SIMPSON
DESERT
NAT. PARK   Birdsville

Windorah

Tambo

Theodore

Bundaberg Sandy
Childers   Cape

Augathella

LAKE
YAMMA
YAMMA

Quilpie

Charleville

Morven

Roma

Miles

Maryborough
Murgon

Fraser
Is.

Noosa

SOUTH   AUSTRALIA

Thargomindah

Warrego R.

St. George

Cunnamulla

Hebel

Balonne R.

Mungindi

Moonie

Goondiwindi

Dalby

Toowoomba Ipswich

Warwick

Stanthorpe

BRISBANE

Gold
Coast

NEW   SOUTH   WALES

N

158

sheep, and warm-hearted crops like sugar, cotton, pineapples and bananas. Lately, tourism is reckoned to be the second biggest money-spinner. Queensland is the only state with three international airports.

For touristic purposes the state can be divided into a dozen or more zones, from wild tropical adventurelands in the far north to the swinging sophistication of the Gold Coast. The busiest gateway to all of this is Brisbane, the sprawling state capital.

Brisbane

Clean and keen, Brisbane is bigger-than-life, the sort of skyscrapered city with a checkered past that you'd expect to find in Texas. The people are not at all modest about the advantages of living here; some are downright smug about their good luck.

With its palm trees and backyard swimming pools, Brisbane maintains a pace so relaxed you'd hardly imagine it was a metropolis with a population well over a million. The sleek skyscrapers, some quite audacious, have gone a long way towards overcoming the "country-town" image, but enough of the old, elegant, low-slung buildings remain as a reminder; some are filigreed Victorian monuments, now done up in bright, defiant colours.

The climate is so welcoming that Brisbane has attracted immigrants from near and far. Just how far is indicated by the schedule of a local radio station, which broadcasts in, among other languages, Arabic, Bulgarian, Croatian, Fijian, Polish, Tongan and "Scandinavian".

In 1859, when Brisbane's population was all of 7,000, it became the capital of the newly proclaimed state of Queensland. The state treasury contained only 7½ pence; but within a couple of days even that was stolen. Old habits of the former penal colony seemed to die hard.

The capital's location, at a bend in the Brisbane River, has made possible some memorable floods over the years, but it sets an attractive stage for

*T*hree generations of architecture compete in the centre of Brisbane.

*M*ap of Queensland.

Australia's third largest city. Spanned by a network of bridges (the first dated 1930), the river continues through the suburbs to the beaches and islands of Moreton Bay. Some of Australia's most celebrated seafood comes from the bay, notably the gargantuan local mud crabs and the Moreton Bay bug. Don't let the name put you off: this bug, related to the lobster, is a gourmet's joy.

City Sights

To begin with the historic heart of town, Brisbane's neoclassical **City Hall**,

Anzac Square is a sunken semi-tropical garden leading to Brisbane's old Central Railway Station.

built of Queensland sandstone, is easy to find because of its inspired spire, 91 m (nearly 300 ft) tall. When the Prince of Wales laid one of the foundation stones in 1920, it was designed to be the tallest building in the country. You can mount the great clock tower for what is still a hard-to-beat panorama, though various skyscrapers now block what used to be an unimpeded 360° view. The building, which houses a library, a museum and an art gallery, has many functions as a community centre but you can't "fight city hall" at city hall: the actual administration of the city has moved to a modern office block.

Up the hill, on Wickham Terrace, stands an unusual historic building, the **Old Windmill**, also known as the Old Observatory, built by convicts in 1829. Design problems foiled the windmill idea; to grind the colony's grain, the energy of the wind had to be replaced by a convict-powered treadmill. The work was so strenuous the prisoners called it the Tower of Torture. Later, the windmill found happier uses as a fire lookout station and a transmitter for early television experiments.

King George Square, next to City Hall, and the nearby **Anzac Square** are typical of the green open spaces with sculptures and fountains that keep the centre of town refreshed. The pedestrian traffic is so heavy in the business district that it's regulated by a line built down the middle of the paving; keep left.

Town plan of Brisbane.

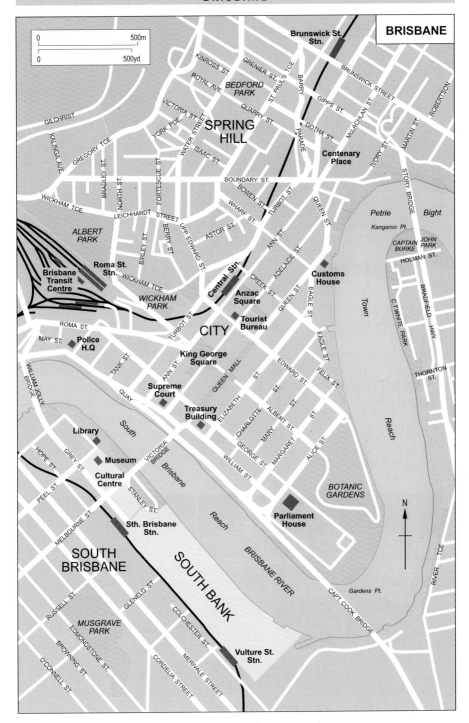

On the Mall

Pedestrians only is the rule in Brisbane's central **Queen Street Mall**, flanked by big stores and interspersed with shady refuges and outdoor cafés. Controversially, the mall has kept many classic façades of old Brisbane buildings, like the filigreed iron balconies of the defunct Hotel Carlton, then painted them in bright colours, tastefully blacking out empty windows.

It ends up something like a film set as the exterior of a multi-storey shopping precinct. On the inside, the Myer Centre is full of light (thanks to many an atrium) and life and temptations, for shoppers, eaters, even movie-goers, as well as children, who love its top-floor fairground rides. It's called the largest city-centre retail development in Australia.

A modern fountain cools the shoppers and snackers in a Brisbane mall.

Queen Street Mall is a crucial place for people-watching. On a fine day, visitors from cooler climes sip a cool drink and watch the lively parade of girls, tanned and fit, in brightly coloured dresses. The local men go about unselfconsciously in sports shirts and shorts—except for the businessmen, wilting in suits and ties. The little restaurants and takeaway cafés feature everything from ethnic curiosities to "gourmet hotdogs".

Landmarks

Twentieth-century history is ensconced in a very solid office building at Queen and Edward streets. In 1942, when Australia felt thoroughly vulnerable, US General Douglas MacArthur established his headquarters on the 8th floor. An inscription says this is where he "formulated the initial plans which led to final victory over the Japanese forces on 15 August 1945". It was MacArthur who accepted the formal Japanese surrender two weeks later. Nowadays it's all very peaceful in the building, called **MacArthur Chambers** in the general's honour, occupied by a bank and

A historic photo of the old Hotel Carlton, one of the victims of an urban renewal scheme. The frilly façade has been preserved as one wall of a vast shopping centre.

organizations as diverse as Weight Watchers and Club Med.

Still in Queen Street, the **General Post Office** is a historic landmark from the 1870s. On the second floor, the GPO Museum contains memorabilia from the earliest days of the colonial postal service, as well as primitive telecommunications experiments.

Brisbane has two **cathedrals**, Anglican and Catholic. St Stephen's Roman Catholic Cathedral, in Elizabeth street behind the GPO, is the older building, consecrated in 1874. St John's Anglican Cathedral, in Ann Street, also in Gothic style, was begun in 1901 and has yet to be finished. There's a secular footnote to this stately church: Queensland's first governor lived in the cathedral's deanery until a proper mansion was built.

Riverside Pleasures

Most Australian capital cities are sited alongside rivers, enhancing their allure. Perth's Swan River may be more beautiful, Hobart's River Derwent more dramatic, Melbourne's Yarra more amusing, Adelaide's Torrens more placid. But the Brisbane River, looping through the city along a most erratic path, is undeniably full of life. In places, highways and factories along its banks mar the picturesque mood. Still, you can sit at a riverside café diverted by all the sailboats, powerboats, commuter ferryboats, barges and floating restaurants and soak up its eternal appeal. For more insight, take a sightseeing boat: the river is so serpentine that the views are always new and surprising. You can't help but envy the people inhabiting the penthouses, even the modest bungalows, along the banks of the Brisbane.

*M*ore than a century old, George Street Mansions uses endless verandahs to screen out the Queensland sun.

From the deanery's balcony, in 1859, the separation of Queensland from New South Wales was proclaimed.

In those days, Brisbane's **Fortitude Valley** was a centre of Scottish emigrants, the first contingent having arrived aboard a ship called *Fortitude*. Nowadays, just ask for **Chinatown.**

Architects and engineers were invited from Guangzhou (Canton) to plan the gardened mall that turned a haphazard collection of Chinese restaurants and shops into a tourist attraction. Since immigration from other areas of Asia has been on the rise, the Chinese no longer have a cultural monopoly in the district.

Where central Brisbane fits into the bend in the river, the **Botanic Gardens** green the peninsula with countless species of Australian and "exotic" (such as American) trees, plants and

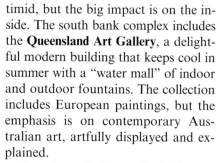

timid, but the big impact is on the inside. The south bank complex includes the **Queensland Art Gallery**, a delightful modern building that keeps cool in summer with a "water mall" of indoor and outdoor fountains. The collection includes European paintings, but the emphasis is on contemporary Australian art, artfully displayed and explained.

Next door, the **Queensland Museum** covers everything from dinosaurs to airplanes, from fish to anthropology; kids don't fall asleep in a museum this interesting. And right outside is "Mephisto", a World War I behemoth—a 30-tonne German tank brought back from France by the Queenslanders who put it out of action.

A 2,000-seat concert hall with tiptop acoustics is the home base of the creditable Queensland Symphony Orchestra, and plays, ballets, operas and musicals occupy the even bigger Lyric Theatre. An intimate 300-seat theatre is used for experimental productions. Riverside gardens, plazas, restaurants and cafés round off the glittering scene. There are guided tours of the art gallery as well as the Performing Arts Complex.

Out of Town
One place to escape the heat and rush of the city is **Mount Coot-tha Botanic Gardens**, on the western edge of Brisbane. The name is derived from an Aboriginal word meaning "mountain of dark native honey". The spacious park features a giant modern dome enclosing some 200 species of tropical plants. Here, too, you'll find Australia's largest planetarium.

flowers. It began as a convict-tilled vegetable garden. A political hothouse, the 19th-century Renaissance-style **Parliament House** overlooking the gardens, is the headquarters of the state's legislative assembly.

Cultureland

Across the low, streamlined Victoria Bridge from the centre of town, the **Queensland Cultural Centre** puts most of Brisbane's cultural eggs in one lavish, modern basket. From afar the project may look architecturally

riding on the back of a German shepherd dog. The sanctuary has kangaroos galore, so tame they come up to you to be fed and, if you insist, petted. You can also get a close-up look at a couple of Tasmanian devils, piggish-looking marsupials and, unlike the koalas, frankly difficult to love.

Farther afield, the **Bunya Park Wildlife Sanctuary**, at Eatons Hill, north-west of Brisbane, stresses the koala-cuddling facilities. Kangaroos, wallabies and emus roam free, and the usually maligned dingo is treated with respect and even affection. Baby farm animals are corralled for the edification of visiting youngsters.

Active and passive animals draw tourists to the **Australia Woolshed** in nearby Ferny Hills. Sheepshearing demonstrations are the highlight, but hearts go out to the sheepdogs, who impress with their intelligence and agility.

An outdoor museum of Queensland architecture, **Earlystreet Historical Village** in Norman Park, features classic buildings in a garden setting. These are the original houses, inns and stores, going back to the early days of settlement, moved to this peaceful place and restored for posterity.

Subtropical surprises await at Lone Pine Sanctuary, mostly noted for its population of cuddly koalas.

By car, bus or taxi, it's only about 11 km (7 miles) to **Lone Pine Sanctuary**, which has one of the country's best-known collections of native animals. By boat the trip is a few kilometres longer. The darlings of the park are the koalas, clinging to their eucalyptus branches. They are awakened now and then to pose for photos in the arms of tourists. They "perform" by

Moreton Bay

East of Brisbane, Moreton Bay is sprinkled with islands. Closest in of the excursion isles, **St Helena Island** was a 19th-century Alcatraz for the toughest Queensland criminals. Now the inmates are mostly seabirds, for it's a national park. Excursion guides point out the ancient Aboriginal seashell middens, the prison vestiges, the trees and the birds.

Despite its proximity to Brisbane, **North Stradbroke Island** is largely unspoiled. Thirty-four km (21 miles) long, it's big enough to squeeze in a permanent population of more than 3,000 and some unobtrusive resorts. In addition to the beaches, the scenery runs to bushland, lakes, mangrove swamps and cliffs. **South Stradbroke Island**, which used to be attached to its neighbour before a storm broke them asunder in 1896, is much smaller and quieter, except for day-trippers from the Gold Coast.

A one-time whaling base, **Moreton Island**, though accessible by helicopter, plane or boat, has no paved roads and fewer visitors than Stradbroke. The island is a vast sandhill, topped by Mount Tempest, 280 m (920 ft) high. But there are forests and lakes and a resort on the west coast and, predictably, more beaches than anyone knows what to do with.

A bridge across Pumicestone Passage makes **Bribie Island** accessible by car or bus from Brisbane, yet it's surprisingly little disturbed by tourism. There's a choice between surfing or calm-sea beaches, scuba-diving or cycling.

Gold Coast

The Beautiful People come from all the world to don the skimpiest swimsuits and laze on the boundless beaches of the Gold Coast. A lot of ordinary mortals come, too, so nobody need get a complex; if all else fails, there's glamour in the setting itself.

South of Brisbane, at day-trip distance if you're rushed, the Gold Coast is a Down Under impression of Miami Beach. It may be overexploited, but it's so dynamic and there's so much to do that you can hardly fault it. And the beach—anything from 30 to 50 km (18 to 31 miles) of it, depending who's measuring—is a winner in any league.

The trip down the Pacific Highway from Brisbane is a study in escapism. In the midst of forest and brushland grows a seemingly inexhaustible supply

*D*ress tends to be informal in the high-rise resort of Surfers Paradise.

Down the hatch in Surfers: fantastic water slides have become commonplace in many countries, but rarely in city surroundings.

of amusement or theme parks. They lure transient fun-seekers with diversions for all the family, such as "computerized animated koala show", "log ride splashdown", and "sheep-shearing exhibitions". **Warner Bros. Movie World** involves a behind-the-scenes studio tour, cartoon characters on film and in costume, and countless movie-themed shopping and eating opportunities. Another of the most popular parks, **Dreamworld**, has 16 rides and nine different "theme worlds"; it's so big they sell two-day passes. Other entertaining establishments have names like Magic Mountain, Lion Safari, Sheep Station and Old MacDonald's Farm. The Gold Coast War Museum advertises "free uniform hire". You enter the "Great White Shark Expo" through monstrous open jaws.

Where It's Happening

The essence of the Gold Coast is **Surfers Paradise**, or, coloquially, Tinsel Town—as lively as any seaside resort in the world. When you're not sunbathing, swimming or, of course, surfing, you can wander through the malls, window-shopping, eating out and socializing. Or go water-skiing or parasailing. Or take a joy ride in an ancient Tiger Moth. Or—how's this for Aussie subtlety?—take what's advertised as a "moonlight booze cruise". The Surfers pace is hectic, and

all their revelry goes on as late as you can possibly last and probably later.

Surfers Paradise is approached through a thicket of petrol stations, fast-food outlets and motels—a reconstruction of the outskirts of many an American city, and in similar taste. The conglomeration has been sky-scrapered in an odd way: tall, slim apartment blocks interspersed with bungalows. It's not a real city at all, except for the pursuit of fun. (Until 1933 the community of Surfers Paradise was known more prosaically as Elston.) The tanned, relaxed, glamorous sophisticates you see on the beach today were pale yokels a couple of days ago; the irresistible sun does wonders.

By way of nature-oriented Gold Coast attractions, **Seaworld** stars frolicking dolphins, with the villainous parts played by performing sharks. Beyond the expectable attractions it's a vast "marine theme park" with live shows, hair-raising fairground rides and a monorail line.

Sanctuaries of Sorts

North of Surfers, a lavish modern resort and residential community, **Sanctuary Cove**, stresses water sports—at sea and on the Coomera River and in swimming pools. Ashore it offers two 18-hole golf-courses, tennis and squash courts, and diversions of more sedentary sorts for the well-heeled guests.

Just south of Surfers, at Broadbeach, **Jupiters Casino** is simply enormous, with more than 100 gaming tables and ancillary facilities such as bars, restaurants and nightclubs. To encourage beginners, they provide

*A*t the Currumbin Bird Sanctuary, a pelican struggles with a problem in its pouch.

video instructions on how to master baccarat or roulette. This Vegas-style, round-the-clock casino also employs guides who speak Japanese.

Back to nature: at the **Currumbin Bird Sanctuary**, huge flocks of brilliantly coloured lorikeets, shrilly chorusing, come to greet the tourists—when food is being served. Currumbin is down towards the southern edge of the Gold Coast, which ends at Point Danger (so named by Captain Cook when he passed by—and almost ran aground—in 1770). A giant memorial to Cook, capped by a lighthouse,

Sunshine Coast

The Sunshine Coast, stretching north from Brisbane, is about twice as beachy as the Gold Coast, but far less feverish. Some of Australia's best surfing is hiding among these less commercial, family-style resorts.

Inland, plantations of sugar cane, bananas, pineapples and passionfruit reach the horizon. The area is also a centre of production of the prized macadamia nut, named after a 19th-century Australian scientist, John Macadam.

The Bruce Highway north from Brisbane skirts Deception Bay, one of those memorable names that wistful explorers assigned to tricky coasts. (Some other evocatively named Australian bays: Weary Bay, Qld, Doubtful Bay, WA, and Disaster Bay, Vic.) From the old highway you get a good look at the **Glasshouse Mountains**, so named by Captain Cook, who could see them from the sea. These strange volcanic outcrops, suitable for mountain-climbing practice, offer a different mood from each vantage point.

The Sunshine Coast resort closest to Brisbane, **Caloundra**, has a beach for every tide. For the historically minded, a smaller-scale replica of Captain Cook's ship *Endeavour* may be visited. And a local museum of "matchcraft" specializes in models painstakingly constructed from thousands of matchsticks.

The euphoniously-named harbour of **Mooloolaba**, climax of the annual Sydney–Mooloolaba yacht race, is the site of an ambitious superaquarium called **Underwater World**. The view from within a transparent underwater

marks the spot, which is the border between Queensland and New South Wales. The modest danger on the NSW side of the line—and the reason the area is so popular with tourists from Brisbane—is the availability of mass gambling opportunities. South of the border the one-armed bandits, or poker machines ("pokies" for short), are kept so busy the cheery clang of coins never stops.

171

Surf-casting on the Gold Coast seems to satisfy this burly fisherman.

tunnel is a crash course in identifying tropical fish—not only multicoloured beauties but monsters of the deep so big they seem worthy of fishermen's lore. Seals are put through their tricks, though they are pointedly treated with dignity, as if to appease critics of animal exploitation.

Down on the Farm

Inland here, you can hardly miss a terribly Australian sort of tourist attraction: the monstrously magnified symbol. A startling example is an immense reproduction of a pineapple, as tall as a house—the come-on for a whole tourist complex. What used to be called simply the Big Pineapple has expanded and changed its name to

Sunshine Plantation. If the 15-m (50-ft) hollow plastic pineapple doesn't fill your quota of kitsch experience, you

Mind the Sun

Everybody loves Australia's heart-warming sunshine, but wise sunbathers know not to overdo it. Apply sun screen to exposed skin and wear a hat. Try to stay out of the sun during the middle of the day; you'll tan quickly enough before 11.00 a.m. and after 3.00 p.m. and run much less risk of painful, potentially dangerous sunburn. The end of the line for sun abuse—ever more common in Australia—is skin cancer.

There's no escape outdoors, even on a cloudy day. And the sand and sea reflect the sun's rays, worsening the problem. Proper sunglasses that screen out the ultraviolet rays are a wise precaution. If you're snorkelling, wear a T-shirt in the water; otherwise your roasted neck and shoulders might glow for days.

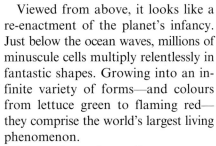

can be driven through the macadamia plantation aboard a genuine Nutmobile.

Agriculture, commerce and tourism coincide, as well, at **Yandina**, home of what's stated to be the world's largest **ginger factory**. Here you can look down onto a sort of tank farm of vats of liquified ginger, and the assembly line, where green-uniformed women cut ginger to size and classify the bits. A shop on the premises does a brisk business selling ginger marmalade, ginger wine, ginger beer, pickled ginger, even—why not?—ginger ice-cream.

The northernmost town on the Sunshine Coast, **Noosa**, used to be a hideaway of fishermen, surfers and beachcombers, but it has been discovered by the trendsetters from Sydney and Melbourne. Noosa Neads, an understated resort at the junction of the Noosa River and Laguna Bay, has the expensive boutiques and stylish restaurants. Noosaville, a quiet, family resort, sprawls from there along the winding river. Noosa National Park, a sanctuary of tall pines, rainforest and underpopulated beaches, occupies the dramatic headland that protects the bay from the sometimes squally South Pacific breezes.

Great Barrier Reef

Australia's biggest playground is nothing like the usual mixture of sand and sea. Pleasures of many sorts abound on the Great Barrier Reef, but at the same time it inspires the most profound thoughts about the world and its inhabitants. The reef is, after all, a miracle by any standards.

Viewed from above, it looks like a re-enactment of the planet's infancy. Just below the ocean waves, millions of minuscule cells multiply relentlessly in fantastic shapes. Growing into an infinite variety of forms—and colours from lettuce green to flaming red—they comprise the world's largest living phenomenon.

The reef stretches as far as you can see and beyond: more than 2,000 km (1,200 miles) of submerged tropical gardens. In among them, the sea is sprinkled with hundreds of paradise islands.

Seen more intimately through a skin-diver's mask, the Great Barrier Reef is the spectacle of a lifetime, like being inside a boundless tropical fishbowl among the most lurid specimens ever conceived. The fanciful shapes of the coral, gently waving in the tide like wildflowers in a breeze, might almost lull you to sleep. But not for long. A blazing blue and red fish darts into sight, pursuing a cloud of a thousand minnows. A sea urchin stalks past, walking on its needles; a giant clam opens its hairy mouth as if sighing with nostalgia for its youth, a century ago.

The reef is alive, the work of millions of minute polyps building on the skeletons of their ancestors. They grow into surreal formations, such as elkhorn, swaying sea fans or an oversized, wrinkled brain. The coral feeds on, and in turn feeds, microscopic algae. The oxygen-producing algae support schools of theatrically tinted fish, like angelfish, butterfly fish and red emperors. These beauties attract the whoppers that fishermen dream of. It all seems a beautiful, incredibly

The Great Barrier Reef stretches 2,000 km (1,240 miles) along the Queensland coast. Coral, algae and tropical fish thrive in symbiosis.

complex master plan. But it only works when the conditions are just right—when the sea is clear, warm and not too deep, for instance, here in the Coral Sea just off the north-east coast of Australia.

On the Reef

In 1770 Captain Cook, who was exploring the Australian coast, stumbled—that's the word—upon the Great Barrier Reef. An unsuspected outcrop of coral gored the *Endeavour*. It was touch and go whether the ship would survive. Patching the holes as best they could, the crew managed to sail across the barrier, and onto the beach at what is now Cooktown, where major repairs were improvised.

There are many ways of appreciating the coral and its fishy visitors. You can stay dry in a glass-bottomed boat, or join a brief cruise aboard a semi-submarine. Or descend into an underwater observatory. If you prefer to remain topside, at certain places and tides you can walk—but not barefoot!—on the coral as it stands exposed. With a mask and snorkel tube you can get close to the whole truth of the underwater world. But the only way to blend totally with the

---

One Step at a Time
Never mind the perils of the deep. Along the Great Barrier Reef it's the shallows that are dangerous. Walking on the reef is a delicate pursuit, not just because you could harm the coral; it could harm you, too. Some coral is sharp, some burns the skin. And hidden where you least expect to step on anything dangerous is the stonefish, armed with very poisonous spines, a nasty beast stealthily camouflaged. By contrast, the firefish is beautiful but just as deadly. Beach-walkers, clearly, must defend themselves by wearing stout boots. And you should keep your hands off coral or a seashell or anything else on the reef unless you're certain it's benign.

---

environment is in a weightless state, diving as long and as deep as you please with scuba gear. If you're not a qualified diver you can take a course at one of the resorts; a week should suffice to win you a certificate.

The Resort Islands

The reef—really a formation of thousands of neighbouring clumps of reefs—runs close to shore in the north of tropical Queensland but slants ever farther out to sea as it extends southwards. Hundreds of islands are scattered across the protected waters between the coral barrier and the mainland. More than a dozen have been developed into resorts, ranging from spartan to sybaritic. But you should keep in mind that only three resort islands—Heron, Green and Lady Elliot—are coral cays. From all the others you have to travel, by sea or air, from 5 to 70 km (3 to 40 miles) to reach the main attraction. Incidentally, if you're anti-island or in a hurry, you can go to the reef on a day-trip from the mainland—by fast boat, light plane or helicopter. There are excursions from towns up and down the coast between Port Douglas and Bundaberg.

Our survey of the character and facilities of the resort islands on and near the reef reads from south to north.

But first, for the record, consider **Fraser Island,** which is just south of the Great Barrier Reef and truly the odd one out. It's vastly bigger than any of the reef islands, and unlike them in almost all other ways. About 120 km (75 miles) long, Fraser is called the largest sand island in the world. But there's more than sand dunes: lakes, marsh, pine forest, rainforest, even

Juicy welcome to paradise is offered to vacationers flying in to Dunk Island.

tremendous cliffs of sand. The island is a state forest and national park, inhabited by animals as unusual as the wild brumby, a "wild" horse that's really quite tame. This is an island for fishing and beachcombing more than swimming (ocean swimming can be dangerous here); and there's no coral to look at. Four-wheel-drive vehicles are obligatory as there are no paved roads. The principal departure points for Fraser Island ferries from the mainland are near Rainbow Beach and Hervey Bay, north of the Sunshine Coast. Package tours are also available from Noosa.

Southern Reef Isles

The southernmost reef island—actually it's south of the Tropic of Capricorn—is **Lady Elliot Island**. This is the only coral isle with an airstrip but it has few luxuries: no telephone, for a start. Activities centre on diving (the amazing undersea sights start right off the beach), reef walks, swimming and windsurfing. Non-divers can get a glimpse of the coral wonders from glass-bottomed boats. A lighthouse has warned away ships for well over a century, but wrecks have nonetheless piled up here—a further attraction for divers. The gateway airport is Bundaberg, a sugar-producing town 375 km (230 miles) up the coast from Brisbane.

Heron Island, heaven for divers, is a very small coral island right on the Great Barrier Reef. Amazing coral and hundreds of species of fish are waiting just outside the door. The fish, from spectacular splangled emperors to creepy-looking moray eels, are friendly. Alternatively, nature lovers can concentrate on the giant green turtles, which waddle ashore between mid-October and March to bury their eggs in the sand. Bird-watchers know Heron Island as the goal of thousands of migrating noddy terns and shearwaters. *Après-dive* activities centre on a bar, a disco and what the brochure calls the only five-star restaurant on the reef. You can fly to Heron by helicopter in half an hour from Gladstone; by launch it takes 90 minutes.

A butterfly takes a flower break on an island of the Great Barrier Reef.

Great Keppel Island is one of the larger resort islands in area and in holiday population. The great white beaches—28 km (17 miles) of them—are simply gorgeous. Although the Great Barrier Reef is fully 70 km (more than 40 miles) away, Great Keppel is surrounded by good local coral, and there's an underwater observatory. For other angles on the sea's secrets in the area, try a glass-bottomed boat, snorkelling or scuba-diving. Landlubbers can keep busy with archery, cricket, horse-riding, tennis and many other active and mildly active sports. Formerly promoted as a resort for young swingers, Great Keppel has been expensively renovated and now aims to please all ages. You can fly to the island from Rockhampton, or take a ferry from Rosslyn Bay, near Yeppoon.

177

Brampton Island, an informal resort with lots of day and night activities, is easily reached by air or sea from Mackay. With forested mountains and abundant wildlife, it's worth exploring the interior of the island on well-laid-out trails. If the many sandy beaches don't suffice, there's a salt-water swimming pool. You can also discover neighbouring Carlisle Island, connected to Brampton by a sand bar which you can wade across when the tide's out. As for scuba-diving, the reef is about 40 km (24 miles) away. But snorkellers can look over the century-old wreck of the SS Geelong in Carlisle waters; its bow is on the beach.

The Whitsundays

Lindeman Island has an airstrip and a nine-hole golf-course on its plateau, from which the view over the Whitsunday Passage is highly recommended. It's a long trip to the reef to dive, but nearby waters are eminently fit for swimming, sailing, windsurfing, jet-skiing and parasailing. Lindeman Island has been exploited as a resort for more than 60 years. In recent times it was refurbished and upgraded as a holiday destination, with the emphasis on comfort rather than size. Some of the islands ban children, others tolerate or even welcome them, but Lindeman goes out of its way with hospitality and activities; at school holiday time the kids can be whisked away to the island's overnight camp.

Palmy islands by the hundreds are scattered along the length of the reef.

179

reef, 65 km (40 miles) to the east, aboard the "world's fastest passenger-carrying catamaran" or by helicopter. Children are kept busy with a Kids Club and a fauna park where the island's rainbow lorikeets not only eat out of your hand but sit on your arm while doing it. Meet the tame kangaroos, too. The resort can arrange for weddings in the island's tiny church— if you run out of things to do. Direct

*T*he tame rainbow lorikeets on Hamilton Island are insatiable junk-food fans.

Hamilton Island. With its jet airstrip, skyscraper apartment towers, eight restaurants, ten bars and what's called the largest freshwater pool in the Pacific, Hamilton is the slickest international resort in the Coral Sea. It's all carefully thought out, from the busy yacht marina and shops to the landscaping around the Polynesian-style cottages. Divers can rush out to the

180

jet flights link Hamilton with capitals as distant as Sydney and Melbourne.

Long Island, close to the mainland and far from the reef, is long (as you guessed) and narrow and hilly. It's a 20-minute boat ride from Shute Harbour or 15 minutes by water taxi from Hamilton Island. Two resorts share the northern portion of Long Island: Contiki (on the site of the old Whitsunday 100 resort), catering to 18-to-35-year-old swingers; and Palm Bay, part way down the coast, a less expensive, secluded retreat. They're within a couple of kilometres of each other, so if any

M ost holiday-makers arrive in the islands by aeroplane or ferry but yachts are equally welcome.

Palm Bay guests become bored with nature they can hike over to Contiki to sample the frenzied night-life.

South Molle Island, one of the bigger resorts, has every imaginable recreational facility except, at last report, horse-riding. Fitness enthusiasts have the use of a gym, a sauna, a spa, and a swimming pool suitable for serious workouts as well as cooling dips. Children, too, are kept busy. The beaches are good, and there are interesting paths for walks through the hilly bush. The Great Barrier Reef, though, is some 60 km (nearly 40 miles) away. Although South Molle is operated by Ansett, it has no airport; you have to

Helicopters speed visitors to hard-to-reach islands and to diving spots on the Barrier Reef itself.

shuttle over from Hamilton by boat or helicopter, or by boat from Shute Harbour.

Daydream Island. The tiniest of all the Barrier Reef resort islands, Daydream snoozes just off shore from busy Shute Harbour, a 15-minute ferry trip. Since beaches are not the island's strongest selling point, they've built a grand swimming pool. The recently renovated resort has accommodation for several hundred guests and a marina.

Hayman Island is the most northerly of the Whitsunday group. (The archipelago was named by Captain Cook, who passed through here on or about the feast of Pentecost.) Reopened in 1987 as a chic, international-class resort, Hayman has a marina for drop-in yachts, and a choice of posh restaurants, bars and shops. It's the only reef resort to offer penthouses with servants' quarters. The long, sandy beach suggests all sorts of

water sports, dutifully catered for by the resort's activities staff. Some tiny, uninhabited isles are so close you can walk out to them at low tide. The usual approach to Hayman is Hamilton Island's jet airport; guests register aboard the champagne-equipped luxury cruisers waiting to take them from there.

Off Townsville

Magnetic Island is virtually a suburb of Townsville, the biggest city in northern Queensland. Many of the island's 2,500 permanent residents commute to work on the mainland by ferry. Being so easy to reach, it's a busy day-trip destination—by sea or helicopter. But Magnetic Island also has plenty of accommodation of all classes, from hotels and holiday flats to backpackers' hostels. Most of the island is a national park, alive with birds and animals. The choice of beaches is enticing, but box jellyfish are a real danger between October and April. Tracks have been laid out for bushwalks ranging from an easy half-hour to a full day. Magnetic Island, "Maggie" to the locals, got its name from the omnipresent Captain Cook, whose compass broke down here—magnetized, he thought.

Orpheus Island. The way to get to this small, exclusive resort is by seaplane from Townsville; on the way you'll get an aerial introduction to the expanse and brilliance of the reef. Orpheus, a national park island, has all the facilities the most demanding guests might desire, including tennis, water-skiing, sailing and windsurfing. Divers can enjoy the island's fringing reef. The resort won't tolerate children under 12.

Hinchinbrook Island basks in a superlative of its own: "The world's largest island national park." A continental rather than coral island, but only 5 km (3 miles) from the reef, Hinchinbrook has a couple of campsites (park rangers issue permits on the mainland) and, at northernmost Cape Richards, a small, relaxed resort. Inland from the smooth sand beaches are craggy mountains worth climbing, tropical rainforest, waterfalls, and bush in which you'll come across wallabies and, less adorably, goannas, lizards and echidnas. Amphibious or seaplanes fly to Hinchinbrook from Cairns or Townsville; or you can get there by boat from the small town of Cardwell, where there's a national parks information centre.

Family Islands

Bedarra Island, in the Family Islands group, has two small, exclusive resorts on opposite sides of the island, within hiking distance of each other across the rainforest. Day-trippers and children are not catered for, and the tariff will put off most other potential visitors. But the very high prices are all-inclusive—not only very comfortable accommodation and classy food but sports equipment and all you can drink. Bedarra is reachable via neighbouring Dunk Island. The nearest mainland town is Tully, noted for its annual rainfall average, the highest in the country. Statistically, Tully is twice as wet as Darwin.

Dunk Island is mostly a national park. But one of the biggest, best-developed resorts fits inoffensively into a corner of the island originally occupied by a World War II radar station.

Getting away from it all, this resident of Dunk Island prefers living in a cottage on the edge of a rain forest in the Great Barrier Reef.

Guests enjoy a big range of diversions from golf, tennis and horse-riding to windsurfing and water-skiing. Dunk's genuine tropical rainforest offers a taste of the eternal: vines struggling to grab the sunlight at the expense of the trees they strangle on the way up. All is silence except for a waterfall, the trickle of raindrops off glistening leaves, the fluttering wings of a brightly plumed bird or a giant Ulysses butterfly. Dunk's airfield has flights from Cairns and Townsville. For sea transport Clump Point and Mission Beach are the key ports.

Fitzroy Island, a 19th-century quarantine station for Chinese immigrants, came into the resort business later than most. Like Green Island, it's a day excursion from Cairns. Accommodation is quite limited but varied—from villas to a campsite. A dining room and

evening entertainment keep the overnight population amused. Fitzroy Island's interior is rainforest; the beaches meet anyone's standards.

North of Cairns

Green Island, one of the three resorts actually on the reef, is popular with day-trippers from Cairns. When the crowds depart, the vacationers occupying its small colony of cabins and lodge units have the tiny 12-ha (30-acre) island, and its throngs of seabirds, to themselves. Green Island's Underwater Observatory, claiming to be the first of its kind in the world, lets you view the coral garden from a dry vantage point 5 m (3 fathoms) deep. In this situation, the fish come to look through the glass at humans in the tank. Another attraction, a short walk inland, is a Marineland with sharks, crocodiles and giant turtles.

Lizard Island. Lying about 30 km (less than 20 miles) off the tropical northern coast of Queensland, Lizard has all the trappings of a fictional escape island: rainforest, mangrove swamps and a couple of dozen delectable beaches. Favoured by

Dry diving: tourists head for the underwater view of the reef through the windows of the Green Island observatory.

millionaires and celebrities, the resort has almost every vacation facility—tennis, windsurfing, sailing—except a nightclub. Which is just the way the guests like it. There are guided tours of the marine research station on the west coast, which is operated by the Australian Museum. The island is almost on the edge of one of Australia's most productive game-fishing zones, where the 500-kg (half-ton) black marlin live; an international tournament takes place in October. Daily flights link Lizard with Cairns.

 Tropical Coast

The coast of mainland Queensland paralleling the Barrier Reef is a fiercely difficult drive along a highway that looks easy on the map. Here are a few highlights, from south to north, heading relentlessly towards the Equator.

Rockhampton sits only a few kilometres north of the Tropic of Capricorn—the line at 23°27' south of the Equator that officially divides the tropics from the subtropics. From here on northwards, you need no excuse to order an icy beer to assuage your tropical thirst. Rockhampton, "Rocky" for short, is known as the beef capital of Australia. The town's genuinely interesting Victorian architecture makes for a worthwhile walking tour.

Mackay is the next substantial town, and even by Australian standards it's a long haul—about 340 km (more than 210 miles)—over Highway 1, a road not particularly noted for its comfort or scenery. Surrounded by dense green fields of cane, Mackay processes one-third of the nation's sugar crop. At the harbour you can tour the world's biggest bulk sugar terminal. Inland from Mackay, in rugged mountain country, is the largest national park in Queensland, **Eungella National Park**. This is probably the only place in Australia where you can see platypuses in the wild. The best time is morning and late afternoon. Other novelties among the wildlife are a bird called the

Eungella honeyeater, a strange lizard and three bizarre species of frog.

Proserpine, another sugar town, is inland from **Airlie Beach** and **Shute Harbour**, lively resorts from which there are boat trips to the Whitsunday Islands. "Prosperpine", a high-flown name, is a variation of the Latin version of "Persephone", the ancient Greek goddess of vegetation.

Townsville

Another 265 km (165 miles) closer to the Equator, and you're in Australia's largest tropical city, Townsville,

In the metropolis of northern Queensland, Townsville, it's hot enough to take it easy in the park.

named after one of its founders, Robert Towns, a businessman from Sydney. With a population close to 100,000, Townsville is the headquarters of the mining and cattle industries of Queensland's interior and a gateway for islands of the Reef.

The historic centre of town, along the river, contains some photogenic old buildings with filigreed iron balconies or stately columns and arches. Townsville is proud of its broad modern pedestrian mall, enlivened by exotic birds inhabiting the tropical trees. And for the ultimate touch of sophistication, a big, glamorous gambling casino stands on reclaimed land along the bay.

Townsville is the home of the James Cook University, specializing in marine studies. For some effortless field work, try the local aquarium, called the world's largest live coral aquarium. Highlight of the **Great Barrier Reef Marine Wonderland**, it has artificial tides to keep the coral and tropical fish happy in captivity. For the real thing, several excursion companies run day-trips to the reef itself. In addition, experienced divers sail 20 km (12 miles) offshore to explore the wreck of the passenger ship *Yongola*, lost in a cyclone in 1911, now a convention centre for fish.

Cairns

Less than half as big as Townsville, the metropolis of Queensland's far north, Cairns, is a cheerful, thriving port laid out in grid style with huge blocks and extra-wide streets. Since it's perfectly flat, bicycles are a good bet here; modern pedicabs, driven by young students and blaring rock music, compete with

Soft Adventure
In a go-ahead town like Cairns the travel agencies open their doors at 7.30 a.m. and keep going until after dark. They sell a fat collection of excursions—to Green Island, inland to Kuranda and the Atherton Tableland, and up the coast to Port Douglas and beyond. There are so many ideas for excitement, from white-water rafting to balloon flights to bicycle tours of the rainforest, that the tourist office calls Cairns the "soft adventure capital of Australia". (Soft adventure, a definite growth area in tourism, is a trade term for thrilling experiences available to non-daredevils. Hard adventure is when you jump out of the balloon.)

Old-fashioned verandahs provide some shade for shoppers along the wide streets of tropical Cairns.

taxis. The distinctive atmosphere derives from an awkward mixture of cultures: a remote country town torn between a pride of luxury hotels and hordes of backpackers. Thanks largely to its tourist throngs, Cairns is full of life, day and night. The excitement begins early in the morning, when coaches prowl among the hotels collecting passengers for excursions by land and sea. Speedy catamarans leave for Green Island and other boats set

An ecologically sound method of touring the charms of tourist-friendly Kuranda.

sail with scuba-divers or fishermen aboard. Big-game fishing is big business in Cairns, where the sportsmen hunt black marlin between August and October. How big is big game? Whoppers weighing 500 kg (half a ton) have been landed, with witnesses and photos to corroborate.

Along the Coral Seafront, a spacious Esplanade shaded by lavish banyans and palms aims to compensate for the muddy state of the shallow sea here. Bathers who have outgrown the hotel pool have to travel a few kilometres up the coast, just past the airport, to find a good beach.

Beyond Cairns

The charming little tourist town of **Kuranda** is best reached by colourful narrow-gauge train. Leaving Cairns and the steamy sugar-cane fields, the century-old right-of-way climbs to cooler temperatures, alternating between tunnels (15 of them) and scenic mountainsides, loveliest at Barron Falls gorge. At the end of the line, the extravagantly botanical Kuranda rail station is a classic in itself, bedecked with potted ferns and tropical plants. The village is well supplied with souvenir shops, cafés, restaurants and other attractions, including a mini-museum of Aboriginal history and art. The Tjapukai Aboriginal Dance Theatre gives two performances a day. Some 2,000 fluttering little wonders with names like the Ulysses Blue and the Cairns Bird Wing inhabit the

Australian Butterfly Sanctuary, where jungle conditions are well simulated. You don't have to go far out of town to enter the rampant rainforest, where ferns grow as big as trees and the trees seem as tall as skyscrapers.

Spectacularly beautiful coastal scenery is the reward along the highway north from Cairns to **Port Douglas**. The perfect beaches on the way are so underpopulated you can easily have one to yourself. When the tide goes out, Port Douglas's **Four Mile Beach** is a wide, hard-packed, almost flat sweep of sand suitable for bike races, jogging, or simply sunbathing. The inauguration of a 300-room, five-star resort hotel on the beach, along with an 18-hole golf-course, a heliport and a marina, signalled a change of tone. But it's not all posh. Even though medium-priced and economical accommodation is now outnumbered, Port Douglas has retained its relaxed, far-north character.

For practical purposes, the nearby sugar-milling town of Mossman is the end of the line. From here northwards it's several hundred hot kilometres to the likeable river port of **Cooktown**, where Captain Cook's battered *Endeavour* was beached in 1770. The James Cook Memorial Museum tells all about it. Cooktown's heyday came almost exactly a century after the *Endeavour*'s departure, when the Palmer River gold rush brought the town's population to some 30,000. Many miners were Chinese; hence the Buddhist shrine in the local cemetery.

The tip of Cape York Peninsula, north of Cooktown, is a vast expanse of marshy terrain, prone to flooding and crocodiles, and negotiable only by the most intrepid adventurers in well-equipped four-wheel-drive vehicles. The rivers are totally impassable from December to March; Coen is the last outpost for supplies and fuel. From the very tip of the peninsula it's scarcely 150 km (less than 100 miles) to Papua New Guinea.

*F*our Mile Beach has been "discovered" by the tourist industry, but there's still more than ample space to spare.

All the Outback You Can Handle on Australia's Last Frontier

The neighbours in the Northern Territory tend to be a long way down the road. "Few and far between" is putting it mildly. It's not so much a case of low population density, more like population rarity. Here only 1 per cent of the Australian population occupies one-sixth of the continent's area. If it gets lonely, some spectacular scenery will keep you company.

At first sight, the deserts, canyons, torrid tablelands and rainforests look uninviting, especially when it's blazing hot. But the grandeur and mystique soon make an impression, and you'll find the wildlife enchanting. Well, maybe not the crocodiles. As for the people, some may verge on the eccentric, as you'd expect in offbeat places, but they welcome the wandering stranger with Outback hospitality, openness and charm.

A Santa Claus
beard is right at home on the range in the Northern Territory.

The population of the self-governing territory is around 150,000. About a quarter of all Territorians are Aborigines, so cultural insights are part of the agenda for foreign visitors. Here you can discover the grandeur and mystery of the most sacred Aboriginal sites.

The climate effectively divides the Northern Territory into two parts. The north, called "The Top End", is lush and very hot. The rest of the Territory, known as "The Centre", has drastically less rainfall. The Red Centre, with its infinite horizons and parched, rugged beauty, fits the stereotype of "back of beyond". But you don't have to rough it. The comfortable air-conditioned motel at the end of the highway is no mirage.

191

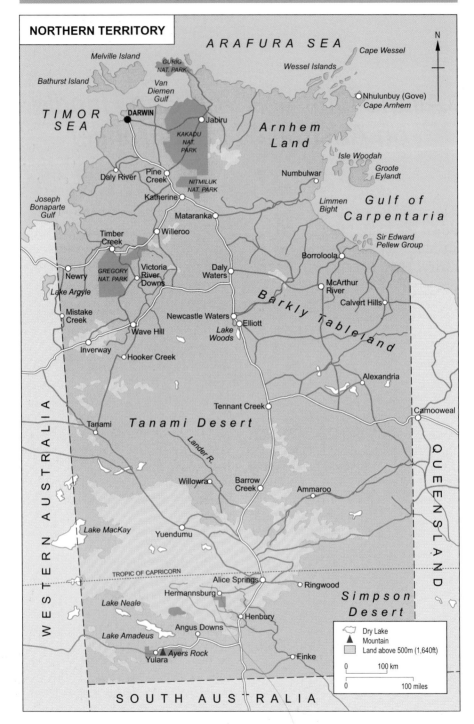

NORTHERN TERRITORY

ARAFURA SEA

Cape Wessel

Wessel Islands

Melville Island

GURIG NAT. PARK

Bathurst Island

Van Diemen Gulf

Nhulunbuy (Gove)
Cape Arnhem

TIMOR SEA

DARWIN

Jabiru

KAKADU NAT. PARK

Arnhem Land

Isle Woodah

Groote Eylandt

Daly River

Pine Creek

NITMILUK NAT. PARK

Numbulwar

Katherine

Limmen Bight

Gulf of Carpentaria

Joseph Bonaparte Gulf

Mataranka

Willeroo

Sir Edward Pellew Group

Timber Creek

Borroloola

Newry

GREGORY NAT. PARK

Victoria River Downs

Daly Waters

McArthur River

Lake Argyle

Barkly Tableland

Calvert Hills

Mistake Creek

Newcastle Waters

Elliott

Wave Hill

Lake Woods

Inverway

Hooker Creek

Alexandria

Tennant Creek

Camooweal

Tanami

Tanami Desert

Lander R.

WESTERN AUSTRALIA

QUEENSLAND

Willowra

Barrow Creek

Ammaroo

Lake MacKay

Yuendumu

TROPIC OF CAPRICORN

Alice Springs

Ringwood

Simpson Desert

Hermannsburg

Lake Neale

Henbury

Angus Downs

Lake Amadeus

Ayers Rock

Yulara

Finke

N

Dry Lake
Mountain
Land above 500m (1,640ft)

0   100 km

0   100 miles

SOUTH AUSTRALIA

192

M ap of the Northern Territory.

Darwin

Australia's northernmost port is a city of sumptuous parks and splendid homes overlooking the sea. Time, violent weather and other disasters have left Darwin not a lot of visible history, but that's secondary when the present is so pleasant. The capital and only real city of the Northern Territory—Darwin's population is around half of the Territory's total—revels in the tropical sun and every sport under

P yramid-shaped casino is good for the tourist business in the reborn Darwin.

it, from cricket and baseball to fishing, sailing and parasailing.

Young and prosperous, Darwin radiates the optimism of the reborn, for the city has survived far more than its share of catastrophes. At a cost of hundreds of lives, it was bombed 64 times in World War II. Rebuilt, it was wiped out by a killer cyclone in 1974. The planners went back to the drawing board to design a bigger and better city.

In Darwin, daytime temperatures average more than 30°C (86°F) virtually all year round. But while transients wilt, the locals know how to withstand the heat. They dress lightly and casually—even businessmen wear shorts to work. Hereabouts, "formal" means wearing shoes; you'll be surprised how many pedestrians stroll the town centre barefoot. To stave off heatstroke and dehydration, Darwin consumes a record amount of frosty beer. Elsewhere in Australia a *stubby* means a

small beer; order a *stubby* in Darwin and you get a two-litre bottle—almost half a gallon. This gives a clue to the Top End sense of humour; the jokes are a pleasant distraction from the heavy-handed heat. And a conservation bonus: empty beer cans wind up as the construction material for a flotilla of fanciful boats competing in Darwin's annual slapstick regatta.

Local chauvinists admit that Darwin, which is about 3,000 km (nearly 2,000 miles) from Sydney and Perth, is "a trifle isolated". But that doesn't seem to deter the eager newcomers arriving from all parts of the country to spend some time or make their lives on the last frontier.

City Sights

Historic buildings are the last thing you'd expect to find in a city wiped out by a modern cyclone. But visitors are taken on a tour of restored 19th-century buildings calling to mind the atmosphere of the pioneering days. Darwin's foundation as a permanent settlement dates back only to 1869, relatively modern history even by Australian standards. Actually, Port Darwin was named in 1839 by an exploration party on the *Beagle,* Charles Darwin's old ship. In 1911 the town, called Palmerston in the interim, changed its name in honour of the evolution man.

Government House, overlooking the harbour, is an elegant example of colonial style, still in use. A series of cyclones and the wartime bombs badly damaged the building (known as the House of the Seven Gables), but it has been put back together in fine form, and is surrounded by lovely tropical gardens. Note the louvred verandahs for keeping cooler in the tropics.

Dating from 1885, the single-storey building called **Brown's Mart** is now a theatre for live plays. You might say the building has a theatrically checkered past. Built as a miner's exchange, it was converted for use as a police station and subsequently served the community as a brothel.

Another unconventional historical monument, the old **Fannie Bay Gaol** opened for business in 1883 and grew into a big prison campus, with everything from a women's wing to a couple of solitary confinement cells. Closed down in 1952, the jail is now a museum, where you can follow the march of penal progress since those rough-and-ready days. The highspot for tourists is on the ghoulish side—the double gallows used to execute a pair of killers in 1952. The location is a sick joke in itself: the prison infirmary. A souvenir shop inside the compound sells jokey coasters, recalling convict days; they are meant to protect your tablecloth from sweating beer cans.

Other restored buildings include the **Victoria Hotel**, a popular drinking venue as reminiscent of Victorian England as its name, and the former **Admiralty House**, now an arts and crafts gallery. A portion of the old Anglican **Christ Church Cathedral** that survived Tracy has been incorporated into the modern building that replaced it.

The New Darwin

For the feel of modern Darwin, drift over to the **Smith Street Mall**, a pedestrians-only shopping area in the heart of the restored city. Here you'll find the government tourist bureau, with

Post-modern style of architecture fits into the scenery in the new Darwin.

maps, brochures and advice on everything from housing to excursions. The shady mall, lined with stores, cafés and restaurants, is the perfect place for sizing up the locals and—always numerous in Darwin—the transients. This may be your first close-up look at Aboriginal people, who often congregate in the mall. If you want to take a photo, be discreet; they don't normally appreciate this kind of attention. Neither, for that matter, do the white but sunbaked Australian "characters" who turn up here with "Outback" all but written on their beards.

Darwin's **Performing Arts Centre**, an enterprising post modernist edifice designed for the tropics, puts theatre, shops, cafés and a five-star hotel under one roof. Another building that looks remarkably ambitious for a town of Darwin's size is the **Diamond Beach Casino**, a white pyramid of a leisure centre surrounding the magnet of gambling. Investors have a choice of traditional games in the sophisticated mould of Monte Carlo or the more folksy Australian style. You can try your hand at two-up, the Aussie game that's as simple as tossing two coins. The excitement grabs participants and hangers-on alike. Above the roulette tables flashes the list of recent winning numbers, an aid to systematic numerologists among the punters. The atmosphere is formal by local standards—shoes and shirts are required.

At the opposite end of Fannie Bay, in the East Point Recreation Reserve, Darwin's **Military Museum** has a collection of World War II relics like artillery pieces and twisted propellors. The museum's headquarters occupies an old command bunker. Another imposing emplacement once housed a coastal defence gun that had a range of 26 km (16 miles), but the weapon itself was scrapped after the hostilities ended. Scattered about the grounds are lesser guns and other reminders that the war was very real in Darwin.

Frangipani and Frantic Fish

Lovers of tropical flowers will be delighted by every little garden around town, but the ultimate display occupies the century-old **Botanical Gardens**, 34 ha (84 acres) of the most fetching, fragrant flowers and plants. In addition to the bougainvillaea and frangipani, the orchids are a special source of pride, and the brightly hued birds that live here are a delightful bonus. The Botanical Gardens amphitheatre is used for all manner of occasions from symphony concerts to Aboriginal dances. Barbecue facilities are thoughtfully provided at the edge of the gardens.

Back to the seaside for something completely different: Doctors Gully, at the northern end of the Esplanade, is the scene of a strange audience-participation ritual, the feeding of the fish. At an establishment called **Aquascene**, tourists wade into the sea at high tide (check the local paper for the time) to hand-feed catfish, mullet, bream and other denizens of the harbour. When a fish big enough to feed several families snatches a piece of bread out of your hand, the experience is worth the admission fee. A maelstrom of insatiably hungry fish turn up here daily for the festivities, after which they return to normal deep-sea pursuits until the next free hand-out. A fish

psychologist could have a field day figuring it all out.

If you'd prefer not to get your feet wet, Darwin has an unusually ambitious aquarium, the award-winning **Indo-Pacific Marine**. It's said to be one of only four of its kind in the world, containing living coral reef communities transplanted from the sea.

Stingers at Large
Wonder why the Darwin beaches are empty when the weather's at its most sweltering? Blame *Chironex fleckeri*, alias box jellyfish. At Indo-Pacific Marine or the Museum of Arts and Sciences you can, with impunity, get close to this sinister character. But the meeting can be deadly dangerous unless there's a window between you and one of these slimy transparent creatures. Between October and May, swimming in the Timor Sea is out of the question, due to the throngs of sea wasps drifting by. They can kill, or at least cause a violently unpleasant shock. The rest of the year, it's still prudent to look out for jellyfish, but the biggest remaining problem for swimmers and divers is probably the shark.

Past and Present

Overlooking Fannie Bay, surrounded by gardens, the Northern Territory **Museum of Arts and Sciences** is the place for a quick briefing on Aboriginal art and culture. Among the strong points: a survey of the work of Albert Namatjira and his sons and friends. Based at Hermannsburg, west of Alice Springs, they were the first acclaimed Aboriginal landscape painters. And there's a stunning collection of Aboriginal bark painting from Arnhem Land and the islands off Darwin. In

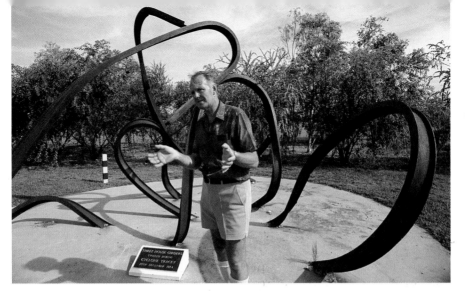

*M*ore eloquent than a poem, wreckage of the 1974 cyclone stands as a monument to Darwin's great disaster.

fact the whole museum amounts to an expertly organized show of almost everything relevant to the Territory's past and present, from archaeology to the natural sciences, plus displays of South-East Asian and Oceanic art.

Most of the tourist hotels are concentrated at the tip of the peninsula leading to the harbour. But Darwin's residential and recreational areas stretch in all directions around the airport at the centre of the metropolitan area. This is handy for airline passengers but less so for the locals, who must go miles out of their way to get from one part of town to another on opposite sides of the runway.

On the Stuart Highway, which skirts the south side of the airport, the Darwin **Aviation Museum** occupies a capacious hangar built expressly to house a B-52 bomber called **Darwin's Pride**, on permanent loan from the US Air Force. The plane, weighing 75 tonnes empty, is so huge that the tail had to be tilted to the horizontal to squeeze it through the hangar doors. You can walk into the bomb-bay of this eight-engined monster. Dwarfed by the Stratofortress, World War II bombers and other aerial memorabilia complete the display.

On the north side of the airport, near the Casuarina High School, is a moving **monument** to the victims of Cyclone Tracy, which killed more than 50 people on Christmas Eve, 1974. It's a "sculpture" of twisted iron girders, like roller-coaster tracks gone wild. No artist produced this abstraction; it's merely the way three girders were contorted when the big wind destroyed a nearby house.

Cyclone Tracy taught everyone a lesson in architecture and engineering. Now esspecially reinforced roof construction is required by law; in theory, anyway, houses should never again go sailing away. Even Darwin's **Chinese Temple**, notwithstanding its sweeping roofs, is guaranteed cyclone-proof. It serves the Buddhists, Taoists and Confucians well.

Fogg Dam, 60 km (37 miles) east of Darwin, is a splendid sanctuary for a dozen species of water bird, coexisting on magical pools. This was the site of the Humpty Doo rice project, a multi-million-dollar scheme to grow rice without the disadvantages of the traditional feet-in-the-mud, aching-back method. According to the plan devised by the efficiency experts, airplanes effortlessly seeded the area at one fell swoop. Countless swarms of birds, not having been consulted, feasted on this manna from heaven as soon as the seeds hit the ground. Riceless, Humpty Doo had a great fall and went out of business. The area is again strictly for the birds—more than 2 million of them, by some counts, during the wet season.

*H*ighrise in the bush: termites erect mammoth "anthills" near Darwin.

Kakadu Park

Bird-watchers, botanists and all other visitors are enthralled by Kakadu National Park, about 220 km (135 miles) east of Darwin. The scenery ranges from romantic to awesome. As an unparalleled outdoor museum of ancient Aboriginal art, the park is on the World Heritage list of places of "outstanding universal value" deserving protection. Timeless paintings on Kakadu's rock ledges brim with mystery and meaning. Some have been there since the era of Europe's Paleolithic cave art.

Nineteen different clans of Aborigines live in the park's nearly 20,000 km^2 (some 7,500 square miles), between the Wild Man and the East Alligator rivers. They lease the land to the National Parks and

East of Darwin

In Australia, nature's ingenuity seems to know no bounds. If you venture into the tropical wilderness east of Darwin you can see natural phenomena called **"magnetic anthills"**. They are widely scattered like prehistoric dolmens in the bush alongside the highway. "Magnetic anthills" is a neat expression describing the insect equivalent of skyscrapers, but, to be accurate, they are neither magnetic nor anthills. These termite mounds, often taller than humans, are always aligned exactly north–south ... for reasons only termites can explain. They look like two-dimensional sand castles.

There's always a convention of water birds at Fogg Dam, but the wet season is the best time. These are spoonbills and egrets.

white-lined honeyeater and white-breasted whistler, to list but three of the species that breed in the park. The stand-out, though, is the jabiru, a stately variety of stork.

In the mangroves you'll see striated heron, little kingfisher, and broad-billed flycatcher. And you can go down the checklist with magpie goose,

Wildlife Service and participate in the park's management; you'll see Aborigines in the uniform of park rangers.

Nature has bluntly divided Kakadu into two worlds: the plains, with their lagoons and creeks, and the escarpment, a stark sandstone wall marking the western edge of Arnhem Land. From the high plateau, waterfalls tumble to the lowlands in the wet season (November to March), when, incidentally, road travel becomes next to impossible. The floodplains entertain water birds by the thousand. The names alone turn laymen into dedicated bird-watchers: white-throated grasswren,

Lilies, birds and crocodiles thrive in the wetlands of Kakadu National Park.

199

black shag, ibis and crested plover. A special delight is the sight of the delicately poised lotus bird, which walks miraculously on the water.

The waterways are rich in the eminently edible barramundi. Less appetizingly, the estuaries are home to the saltwater crocodile, which preys on barramundi, birds, small animals and, on special occasions, humans. Kakadu is Crocodile Dundee country; in fact thanks to the film, which was shot here, the national park incurred a big increase in tourist traffic. Accommodation used to be on the basic side in the park, mostly camping sites, but now there's even a four-star hotel at Jabiru. Seen from the air the installation resembles a giant crocodile, no less.

Bigmouth
Maybe it's because they've been roaming the earth since the time of the dinosaurs, but crocodiles receive a lot of respect. Awe aside, they are protected under Australian law. Please don't pester them.

The saltwater crocodiles of Kakadu National Park eat anything they can wrap their teeth around. Every so often they devour a boatsman, bather or wader, or someone who comes too close to the bank of a river or marsh. Although "salties" can grow to a length exceeding 6 m (20 ft), they often escape notice as they snooze almost submerged in a swamp.

Kakadu's Rock Art
Ancient Aborigines left impressive works of art—rock paintings in styles both primitive and eerily sophisticated—at hundreds, perhaps a thousand, different places in the park and Arnhem Land beyond. The Northern Territory Museum of Arts

*M*ythological figures on the cliffside of Kakadu's Anbangbang Gallery, one of thousands of archaeological sites in the park.

and Sciences considers this to be the greatest body of rock art in the world. Furthermore, the ritual significance of the paintings has endured for many thousands of years.

The earliest legacy consists of arrangements of handprints and the imprints of objects that were dyed and thrown for decorative effect at cliff walls and cave ceilings. Many centuries later, abstract-expressionist artists reinvented a similar splashy technique.

The next generation of prehistoric artists concentrated on the figures of animals. Among them is a curious variety of anteater believed to have become extinct perhaps 18,000 years ago, a valuable clue to the age of some of these paintings. The same school of artists painted stick-figure humans in hunting and battle scenes. They used ochre pigments for colour.

Later artists brought movement to their pictures—for instance, hunters caught in the act of throwing spears or boomerangs. A few thousand years after this, Aboriginal artists developed a remarkable style, now called X-ray painting. The profile of, say, a fish is clearly painted but instead of its scales we see its bones and internal organs, with the emphasis on edible or otherwise useful parts.

After Australia was colonized, the white man, too, became a subject for Aboriginal artists. There are pictures of the sailing ships the British arrived in, and caricatures, scarcely flattering, of the new settlers holding recognizable muskets.

Katherine Gorge

The most spectacular natural attraction of the Top End of the Northern Territory, Katherine Gorge is about 350 km (220 miles) "down the Track" from Darwin. "The Track" is what they call the highway linking the Timor Sea and Alice Springs, in the Red Centre of Australia. Originally a rough path fit for bullock carts and camel trains servicing the overland telegraph line, the route was upgraded by the Americans in World War II to supply Darwin, which was dangerously isolated and under air attack. Now it's a proper, year-round, sealed road, the Stuart Highway.

Refugees and the wounded were evacuated down the Track, first to Adelaide River, about 110 km (70 miles) south of Darwin, an important military staging post at the time. Memories are strong on the outskirts of the village, where a pleasantly landscaped war memorial cemetery contains the graves of 432 military and civilian casualties.

The town of Katherine, founded as a telegraph relay station, became a crucial stop on the railway. The cattle now grazing the area have a comfortable life, but their ancestors walked all the way from Adelaide in the 1870s, a tremendous odyssey for the cowboys and shepherds, as well.

Exploring the Gorge

Katherine Gorge is, to be precise, not a single gorge but a series of 13 gorges. During the wet season (from November to March) the torrents, waterfalls, whirlpools and rapids give an impression of thundering power. But it's uncomfortably hot and humid, and sometimes the nonstop rains cut off the roads. So Katherine Gorge National Park is best visited in the dry season (April to October), when the water flows at a relative trickle. Flat-bottomed boats cruise the river, which reflects sheer cliffsides; walks and hikes offer other perspectives.

Among the sights are Aboriginal wall-paintings portraying kangaroos and other native animals bigger than life-size. Live kangaroos may be seen in the park, as well as the echidna (spiny anteater) and the dingo. Adding a tremor of excitement, there are glimpses of a freshwater variety of crocodile called Johnstone's Crocodile.

Unlike the "salties" of the north, though, these fierce-looking reptiles are timid fish-eaters; tourists do not figure on their menu. Bird life is colourful: hooded parrots, black cockatoos, and agile rainbow birds.

Like Kakadu, the Katherine Gorge park once again belongs to the local Aboriginal people. The Jawoyn people lease the land back to the Northern Territory Conservation Commission.

Tennant Creek

Two-thirds of the way down the Track from Darwin to Alice Springs, the mining town of Tennant Creek commemorates its gold-rush history with a carnival every May. Tennant Creek was behind the times, for its gold wasn't discovered until the depression year of 1932. After the gold thinned out, copper was found, so they have lived happily ever after. The biggest monument to the bonanza is a big hole in the ground. Legend says that Tennant Creek, a popular, comfortable overnight stop for long-distance travellers, was founded by accident when a truck full of beer suffered a fatal breakdown. While drinking the cargo to lighten the load, the crew opened a pub on the spot, and settlers were attracted from miles around.

A natural curiosity in the Outback about 100 km (60 miles) south of Tennant's Creek, the **Devil's Marbles** are huge granite boulders that mean a lot to the Aborigines. The boulders seem precariously perched on other rocks. It doesn't matter what geologists say about erosion and other mundane explanations, the Aborigines believe these "marbles" are the eggs of the Rainbow Serpent.

Alice Springs

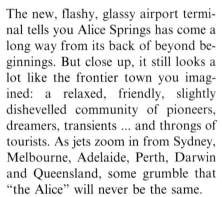

The new, flashy, glassy airport terminal tells you Alice Springs has come a long way from its back of beyond beginnings. But close up, it still looks a lot like the frontier town you imagined: a relaxed, friendly, slightly dishevelled community of pioneers, dreamers, transients ... and throngs of tourists. As jets zoom in from Sydney, Melbourne, Adelaide, Perth, Darwin and Queensland, some grumble that "the Alice" will never be the same.

The Northern Territory's second biggest population centre has more than 24,000 inhabitants. When it comes to climate, they are extremists. In the summer it gets as hot as 42°C (107°F) but, mercifully, the nights in June, July and August require a sweater or two. Chances of seeing rain are slight. The Henley-on-Todd Regatta, a whimsical fixture each August, is run on the sandy bed of the sometime Todd River, a wide wadi gullying through the centre of town. The boats, of many classes, are all bottomless, hilariously propelled by the racing legs of their crews.

"The Alice" first grew around a waterhole discovered in 1871 by the surveying party stringing the first telegraph line from Adelaide to Darwin—and from there to the rest of the world. Alice Springs was named after Alice Todd, the wife of South Australia's Postmaster General. He won a knighthood for pushing through the project; locally, the Todd River immortalizes him.

Camels, traditionally jockeyed by experts from Afghanistan, brought the equipment for the telegraph relay

A mural recalls the completion of the railway line between South Australia and Alice Springs in 1929. More recently, good airline connections with many cities have really put "the Alice" on the tourist map.

station built at Alice Springs and the supplies to keep the technicians alive. When the termites devoured the first telegraph poles, replacements—heavy iron poles manufactured in Britain—also had to be transported by camel train.

Telegrams aside, Alice Springs remained isolated until World War II, when it was abustle with troop movements and evacuees from the north. After the war, until the 1960s, it was little more than a crossroads market town. Now the biggest outpost of civilization for a thousand miles around,

"the Alice" is thriving as a staging post for tourist jaunts throughout the Red Centre, with more hotels and motels of three stars and up than Darwin.

A Walk in The Alice

Like many an Australian town, "the Alice" is bigger in area than you might expect, but the essential atmosphere can be taken in on a walking tour. In the main street, **Todd Street**, you'll find the Northern Territory Government Tourist Bureau, with maps and brochures. Nearby are historic buildings like the **Old Stuart Town Gaol** from the beginning of the 20th century, with "his" and "hers" dormitory cells, and **Adelaide House**, built in the 1920s as the first Alice Springs hospital, now a museum.

Panorama "Guth" on Hartley Street is the realization of a dream by a Dutch artist, Henk Guth—a monumental 360° panoramic painting of the local landscape, 60 m (200 ft) in

Playing in the hot sun, musicians attract no more than a modest crowd in the centre of Alice Springs.

circumference. Downstairs is a museum of outstanding Aboriginal art and artefacts.

The **Flying Doctor Service**, which brings health care to the farthest cattle ranch, began here in 1928. You can take a tour of the base, on the south side of town. Another service which eased development of the Outback, the **School of the Air**, a radio link with isolated pupils, has its headquarters on Head Street.

A couple of kilometres north of town, an unspoiled park surrounds the restored **Telegraph Station**. This was the most important relay station on the line. Before the wires were strung a message could take three months to

Where it all began: the Alice Springs Telegraph Station, a vital relay point along the first wire linking Adelaide and Darwin—and from there the rest of the world.

reach London from Adelaide. The relics here give a glimpse of 19th-century technology and the lonely life of the telegraph pioneers.

Diversions

South of "the Alice" on the Ross Highway, a **camel farm** offers rides atop swaying beasts, the descendants of the camels that supplied the pioneers. Every May the local Lions Club sponsors the Camel Cup, a festive day of camel races at Blatherskite Park. The animals, launched from a kneeling start in a cloud of dust, run as fast as racehorses, though less gracefully. Camel connoisseurs say they are less temperamental than horses.

You may be surprised to find that a town like Alice Springs has an "international standard" **casino**. For seven nights a week, up until 1.00 a.m.,

Before the railway, Alice Springs was supplied by camel trains. Now one burden of the beasts involves racing around a track—always a bizarre sporting spectacle.

enthusiasts have a choice of blackjack, roulette and a sophisticated version of the Australian game of two-up, along with the excitements of poker machines and keno, a game resembling bingo.

An eccentric enterprise south-east of town is the only winery in the Northern Territory. **Chateau Hornsby** produces about 25 tonnes of grapes per year. In this hostile desert climate the vines have to be irrigated daily. The resulting wines, with quaint names like Alice Springs Shiraz and The Ghan Moselle, are available to be sampled on the spot.

A popular excursion from "the Alice" concentrates on **Standley Chasm**, 50 km (30 miles) to the west. This passage through the MacDonnell Ranges dwindles to the narrowest gap. The walls are so high and steep that the sun penetrates the bottom only fleetingly at midday. Slender trees bravely sprout from the rockface high above, reflected in the cool, still water of a natural pool at the far end of the gorge. In the "wet" season, from November to March, rainwater can suddenly flood the chasm.

Ayers Rock

The world's best-known rock is as photogenic as any film star, but moodier. As the sun begins to sink beyond the rim of the desert, the crowds with their cameras gather by car and bus along "Sunset Strip", the tongue-in-cheek name for a dusty stretch of improvised parking lot. Watching Ayers Rock undergo its striking changes of colour, the onlookers are not solemn but rather festive, friendly and relaxed ... in fact, very Australian. They are fulfilling an Australian dream, getting to know this mystical, 500-million-year-old rock that rises from the red heart of the country.

The wonderful rock, seemingly dropped by divine design in the middle of nowhere, actually protrudes from a buried mountain range. About 350 m (1,150 ft) high and some 8 km (5 miles) around, it is even more impressive than the dimensions suggest. Standing alone in a dead-flat landscape, and tinted as bright as your imagination, the monolith lives up to its reputation. You'll need no complicated explanations to understand why the Aborigines consider it sacred.

The Aborigines have owned Ayers Rock (they call it **Uluru**) under Australian law only since 1985; the small local Aboriginal community leases it back to the government for use as a national park in return for a healthy income and participation in its management. The hand-over of the land created a raging controversy; vociferous opponents advertised the slogan, "The rock belongs to *all* Australians."

For the Aborigines it's not just a rock, it's a vital aspect of the Dreamtime, encompassing the creation of the earth, linked with the life of the present and future. Various parts of the monolith are qualified as sacred sites; they are signposted, fenced off, and definitely barred to outsiders.

The Longest Rigs

Of all the perils of driving in the Northern Territory's Outback, the most visible is the road train sending up clouds of exhaust fumes and dust. A mighty truck pulling two or three full-sized trailers can measure 50 m (165 ft) from kangaroo-catcher to tail. It's marked "road train" front and rear to warn that this is no ordinary vehicle. Trying to overtake one requires patience, strong nerves, and at least a full kilometre (1,100 yd) of empty road ahead. Fortunately, the drivers are courteous professionals who'll give you a fair chance. In exchange, they ask you to understand that their momentum makes sudden manoeuvres very dangerous. If somebody has to yield, it had better be you.

Viewing the Rock

The most inspiring views of the rock are to be seen at dawn and dusk. It's worth getting up at six in the morning to stake out the mighty silhouette from 20 km (12 miles) away, waiting for the sunrise. As first light strikes the lonely monolith it catches fire, glowing red, then orange, finally seeming to emit rays of wondrous power. Only then the desert world comes to life: a hawk squawks, a rabbit rustles the brush, and hordes of pesky flies begin to buzz. Insect repellent helps, but the flies seem to outnumber the people 20 to one. Maybe this is why Aboriginal legends mention bothersome flies.

The Great Aussie Salute

Waving your hand in front of your face becomes second nature in the Outback, like a horse flicking its tail. "The Great Australian Salute", as the involuntary gesture is wryly known, aims to disperse the aggressive bush flies. The reason the little buzzers harass people is their thirst; they hope to lap up some moisture from human perspiration, saliva or tears. Aside from hand signals, those silly hats with bobbing corks are the only remedy. But you'll be relieved to know that scientists report there are fewer flies in the bush these days, thanks to colonies of African dung beetles assigned to reduce the insects' food sources.

If you're fit you can join the crowds climbing the rock. A few hours suffice for the round trip via the marked trail, which has a protective chain to grab when the going gets too steep or windy. The ascent requires no mountain-climbing experience or equipment. But do wear sensible rubber-soled shoes and carry drinking water. From ground level the climbers attaining the summit look like a line of very tired ants.

Another worthwhile way to get to know the rock is to join a walking tour led by a park ranger, which circumnavigates the base. Up close, the monolith discloses its variegated surface: caves, dry rivulets, furrows and burrows, wounds and gashes, and what might be taken for fanciful engravings 60 m (200 ft) tall.

Like a line of ants, tourists follow the protective chain on the trail to the top of Ayers Rock.

Sunrise puts the monolith of Ayers Rock into one of its several awesome moods (previous page).

The Olgas

Only 36 km (22 miles) by road west of Ayers Rock, and visible from its summit, is another stupendous rock formation, the **Olgas**. From afar, Mount Olga and its satellites look like

The Olgas, more complex than Ayers Rock, also provide a moving sight as the sunlight changes. Climbing is complicated.

a scattering of dinosaur eggs or sleeping elephants, but they're even higher than Ayers Rock. Here, too, dawn and dusk colour the most fascinating views, the fantasy shapes changing with the hues and the movement of the shadows. The Aboriginal name is **Katatjuta**, meaning "many heads", and you can guess that the sand-blown rocks have profound meaning in the native culture.

You can get to know the Olgas by a choice of hiking routes. The popular trail from the Katatjuta car park up to the lookout is officially called "suitable for family enjoyment", but it's steep and tricky enough to deter the very youngest and oldest generations.

Yulara Development

To cope with hundreds of thousands of visitors each year at Ayers Rock, a

After a hot day's slog in the desert, the Yulara development is an oasis of comfort and luxury.

comprehensive resort has been built. It could have been a disastrous blot on the landscape, but the **Yulara Resort** fits in benignly, 20 km (12 miles) from the rock. Almost camouflaged, the complex is too low-slung to detract from the majesty of the surroundings.

The facilities start with hundreds of sites for tents and caravans, and go up to a five-star hotel with gardens, pool, spa, restaurants and bars, television and in-house video; and of course all the rooms are air-conditioned. It makes for quite a change after a day slogging through the desert. The permanent party of hundreds of people running Yulara was recruited in many parts of the country. There is a school for their children and local Aboriginal children. In other resorts the staff quarters tend to be hidden from sight,

but they are so luxurious at Yulara that they're set in the midst of the prime tourist area.

The **Visitors' Centre** in the hotel-and-shopping complex offers information, literature and audiovisual shows explaining the desert, the wildlife, geology, mythology, and other angles to enhance your appreciation of the Red Centre.

Several airlines serve Yulara, and the views of the desert on the way are spellbinding. Otherwise you can take a bus or drive; it's about 450 km (360 miles) by paved road from Alice Springs, a whole day to become acquainted with the desert in its many forms—flat and desolate, or covered with scrub, thinly forested or, more rarely, sand undulating in postcard-worthy dunes.

The best time of year to visit is between May and October, when the days are sunny and warm and the nights refreshingly chill. In January, by contrast, the mean maximum temperature is 36.6°C (98°F), not quite conducive to hiking.

Aboriginal Art: from Cave Men to Prodigies

Centuries before the expression "multi-media art" was coined, Australia's Aboriginal artists were creating it. The canvas for their paintings could be anything from a cliff-face to tree bark to a human body; for paint they used mysterious mixtures of minerals and vegetables, and sometimes blood. For the modern viewer the results can seem vaguely sinister, or just puzzling, or thoroughly charming.

The first Australian artists—tens of thousands of years ago—engraved their pictures on cave walls, using their fingers to dig outlines in soft surfaces, hammering the design in harder rock with their Stone-Age tools. (The tools didn't change much until the arrival of the colonists in 1788.) Their subjects

were men and women, animals including larger-than-life kangaroos and koalas, and, in rare cases, cartoon-style faces. Everything had a meaning according to the ritual.

Cave painting began with the most elementary designs: hands dipped in dye and pressed against the stone, or the negative version—stencilled hands. Also very basic were the imprints of dyed objects thrown at a wall. (Much later, splashing paint onto a canvas in a similarly free-wheeling way was to bring fame and serious money to some modern artists in the northern hemisphere.)

The representational paintings that followed covered the subjects of the Dreamtime legends of the creation of the earth, portraits of ancestors, and depictions of ritual ceremonies in progress. Lively were the hunting scenes and close-ups of the desired animals, birds and fish, designed to bring luck to the hunters. The artists showed imagination and initiative in the pigments they used, from charcoal and red rocks to the coloured dust found inside ants' nests. Where needed colours couldn't be manufactured locally, artists traded with distant suppliers.

The subject matter expanded and acquired sophistication. There were totally convincing crocodiles, snakes and turtles, and hunting scenes with candid action—for instance, a boomerang at the instant of launching. Another innovation was the use of abstract marks around certain figures, like a modern cartoonist's squiggles representing a character's surprise or confusion or fear.

"X-ray painting", as it is now called, was an imaginative development, in which a recognizable fish or crocodile was shown in cutaway mode, accurately highlighting internal features of interest to cooks or butchers, such as bone structure and organs. The same was done, later, for inanimate objects—for instance a rifle, with a bullet shown in profile in the breach. After the First Fleet arrived, astonished native artists watched big sailing ships disgorging gunslinging Englishmen, and painted historical documents of what they saw.

Art in motion: body-painting has been an Aboriginal art form over the centuries.

Painting on Bark

In several areas of Australia the easy-to-strip bark of *Eucalyptus tetradonta*, coloquially known as the Darwin stringybark tree, has long been the canvas for Aboriginal art. Bark painting

Abstract or surreal, modern Aboriginal art is evermore highly prized by collectors in Australia and abroad.

originated in the Northern Territory's Top End, it's thought, as a pastime for the long rainy season, and a way of decorating the wet-weather huts. Some artists fill every inch of the bark, combining figurative art with abstract background decorations. But they always tell a story, from the biographies of mythological characters to events in the lives of contemporary tribesmen. Other artists specialize in wood carving—big ceremonial poles or grave posts, brightly painted to represent the deceased's ancestors and contemporaries.

In recent times, missionaries, anthropologists and other well-meaning visitors suggested to some of the painters that their art had an economic value. Thus Aboriginal painters turned professional, sharing the traditional

pictures with museums, galleries and art lovers at home and abroad. Nowadays the stars of Australian art can't work fast enough to meet the demand, and galleries ask tens of thousands of dollars for their latest *œuvres*. Artists who once decorated sand floors with mythological scenes for ceremonial use have been converted to the convenience of hardboard or canvas, and pots of acrylic paints instead of the primitive ochres. (They still squat, using no easel, with the painting flat on the ground.) Some of their work looks like a desert-coloured elaboration on the dots of pointillism with geometric forms superimposed. The subject might be a sort of road map of the mythical journey of a Dreamtime ancestor. But there's always a story. Those concentric circles could represent initiates sitting around camp-fires; look closely and you'll see the spears and boomerangs they will throw to prove themselves. In the Aboriginal world of symbols, there's nothing abstract about these dots, circles and spirals.

An x-ray version of a fish dominates a Kakadu cave painting, along with a turtle and (upper right) a hand.

NO MINUTE GONE COMES EVER BACK AGAIN
TAKE HEED AND SEE YE NOTHING DO IN VAIN

Bursting with Natural Wealth, Wild Flowers and Enthusiasm

In a state bigger than Texas and Alaska combined, there's plenty of room for a flowering countryside so fetching you won't want to leave. Yet most of the terrain of Western Australia is frankly forbidding—desert, semidesert or otherwise difficult if not impossible. Nature compensated: the parched earth sparkles with minerals.

Gold brought the first bonanza, in the 1880s and '90s, followed by treasure troves of nickel, bauxite and iron, even diamonds. Much more appealing are the visible riches: the hardwood forests, orchards and vineyards. And, since the climate is so sunny, it's only fair that there's a beach for every mood along the 6,400 km (4,000 miles) of coastline, extending from the tropics to the eminently temperate south.

Long ago and far away was Tudor England: a Perth shopping centre capitalizes on a fantasy of nostalgia.

The bulk of the population of more than 1½ million has gravitated to the Mediterranean climate around the beautiful capital city, Perth. Closer to Jakarta than to Sydney, Perth faces the Indian Ocean with an open, outward-looking stance. The cares of the big population centres of eastern Australia seem worlds away.

The first European to set eyes on Western Australia (in 1616) was Dirk Hartog, a Dutch navigator making his way from the Cape of Good Hope to Java. Soon, other Dutch travellers touched base, and one of them reported spotting what we know as a wallaby; he thought it was a giant cat with a pouch for its kitten. Later in the 17th century, the British adventurer William Dampier happened upon

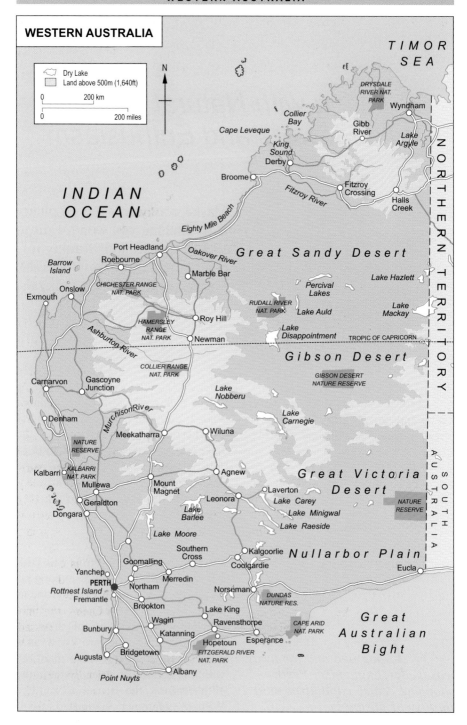

WESTERN AUSTRALIA

Dry Lake
Land above 500m (1,640ft)

0   200 km
0   200 miles

N

*TIMOR
SEA*

DRYSDALE
RIVER NAT.
PARK

Wyndham

Collier
Bay

Gibb
River

Lake
Argyle

Cape Leveque

King
Sound

Derby

*INDIAN
OCEAN*

Broome

Fitzroy River

Fitzroy
Crossing

Halls
Creek

Eighty Mile Beach

Port Headland

Oakover River

Great Sandy Desert

Barrow
Island

Roebourne

Marble Bar

Lake Hazlett

Onslow

CHICHESTER RANGE
NAT. PARK

Percival
Lakes

Exmouth

HAMERSLEY
RANGE
NAT. PARK

Roy Hill

RUDALL RIVER
NAT. PARK

Lake Auld

Lake
Mackay

Ashburton River

Newman

Lake
Disappointment

TROPIC OF CAPRICORN

COLLIER RANGE
NAT. PARK

Gibson Desert

Carnarvon

Gascoyne
Junction

GIBSON DESERT
NATURE RESERVE

Lake
Nobberu

Murchison River

Denham

Lake
Carnegie

Meekatharra

Wiluna

NATURE
RESERVE

KALBARRI
NAT. PARK

Kalbarri

*Great Victoria
Desert*

Mullewa

Agnew

Mount
Magnet

Laverton

NATURE
RESERVE

Geraldton

Leonora

Lake Carey

Dongara

Lake
Barlee

Lake Minigwal

Lake Raeside

Lake Moore

Southern
Cross

Kalgoorlie

Nullarbor Plain

Goomalling

Coolgardie

Eucla

Yanchep

PERTH

Merredin

Rottnest Island

Northam

Norseman

DUNDAS
NATURE RES.

Fremantle

Brookton

Lake King

*Great
Australian
Bight*

Wagin

Ravensthorpe

CAPE ARID
NAT. PARK

Bunbury

Katanning

Hopetoun

Esperance

Augusta

Bridgetown

FITZGERALD RIVER
NAT. PARK

Point Nuyts

Albany

NORTHERN TERRITORY

SOUTH AUSTRALIA

Shark Bay, near Carnarvon, and could hardly wait to leave: the land seemed hopeless for farming, there was no drinking water, and he dismissed the Aborigines as "brutes".

The British Era

More than 200 years after Hartog's discovery of Western Australia, the British finally got around to colonizing it. The site chosen, on the Swan River, was to become Perth. However, what the Colonial Office considered a good idea turned out to be less brilliant in practice. It would take more than the scenery and climate to attract settlers to what seemed, even by Australian standards, the end of the world. Problems of development persisted: poor communications, financial difficulties, and a shortage of workers. Prospects for the new frontier became so precarious that the colony's leaders had to appeal to London to send out forced labourers—convicts.

Still nothing really worked in Western Australia until the gold rush toward the end of the 19th century. Then the population quadrupled in ten years. Once launched on the road to prosperity, there was no stopping the largest state, more than ten times the area of Great Britain. Its isolation finally ended in the early years of the 20th century when the transcontinental railway linked Perth and Sydney. New mineral deposits kept turning up,

*W*estern Australia
showing the main features.

climaxed in the 1970s by jackpots in natural gas and diamonds. The WA mood was buoyed to new heights in 1983, when the yacht *Australia II* wrested the America's Cup from the US for the first time in 132 years. The fame, if not the cup, lingers.

Perth

Innovative and neck-strainingly tall, sleek new skyscrapers compete for supremacy over central Perth, as if to prove that Western Australia's optimism is boundless. If this city were a person, you might imagine it had been born with a silver spoon in its mouth: a handsome, clean-cut youngster with every possible advantage, inevitably growing up to become an unqualified success in life.

Although history refutes the silver spoon theory, you can't miss Perth's easy self-confidence. The people are relaxed, hospitable, anxious to help the stranger. They are proud of their efficient town and its up-to-date facilities and the great sailing, swimming, surfing and fishing on the doorstep. They won't fail to inform you that this tidy city of parks, sprawling magnificently along the looping river, is Australia's sunniest state capital.

Sunshine aside, Perth has called itself "the city of lights" since the early days of the American manned space programme. As John Glenn, the first American to orbit the earth, passed overhead, middle-of-the-night Perth switched on every light bulb in town. It was a typically friendly gesture, brightening the lone astronaut's flight and putting Perth's name in lights.

A rainbow aims its beam at Australia's "city of lights". Like other capitals, Perth's racial complexion has become multicoloured.

City Sights

Few get a chance to enjoy a spaceman's perspective, but the view over Perth from **King's Park** is a good compromise for sizing up the city below. These 400 ha (1,000 acres) of natural woodland and wild flowers, manicured lawns and picnic sites, solemn monuments and lively playgrounds, occupy the top of a bluff called Mount Eliza, right on the edge of the city centre. From up here you look down on the wide Swan River as it meanders towards the sea, the business district with its gleaming skyscrapers, and the complexity of the well-landscaped municipal freeway system.

The Swan River begins about 240 km (150 miles) inland in the wheatlands of Western Australia. For most of its journey, under the name of the Avon River, it is only seasonally navigable, and occasionally downright treacherous. But here, with the Indian Ocean close enough to salt it, the Swan widens into a lake, and invites reflection ... and flotillas of breezy sailing boats.

Near the riverside in the centre of town, the **Old Courthouse** really is old, especially by local standards. Built in Georgian style in 1836, it qualifies as the oldest public building in Perth. **Stirling Gardens**, surrounding the courthouse, is a restful hideaway. A monument here looks like a giant shish kebab impaling all of the minerals produced in Western Australia; but don't

Town plan of Perth.

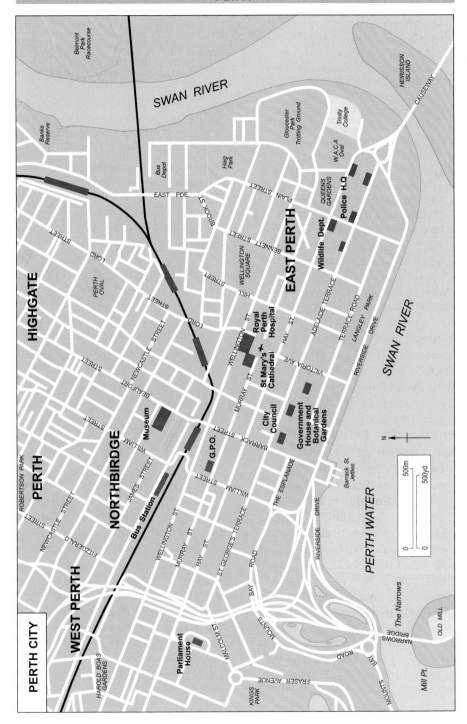

PERTH CITY

SWAN RIVER

Belmont Park Racecourse

Banks Reserve

HEIRISSON ISLAND

CAUSEWAY

Gloucester Park Trotting Ground

Trinity College

Bus Depot

Haig Park

W.A.C.A. Oval

EAST PDE.

BROOK ST.

PLAIN STREET

QUEENS GARDENS

Police H.Q.

STREET

HIGHGATE

LORD

PERTH OVAL

STREET

BENNETT STREET

WELLINGTON SQUARE

HILL STREET

EAST PERTH

Wildlife Dept.

ROBERTSON PARK

PERTH

NEWCASTLE STREET

BEAUFORT

STREET

WELLINGTON ST.

Royal Perth Hospital

St Mary's Cathedral

HAY ST.

ADELAIDE TERRACE

TERRACE ROAD

LANGLEY PARK

VICTORIA AVE.

SWAN RIVER

STREET

STREET

FITZGERALD

NEWCASTLE STREET

WEST PERTH

NORTHBIRDGE

WILLIAM

Museum

MURRAY ST.

BARRACK STREET

City Council

Government House and Botanical Gardens

G.P.O.

JAMES STREET

Bus Station

STREET

WILLIAM

THE ESPLANADE

Barrack St. Jetties

N

500m

500yd

WELLINGTON ST.

MURRAY ST.

HAY ST.

ST. GEORGES TERRACE

ROAD

BAY

PERTH WATER

RIVERSIDE DRIVE

The Narrows

OLD MILL

HAROLD BOAS GARDENS

Parliament House

MALCOLM ST.

MOUNTS

FRASER AVENUE

BAY ROAD

NARROWS BRIDGE

Mill Pt.

KINGS PARK

MOUNTS

expect to find gold or diamonds on the skewer—they don't seem to count.

Historic and Otherwise

Town Hall, at the corner of Hay and Barrack Streets, was built in the 1860s by convict labour. If you look closely at the outline of the windows of the tower, you may perceive the design of broad arrows—the prison symbol that was stencilled on convicts' uniforms.

Similarly historical in inspiration, but even less antique than the Town Hall, **London Court** is a 1930s shopping mall in a 16th-century style, leaded windows and all. One of the clocks is a smaller replica of Big Ben. The twee Tudor shopping court fits in quite happily with the modern stores and interconnecting **shopping malls** radiating from Hay and Murray streets, the main shopping zone of Perth. Cars are prohibited here, so the window-shopping is very relaxed. The area is usually animated by buskers—street musicians, magicians, jugglers or mimes—and fast-talking pedlars.

Next to the stately General Post Office in Forest Chase mall, the state **tourist office**, called the Holiday WA Centre, is an abundant source of brochures, maps, tickets, tours and bright ideas cheerfully dispensed.

In a city as young as Perth, with slim new office buildings soaring skyward out of all proportion to the older buildings, the historic structures which have escaped the developer's demolition ball are proudly pointed out to visitors.

Government House, on the main street, St George's ˙ Terrace, is the official residence of the state governor. Its Gothic effects date from the 1860s. Built by convicts, the house is used nowadays for state occasions and as a place to put up visiting VIPs.

The elegant terrace leads straight to the **Barracks Archway**, the last vestige of a headquarters building of the 1860s. This crenellated three-storey structure has been preserved as a memorial to the early colonists. Behind the brick archway you can see **Parliament House**, where the state legislature holds forth. Guided tours are offered, more comprehensive when the lawmakers are away.

Over the Bridge

On the other side of the railway tracks—you can cross the unusual Horseshoe Bridge by foot or car—stands the **Old Gaol**, built by and for convicts in 1856. Now it's part of the **Western Australia Museum**. In addition to penal relics of the Wild West days, the museum contains a good collection of Aboriginal rock paintings, head-dresses and weapons, as well as a meteorite weighing in at a

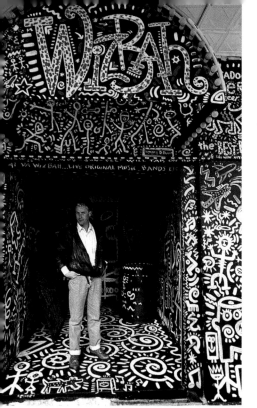

A Perth nightclub offers beer and music, but can it be called art?

hefty 11 tonnes. A Henry Moore sculpture adds cultural gravity to the place where the gaol's gallows used to be. The **Western Australia Art Gallery**, close by, exhibits paintings from several continents, but the emphasis is on Australian art.

Also north of the city centre is the **Northbridge** district, full of restaurants of many nationalities, pubs and nightclubs, ample proof that there is indeed life after dark in Perth. Alternatively, the sparkling white **Burswood Casino** complex, on reclaimed land near the Causeway Bridge, has over 140 gambling tables, plus a cabaret, restaurants and bars. To maintain standards, the casino enforces a sweeping ban on people wearing "jeans, denim, runners, joggers, sandshoes, thongs and sleeveless or collarless shirts." Attached to the gambling den are a luxury hotel, entertainment and convention facilities, and a sports centre that can cram in 14,000 fans. The puffy-domed Superdrome can handle any sort of sporting event from tennis championships to motorbike racing on imported dirt.

Back in the centre of town, you can hardly miss the modern **Entertainment Centre**. Not quite Perth's answer to the Sydney Opera House, this roundhouse landmark can accommodate 8,000 fans for rock concerts or more sober spectacles. Another cultural focus is the modern **Concert Hall** in St George's Terrace, headquarters of the state's symphony orchestra. And for stage plays, opera and ballet, the most atmospheric house is **His Majesty's Theatre**, restored to its sumptuous Edwardian standard.

To the Coast

It's only 19 km (13 miles) down the river from Perth to the capital's Indian Ocean port, Fremantle—an enjoyable outing on one of the cruise boats that ply the **Swan River**.

The river tours begin in the centre of Perth, at the Barrack Street Jetty. On the south side of the Narrows Bridge, note the **Old Mill**, an imposing white windmill in the Dutch style, from the first half of the 19th century. Perfectly restored, the colony's first flour mill is open for visits, but check the limited schedule.

A short ferry ride from the jetty, plus a five-minute walk, leads to the

Zoological Gardens in Labouchere Road, South Perth. For newcomers to Australia, this is the obvious place to get on first-name terms with the kangaroos, koalas, emus and echidnas. You can surround yourself with birds in a walk-through aviary and tiptoe in the dark through a nocturnal animal house, where the resident animals are tricked into playing their night games in the daytime. If the native beasts leave you unmoved, the zoo still makes a pleasant park-and-garden visit.

Down the riverside beyond the windmill spreads what looks like another of those transplants from Europe. The campus of the **University of Western Australia** was built and landscaped in Mediterranean style, from the shrubs right up to the orange-tiled roofs.

Matilda Bay harbours only a relative handful of the swarms of sailing boats that call the Swan River home. During World War II this was a base for Catalina flying boats. The bay is the site of the Royal Perth Yacht Club, where the America's Cup was treasured behind bulletproof glass from 1983 until it was lost to the United States in 1987.

The coastline of the **Dalkeith** district, near Point Resolution, is reasonably enough called Millionaires' Row. The view of these mansions from the river perspective just might evoke a dash of envy; even millionaires from out of town could turn jealous. The guided tour commentary goes on at great length about the cost of the houses, the fame of their owners, and the foibles of the owners' private lives.

Freshwater Bay was named by the crew of HMS *Beagle,* the survey ship made famous as the vehicle for Charles Darwin's researches into nature. After this bay, and a zig and a zag, the river tapers to a relatively narrow-gauge artery crossed by two bridges. Long-suffering convict labour built the first bridge at this site in 1866. It proved a boon to one of its creators, a celebrated outlaw named Moondyne Joe, an escape artist. The night before the ribbon-cutting ceremony, he broke out of Fremantle Prison and gave himself the honour of becoming the first, if unofficial, pedestrian to cross the Bridge Over the River Swan. He made a clean getaway.

Fremantle

A Mediterranean-style sunniness combines with Victorian-era quaintness to give Fremantle its special character—cosmopolitan, yet as down-to-earth as its classic examples of convict architecture. Although it's a serious international port for passengers and cargo, you'll remember the colourful city for its casual charms.

For years Fremantle—"Freo" to abbreviation-prone Aussies—lay becalmed, a long way from the big time of tourism. Then came the America's Cup saga and a saturation of world attention. New pride inspired the townsfolk in a sparkling campaign to restore the old terraced houses and other relics in time for the 1986/87 defence of the Cup. At the same time, the marina facilities were vastly expanded.

Whether you think of Fremantle as a yachting base or a workaday port, you'll want to see the sights of the harbour. There are dream yachts, trawlers, ocean liners and cargo ships of every stripe. You may see one of the

Sunny and cheerful, Fremantle has become more famous but no less friendly.

special sheep ships, loading tens of thousands of sheep from all over Western Australia, bound for the Middle East. Dogs help the shepherds direct truckloads of reluctant "passengers" to their berths. The sheep live on pellets of food for the four-week journey in sub-tourist class.

Fremantle's highest point is **Monument Hill**, in War Memorial Park. There are three memorials here, including one for the US personnel based in Fremantle who died in World War II. Another, an actual periscope, commemorates the British and Allied submarine crews who perished in the same conflict. This is the place to watch the sun set over the Indian Ocean.

Back near the waterfront, and wasting an enviable view, the 12-sided **Round House** looks like the forbidding, windowless prison it used to be. Actually, visitors find it much more cheerful from the inside, with its sunny courtyard, though the inmates might not have agreed. Built in 1831, the Round House specialized in the lesser criminals, but it was the site of the state's first hanging; generally, incorrigibles were simply shipped off to the rigours of Tasmania.

Museums

The building containing the **Western Australian Maritime Museum** was constructed by convicts to house the Commissariat, the bureaucracy in charge of them. Here's a chance to see some shipwrecks, most notably the wooden hull of the 600-tonne *Batavia,* flagship of the Dutch East India Company, which went aground in 1629. Meticulous restoration work is under way to reassemble this rare example of 17th-century shipbuilding technology. What makes the exhibits more fascinating than usual is the postscript to the wreck, an appealingly bloodthirsty tale of mutiny and murder among the survivors.

A wide-open space beyond the Maritime Museum, the **Esplanade** is shaded by Norfolk pines and a sprawling Moreton Bay fig tree. A monument here immortalizes Captain Charles Fremantle, who in 1829 claimed for King George IV the west coast of what was then New Holland.

The **Fremantle Museum and Arts Centre**, at the other end of town, occupies yet another convict-built complex. It first served as an asylum for deranged prisoners, then a training centre for midwives, later an old women's home, and in World War II it found new life as a headquarters of the US Navy. Demobilized and brightly restored, the Colonial Gothic building now contains exhibits on the history of Fremantle and its people.

If you can make it to Fremantle on a Friday, Saturday or Sunday, browse around **Fremantle Markets** at South Terrace and Henderson Street. Stalls of fresh fruits and vegetables, arts and crafts and bric-a-brac fill the century-old market hall, where you can also sample many a cosmopolitan cuisine. Entertainers stake out the pedestrians-only street outside.

Rottnest Island

Here's another of those brash Australian abbreviations: "Rotto". Not a very appealing nickname, but then "Rottnest" doesn't conjure up a lovely getaway island, either. Even in the original Dutch, the name does the island a rotten injustice. It seems that Commodore Willem de Vlaming, who landed here in 1696, confused the indigenous quokkas (a sort of undersized wallaby) with some imaginary species of rat. So he called the island Rottnest, or rat's nest. In spite of this unkind mistake, the Dutch explorer considered Rottnest an earthly paradise. You'll probably agree.

A good reason for going over the sea to Rottnest (18 km or 12 miles from Fremantle) is to see the fetching little quokkas, with babies in the pouch like their kangaroo cousins. These friendly marsupials accept hand-outs from visitors. Other attractions are peacocks and pheasants, which were introduced when the governors of Western Australia used the island as a summer residence. You can also spot dozens of other species of birds, like the curlew sandpiper, the red-necked sting and the osprey. Since 1941 the island has been a wildlife sanctuary, where it's forbidden to tamper with any of its natural resources, even the snakes.

Once, incredibly, this was a prison island; you can tour the old convict buildings. Otherwise, Rottnest is as quiet as an idyllic, barefoot sort of isle ought to be. The number of cars is severely curtailed, and skateboards are emphatically banned. Bicycles are the most popular way of exploring the 40 km (25 miles) of coastline, with opportunities for swimming, snorkelling, fishing and boating.

The island can be reached from Perth by commuter plane, ferryboat or hydrofoil.

Daytrips from Perth

Excursion companies offer an enterprising list of day tours for visitors to Perth who want to see the area's natural curiosities. Because of the distances involved, the three most popular outings take at least 12 hours each. As is the custom, there's always time out for food, shopping and, in season, flower-watching.

The Pinnacles

The imagination runs wild in **Nambung National Park**, approximately 250 km (155 miles) north of Perth. Myriad

Limestone pillars of the Pinnacles rise from the desert in mysterious formations in Nambung National Park.

limestone pillars protrude like stalagmites from the desert floor—more than 400 ha (nearly 1,000 acres) of fantastic formations. The wind that created these evocatively eroded pillars comes and goes—it may have stilled completely during your visit to the site. By the next day, though, it's a sure bet the wind will have erased your footprints in the yellow sand, along with the prints of the kangaroos loping into the bush. A circular walking trail 500 m long (about ⅓ mile) has been laid out among the pinnacles, including some lookout points affording perspective. Clearly, a formation that looks like a

giant kangaroo from one side may look like an abstract sculpture from another angle; it's all in the mind. The exhibits range up to 4 m (13 feet) in height.

A bumpy, unsealed road leads to the Pinnacles; four-wheel drive is no longer required. Though you can't see the sea from the Pinnacle Desert, the national park borders on the Indian Ocean, where sugar-white sand beaches are protected by reefs. Picnic facilities are laid on at Kangaroo Point and Hangover Bay.

The nearest town, **Cervantes**, is only remotely, if at all, connected with the author of *Don Quixote*, Miguel de Cervantes Saavedra. "Cervantes", in fact, commemorates an American whaling ship of that name, wrecked here in 1844. The town's rock lobster fishermen are now outnumbered by holidaymakers, but the lovely white beach is big enough for everyone.

On Perth's Doorstep

Only 51 km (32 miles) north of Perth, on the coast, **Yanchep National Park** is known for its limestone caves, wild flowers and eucalyptus forests fragrant with flaky-barked red gums (or *marri*) and the strong-timbered *tuart*. Nature also provided plenty of kangaroos, but the koala colony had to be imported from Victoria. There is also an island-studded lake called Loch McNess, named after a local philanthropist, Sir Charles McNess. Don't bother looking for a Loch McNess monster. Along the ocean, **Atlantic Marine Park** features performing seals and dolphins, and you can observe the greedy festivities as intrepid employees hand-feed sharks and stingrays.

A classic photo opportunity: tourists stroll beneath the giant frozen surf of Wave Rock.

To Wave Rock

A natural phenomenon reckoned to be $2^1/_2$ billion years old, Wave Rock is 344 km (214 miles) east of Perth. It's a long way to go to look at a rock, but few who do are disappointed.

The trip starts on the eastern fringe of the city, where the highway climbs into the **Darling Range**. Here at the beginning of the great inland plateau, amidst the tall trees and wild flowers, are lookout points for views of the city and the sea. Waterfalls, brooks and dams refresh the relaxing scene.

Farther east, the green expanse of the **Avon Valley** provides pasture land for cattle and grows the grain to feed Perth and beyond. One of the early settlements in the 1830s was the very small town of **Toodyay**, now classified as a historical monument. As in many old Australian towns, the jail is a landmark. It was a case of locking the door after the star convict fled; in this case,

the 1865 prison replaced the old jail from which the noted fugitive Moondyne Joe made one of his ingenious getaways.

The colony's first inland settlement, the pretty town of **York**, is proud of its history. More than a dozen 19th-century buildings have been restored; several now serve as museums. You can tour the old courthouse, conveniently linked with the old police station and prison cells, where the inmates' graffiti, both obscene and despairing, are preserved behind glass. The Castle Hotel, on the opposite side of Avon Terrace, is called the oldest hotel still operating in the state. Several other 19th-century hotels have also been revivified. Maximizing the effect of a corner site, the Town Hall, built in 1911, has a pompous colonnaded entrance topped by a clock tower. Just outside town, one of the early farms has been restored to a "living museum" in which you can watch blacksmiths and wheelwrights at work. Clydesdale horses still plough the fields.

Rocky Fantasy

Near the small, progressive town of Hyden, in the wide open spaces where the wheat, oats and barley grow, looms **Wave Rock**. The rock takes the form of a stupendous surfer's wave, as tall as a five-storey building, eternally on the verge of breaking. The vertical colour bands, which add much to the general effect, are contributed by the minerals which have been washed down its face. Having one's picture taken under the impending splash is one of the state's most popular tourist activities. Mildly energetic visitors can also climb to the top. There, on the edge, slabs of concrete arrayed like a Chinese Wall restrain rainwater, which is fed into an adjoining dam. Completing the roster of attractions here: a wildlife sanctuary, a golf-course and a full-sized swimming pool, extraordinary for an obscure, water-shy place like Hyden.

Other unusual rock formations in the area have expressive names like Hippo's Yawn and The Humps. Excursions to Wave Rock often include a visit to **Mulka's Cave**, a small cavern adorned with Aboriginal wall paintings and suffused with legend.

The South-West

Excursions to the south-western corner of the state encompass a delightful variety of scenery: beaches, vineyards, orchards and soaring **jarrah forests**. Where the water-table is high, you'll see stands of paperbark trees; you could strip off a layer of the papyrus-style bark and write a letter. But the most impressive tree in the region is the jarrah, a giant variety of eucalyptus celebrated for its durable red timber. The lower half grows straight and clean as a telephone pole, with all the branches emerging at the top.

One of the curiosities of the region is its underground wealth. This is bauxite country; so much of the mineral (vital in the production of aluminium) occurs here that the leftovers are used in the surfacing of the roads. The bauxite is transported along "the world's longest conveyor belt", running for about 50 km (more than 30 miles). The belt, which crosses above the "aluminium-paved" roads, is as much a part of the forest scenery as the lumbermen's trucks.

Look, Don't Pick

The state flower of Western Australia is the red-and-green kangaroo paw, one of the delights of the bush in springtime. So splendid is the outburst of wild flowers between mid-August and mid-November that coachloads of camera-armed tourists fan out from Perth in search of pink kunzeas, bright yellow creeping banksia and multi-coloured wild orchids. Isolated from the rest of the world by desert and ocean, Western Australia is a hothouse of unique or rare species.

Driving through the countryside in springtime, a field in flower can be breathtaking. If no blast of colour hits you from the side of the road, it's still worth stopping and scrutinizing the wonders hidden in the bush: flowers of the most delicate hues and bizarre plants, gnarled or rigidly defensive. Look but don't pick them, lest you upset nature's balance.

Some tours also visit the Muja open-cast coal-mine, not quite the sort of view you might have expected, but remarkable by any standard. At the end of a shift you can watch the ballet performed by dozens of ore-carrying behemoths, their movements tightly coordinated as they converge on the parking lots.

The sunny seaside resort of **Mandurah** attracts swimmers, boatsmen and fishermen. The Harvey Estuary and the Peel Inlet provide great expanses of calm water for yachtsmen and windsurfers alike. King prawns and blue manna crabs abound in these waters, along with herring, mullet and pilchard. By no great co-incidence, the estuary is a vital breeding ground of those strange birds, pelicans.

Bunbury, farther south, the state's biggest country town, is now officially a full-fledged city. Notwithstanding the industrial activities in the port, Bunbury's Koombana Bay is a favourite place for dolphins to visit. It's forbidden to feed the animals, but you can swim along with them and make friends. Lighthouse fans head for Apex Drive and the black-and-white-checked Bunbury Lighthouse. The light is 25 m (83 ft) above the ground.

Busselton, a popular resort dominating Geographe Bay, had the country's longest wooden jetty, nearly a century in the construction, but the pier lost its head to a cyclone. Collectors of Busselton superlatives now have to be satisfied with St Mary's Church, the oldest (1845) stone church in Western Australia.

For Wine Lovers

Beachy Busselton leads to the wine-growing area around **Margaret River**, a small town on the river of the same name. There's a memorial to a 19th-century heroine, Grace Bussell, who rescued 48 survivors of a shipwreck down the coast. A member of the family that founded Busselton, she was only 16 years old on the historic day.

The Margaret River region has one of the country's up-and-coming concentrations of vineyards, where estates big and small, mostly relatively new, are producing admirable reds and whites. Cellar-door wine tastings are almost bound to be on the agenda.

A better-known destination on the wine-lover's map of Western Australia, the **Swan Valley**, is only about half an hour's drive north-east of Perth. The area has long been noted for its small,

230

family-run vineyards, which produce most of the state's red and white wines and fortified dessert wines. The wine-making tradition in the Swan Valley dates back to the 1830s, before Victoria and South Australia entered the business. If wine-tasting and driving seem incompatible, you can take a coach tour of selected vineyards from Perth, or an even more leisurely cruise on a Swan River boat with stops at one or two wine cellars.

South Coast

The site of the attractive town of **Albany** was settled on Christmas Day, 1826, making it older than Perth. Albany overlooks King George Sound, an anchorage twice as big as Sydney Harbour. This strategic position seemed to require a military base, but in the event, life was so hard that the outpost shut down after five years. Later in the 19th century the port began to prosper from the whaling industry. Albany subsequently specialized in fuelling steamers travelling between Britain and Australia's east coast. You can visit impressive colonial buildings, and the Old Gaol, and enjoy the sweeping views from the top of the town.

The whaling connection, broken as recently as the 1970s, is remembered east of town in the **Cheynes Beach Whaling Station**, now a museum.

Highway 1, which circumnavigates the whole continent, heads eastward from Albany to Ravensthorpe, a former gold and copper mining centre, and on to the port of **Esperance**. The name refers to the French frigate *L'Esperance*, meaning "The Hope", which mapped these waters in 1792. Modern technology has developed a promising farming area in the Esperance hinterland, but most tourists keep their eyes on the Recherche Archipelago (the French, again) and its entrancing seascape. Sea lions sunbathe on the islands, and sometimes on mainland beaches as well.

From Esperance the highway makes a dog-leg to Norseman, a gold-mining town big enough to have a tourist office. Eastward from Norseman it's clear sailing across the awesome Nullarbor Desert to Ceduna, SA— 1,232 km (765 miles) until the next three-star hotel. Or you can continue northward 167 km (104 miles) to Western Australia's equivalent of El Dorado.

The Gold-fields

Fortunes were made or lost overnight back of beyond on Western Australia's Golden Mile. Physically, the scene may not inspire flights of poetry. There's nary a tree, just desert and scrub, dilapidated shacks, and the skeletons of mining superstructures. You'd hardly guess, but the gold-fields are still booming, thanks to new technology and deeper digs.

Kalgoorlie, about 550 km (340 miles) by air from Perth, retains the atmosphere of the riotous gold-rush town it was in the 1890s. The streets, laid out in a grid, were built wide enough for stagecoaches or camel trains to U-turn. Like a Wild West movie set, there are verandahed saloons for every occasion. In a pawnbroker's window, a used metal detector tells a short, sad story of failure. If this doesn't discourage

The almost total lack of water was the first desperate hardship to face the thousands of prospectors who rushed into the gold-fields when Hannan's news spread. Disease and death by dehydration took a heavy toll. A brilliant and daring solution was found by an Irish engineer, Charles Yelverton O'Connor, who built a 560-km (350-mile) pipeline from a reservoir near Perth. You can still see the big above-ground pipes along the road, similar to the oil pipelines that became common many years later; he even succeeded in pumping the water uphill. Wounded by criticism of the project, C.Y. O'Connor killed himself before the first drop of water reached Kalgoorlie; he is honoured by a bronze statue on the seafront in Fremantle.

Living Legends

As the prospectors came in from the surrounding desert with their sudden wealth, Kalgoorlie became a rip-roaring supplier of wine, women and song. The pubs were legion; many retain their frontier atmosphere. Another old mining tradition is the red-light district of Hay Street, where the camp-followers still hold forth, on display to this day in the window-seat manner of Amsterdam. As for gambling, the town doesn't have a casino, but a few kilometres out in the country "Australia's only legalized bush two-up school" flourishes from midday to sundown.

*A*mong the historic sights in Kalgoorlie: a narrow saloon, now a museum.

you, join the optimists scanning old worked-over sites in search of forgotten nuggets. The occasional whopper still turns up.

The first big strike of Kalgoorlie gold came in June, 1893, when an Irishman, Patrick Hannan, stumbled onto enough glitter to shout about. Paddy Hannan has never been forgotten in Kalgoorlie. A bronze statue of the bearded prospector adorns the main street, which bears his name; the water bag he carries serves as the municipal water fountain.

In the centre of the Golden Mile, the **Hainault Gold Mine** has taken on a new lease of life as an underground monument. Three or four times a day, seven days a week, retired miners take tour groups down to the depths in a

A Tale of Heads and Tails

Unlike the posh pursuits of roulette or baccarat, the game of Two-Up requires little equipment and can be instantly dismantled at the first blast of a police whistle. They say that old-time convicts invented it. The rules could hardly be simpler. The ring-keeper appoints one of the players as "spinner", to toss two pennies. The spinner's goal is to toss two heads. Most of the betting on his chances of success takes place "on the side", informally, between onlookers. In the bush, scrupulous honesty reigns, and verbal bets are considered debts of honour.

The Kalgoorlie Two-Up School, which the casual traveller might mistake for a cockfight ring in some obscure Latin country, involves bets ranging from $10 to a car or house. The game goes on daily except once a fortnight—miners' payday. By popular demand of the miners' wives.

Coolgardie, 40 km (25 miles) west of Kalgoorlie, proudly bears the slogan of "ghost town". In fact, ghosting is its principal industry, and if there's a bit of melancholy in the air, it must be good for business. The historical markers seem to outnumber the population.

Gold was discovered at Coolgardie a year before Paddy Hannan's big strike at Kalgoorlie. By the turn of the century Coolgardie's population was 15,000. You can see how prosperous the town was from the elegance of the Victorian-era buildings, most notably the three-storey arcaded headquarters of the **Gold-fields Museum**. This institution is stacked with exhibits detailing the difficult life and work of the prospectors.

Any good ghost town needs an interesting cemetery, and the inscriptions on the headstones in Coolgardie's graveyard tell revealing stories of the

claustrophobic cage to show how the seams were blasted and the gold extracted. The Hainault Mine has earned its place in Australia's history, as from 1920 to 1947 alone it produced 35 tonnes of gold.

Exhibits in an open-air museum in Coolgardie include an ancient truck and a Ned Kelly-style suit of armour.

harsh frontier life. Among the Afghani camel drivers buried here, one is listed as the victim of a murder.

Up the Coast

The best time to visit Western Australia's Mid-West region must be early spring—wild flower season—from July to September. Local tourist offices along the way issue maps and brochures for flower-spotters. Whatever the season the coastline is a thriller and the small, historic towns are full of interest.

Geraldton, the region's main port, calls itself "Sun City", not immodestly, for it claims an average of eight sunny hours per day all year round. Statistics like that go down very nicely with travellers in search of endless white Indian Ocean beaches, of which the area is over-endowed. The earliest visitors were Dutch—the victims of 17th-century shipwrecks; cannons and coins and all the details are on show at the Geraldton Museum. By far the town's most imposing church, St Francis Xavier Cathedral, was designed in a mixture of Spanish and Byzantine styles by a 20th-century architect-priest, Monsignor John Hawes. The Anglican cathedral is more austere. At Fisherman's Wharf, where the rock lobstermen unload their catch, you might be inspired to try a seafood lunch.

Kalbarri, 166 km (103 miles) north of Geraldton, is a popular resort for fishing, surfing and seeing the scenery. The best of the sights are within **Kalbarri National Park**, 186,00 ha (more than 700 miles²) of wildflowers, eucalyptus and acacia, kangaroos and emus. Uniquely, the park encompasses some gorgeous gorges carved out of the sandstone by the Murchison River fighting its way to the Indian Ocean.

Shark Bay, where Dirk Hartog, the Dutch explorer, first set foot in Australia in 1616, would be delightful if only for its perfect beaches, lagoons and coves, but it's not the sharks that put Shark Bay on the map, it's the dolphins. **Monkey Mia** is the only place in the world where wild dolphins hanker after human company to the extent that they come to the edge of the beach virtually every day just to play. These are no dolphin-show performers, they're free-willed, seagoing mammals who enjoy these particular shallow waters. They like people so much they sometimes offer a fish as a gift. Scientists, too, are fascinated by the goings-on; studying their behaviour, they can identify hundreds of the local dolphins individually. Interesting, too, is the behaviour of the humans who frolic with the grinning extroverts of the Monkey Mia dolphin society.

Echoes from Space

The desert reaches almost to the coast at **Carnarvon**, a mining and farming centre better known for its role in the space race, when it was a ground station of America's NASA. The monument to those exciting days of astronauts circling the earth and then landing on the moon is the Big Dish, a communications antenna nearly 30 m (100 ft) in diameter.

Antennas that dwarf the Carnarvon dishes are the landmark up the coast at **Exmouth**, a new town adjoining a US Navy base near a mothballed RAAF station. The VLF (for Very

Low Frequency) antenna field, a truly titanic project, is a forest of radio masts more than 300 m (1,000 ft) tall. The array is said to make possible communications with submarines submerged in the Indian Ocean and the Western Pacific. Although there are large prohibited zones on the peninsula, tours can be organized.

The English buccaneer William Dampier, who came this way late in the 17th century, is remembered, obliquely, in the industrial port of **Dampier**. Actually, the town was named after the Dampier Archipelago, a family of more than 40 islands just offshore. Giant ore carriers come here to haul away iron ore. Another big export is salt, produced in a 9,000 hectares (35 square miles) artificial salt lake under the pervasive influence of the tropical sun, creating Australia's highest evaporation rate. You can book a tour of the port.

Another very serious port where stupendous industrial installations are on view, **Port Hedland** entertains the world's largest ore carriers. The municipal tourist bureau can put you on a tour of the facilities. Some 40 million tonnes of ore pass through here in a year, supplemented by a couple of million tonnes of salt. Port Hedland has come a long way since the days when the bay was a base for pearl luggers. Before you make your travel plans, you ought to take into account that the average maximum daily temperature in summer in Port Hedland is 36°C (96.8°F).

Broome

The old pearling port of Broome, on a vast, thinly populated peninsula, has a romantic past. It once supplied 80 per cent of all the world's mother-of-pearl. Divers from Japan, Malaya and the Philippines went out on hundreds of boats, diving for the oysters and, not so incidentally, the pearls sometimes found within them. It was a dangerous business for the divers, thanks to storms, shark attacks and decompression sickness, "the bends", little understood at the time. Broome's roomy, well-kept **Japanese cemetery** gives an indication of the fatality rate.

A bit of the oriental aura lingers in modern-day Broome, even if the mother-of-pearl business went down the drain with the introduction of cultured pearls and plastic buttons. **Chinatown** is what they still call the business district, though the old pearl sheds now house tourist-oriented shops—selling cultivated pearls. Until a barrier was built in recent years, part of Chinatown was always flooded at peak tide; customers at **Sun Pictures**, possibly the world's oldest operating open-air cinema, had to wade in.

The Nation's Hothouse

If you're escaping from winter at home, Australia's most effective antifreeze may be found in **Marble Bar**, about 200 km (125 miles) inland from Port Hedland. Just spend a minute or two in the sun in the continent's hottest town. The most celebrated heat-wave here, never surpassed, was 160 consecutive days above 37.8°C (100°F) in 1923–24. On a day-to-day basis, a summer top of 40°C (104°F) is rather common. When gold was discovered here in 1891 thousands settled in Marble Bar in spite of the climate. Now only a few hundred people persevere, feverishly.

For reminders of the port's heyday, and all you'll ever need to know about pearling, see the collection at the Broome Historical Society **Museum** in the old Customs House. For insight into the modern cultured-pearl industry, sign up for an excursion to the Willie Creek **pearl farm**, 35 km (22 miles) north of Broome, mostly on unpaved red-dirt track.

Broome's touristic pearl is **Cable Beach**, a luxurious resort across the peninsula. It's an island in itself.

The Kimberley

Broome is a principal gateway to the Kimberley region, a rugged, largely uninhabited land three times the size of Britain. The main industry is farming—sparse as the grass may seem, it supports great herds of cattle. The other natural resource supplies one of the world's richest diamond mines.

The Argyle mine produces a sizeable heap of pink diamonds—a coveted rarity in the gem world—as well as mountains of industrial diamonds, used for grinding and drilling. Humans look like Lilliputians beside the machines that move the ore to the Argyle processing plant, where millions of carats per year are yielded. This otherwise inhospitable area is thought to hide as much as half of all the diamonds on earth. The astonishing potential of the Argyle diamond field wasn't discovered until 1979. Full-scale production began in 1985.

Before the diamond boom, the nearest town, **Kununurra** (an Aboriginal word meaning, appropriately, "big waters") was best known as a dam site. It's the centre of the far-reaching Ord River Scheme, which changed the character of the region, bottling the monsoon-flooded river and distributing the water for irrigation purposes in the dry season. The project created Lake Argyle, containing nine times as much water as Sydney Harbour. A holiday village overlooking this immense reservoir is a centre for swimming, fishing, boating and hikes. The best season is from May to September, when the days are warm and the nights comfortably clear.

Other parts of the Kimberley have precious stones, too—but not of the Argyle diamond variety. These great rocks, estimated to be a couple of billion years old, rate among the earth's very ancient geological specimens. Cliffs and gorges provide the spectacle along the Fitzroy River, which either ripples or rages, depending on the season. **Geikie Gorge National Park**, just outside the hamlet of Fitzroy Crossing, is one of seven national parks in the Kimberley.

Another regional highlight is **Purbululu National Park**, featuring the astonishing **Bungle Bungle** rock formations, shaped rather like beehives, striped orange and black. Four-wheel-drive vehicles are required, but even they can't get through in the wet season, so the park is closed from January to March. The easy way to solve the problem is to sign up for one of the marvellous scenic flights.

Hundreds of species of eucalyptus thrive everywhere in Australia, even in the almost waterless Outback near Kalgoorlie.

A Festive, Varied State Founded by Idealists

A bit of everything that makes Australia so appealing can be found in the sprawling state of South Australia: beaches, forests, rivers, modest mountains and cheerful towns. There are plenty of wide open spaces, as well, including a cattle ranch the size of Belgium. However, it is history which sets South Australia apart.

South Australia was founded, in 1836, as a planned community run by wealthy idealists. Nothing so gross as convict settlers here; transportation of criminals was against the colony's laws. The "free settlers only" tag is a source of local pride. Sobriety and morality were keystones of the master plan, giving rise to a reputation of stuffy puritanism, though in relatively recent times the influence of the "wowsers" (bluenoses or prudes) has faded. For example, Australian nudists

The vineyards and the farm houses are carefully tended in the beautiful Barossa Valley.

legally conquered their first beach just outside Adelaide, and killjoys would have turned up their noses at the Barossa Valley wine festival and the screaming tyres of the Adelaide Grand Prix.

Driving almost anywhere in South Australia beyond the towns, kangaroos may cross your path (a real problem for motorists at twilight). Be on the lookout, as well, for any stray hairy-nosed wombat. This shy vegetarian, about the size of a piglet, is the state's official animal symbol. The hairy-nosed wombat is just as cuddly as any koala but lacks the public relations organization.

Like the amiable wombat, South Australia is self-reliant. Everything the state needs can be found within its

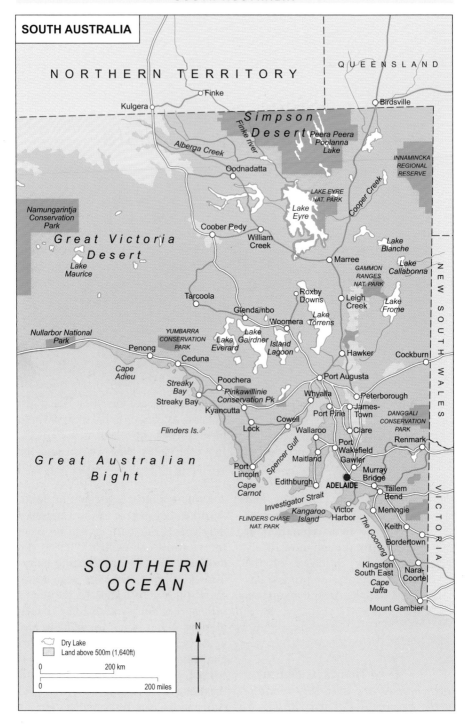

SOUTH AUSTRALIA

NORTHERN TERRITORY

QUEENSLAND

Finke
Kulgera
Birdsville

Simpson Desert
Finke river
Peera Peera
Poolanna
Lake

Alberga Creek
INNAMINCKA
REGIONAL
RESERVE

Oodnadatta

Cooper Creek

LAKE EYRE
NAT. PARK
Lake
Eyre

Namungarintja
Conservation
Park

Great Victoria Desert
Coober Pedy
William
Creek
Lake
Blanche

Lake
Maurice
Marree
GAMMON
RANGES
NAT. PARK
Lake
Callabonna

Tarcoola
Roxby
Downs
Leigh
Creek
Lake
Frome

Glendambo
Woomera
Lake
Torrens

Nullarbor National
Park
YUMBARRA
CONSERVATION
PARK
Lake
Everard
Lake Gairdner
Island
Lagoon

Penong
Hawker
Cockburn

Ceduna

Cape
Adieu
Poochera
Port Augusta

Streaky
Bay
Pinkawillinie
Conservation Pk
Whyalla
Peterborough

Streaky Bay
Kyancutta
Port Pirie
James-
Town
DANGGALI
CONSERVATION
PARK

Flinders Is.
Lock
Cowell
Wallaroo
Clare

Port
Wakefield
Renmark

Great Australian Bight
Port
Lincoln
Maitland
Gawler

Cape
Carnot
Edithburgh
ADELAIDE
Murray
Bridge
Tailem
Bend

Investigator Strait
Kangaroo
Island
Victor
Harbor
Meningie

FLINDERS CHASE
NAT. PARK
Keith

The Coorong
Bordertown

SOUTHERN OCEAN
Kingston
South East
Cape
Jaffa
Nara-
Coorte

Mount Gambier

NEW SOUTH WALES

VICTORIA

N

Dry Lake
Land above 500m (1,640ft)

0   200 km

0   200 miles

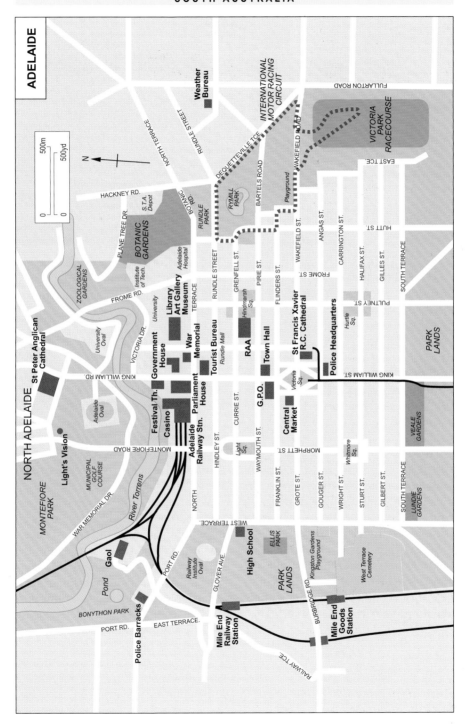

Modern sculptural ensemble mirrors the bright good cheer of Adelaide.

borders: coal from the open-cut mines of Leigh Creek, gas under the north-eastern desert, grain and cattle through hundreds of miles of latitude, fish from the Southern Ocean and world-class wines from scenic vineyards.

The sights of South Australia are as varied as its resources: the rugged grandeur of the Flinders Ranges, the dunes of the Simpson Desert, the green banks of the Murray River, the surf of the Great Australian Bight.

Spread out across 1,000,000 km² (380,000 miles²), South Australia occupies one-eighth of the entire continent. But the inhabitants number only about one-twelfth of the nation's total.

Map of South Australia (page 240) and town plan of Adelaide (page 241).

And most of these may be found far from the inconveniences of the desert, living contentedly in the graceful capital city, Adelaide.

Adelaide

Although its population is less than a million, Adelaide has the metropolitan monopoly: it's 30 times bigger than any other town in the state. Some say this is the most livable city in all Australia, and it aims to become one of the world's high-tech capitals, as well.

With its efficient, modern international airport, Adelaide qualifies as an important gateway, and a most cheerful introduction, to the state and to the entire country. The sunny Mediterranean climate (which helps explain Adelaide's prominence as a film production centre) beams on the many parks and gardens, the elegant squares and broad boulevards.

Adelaide is a relatively sophisticated capital, where culture and good living are important elements of the local scene. There is a very significant art

museum and the world's largest collection of Aboriginal artefacts. The city puts on an international festival of the arts every other year; every single day the locals pay tribute to international culinary art, supporting more restaurants per mouth than any other Australian city. As for night-life, the agenda encompasses rock concerts, nightclubs, discos, strip shows and a casino, with a big new entertainment centre to handle the mob scenes. It's come a long way since the days when outsiders joked, "I went to Adelaide once but it was closed."

Adelaide was founded two generations after the settlement of Sydney, in the reign of King William IV, and named after his queen, the former Princess Adelaide of Saxe-Meiningen. Although the southern coastline had been well charted, the idea of building a city beside the Torrens River didn't catch on until the 1830s. Before the first earth was turned, the city was planned on paper, street by street and park by spacious park. According to the plan, the business district covers the area of 1 square mile (2.6 km²), precisely. This urban model, with its built-in green belt, was a winner in its time, and so it remains in a world gasping for breath and fighting for elbow room.

A long way from the Outback, a folk singer and his guitar require separate but equal microphones in Adelaide.

City Sights

The most stately of Adelaide's streets—and that is a considerable superlative here—is **North Terrace**, which delineates the northern edge of the business district. North Terrace is lined with trees and distinguished buildings—mansions, museums and churches as well as a casino and convention centre. Along the boulevard are a variety of heroic statues, monuments and memorials, and a stone trough in memory of the horses killed in World War I.

Between the Terrace and the gently sloping, landscaped bank of the river, the **Adelaide Festival Centre** calls to mind Sydney's Opera House, but with angular planes instead of billowing curves; Adelaide also truncated Sydney's lavish price tag. The relatively budget-priced, 20-million-dollar complex has a theatre for every occasion.

South Australia was founded by idealistic pioneers, not convicts. The early hardships of the settlers are re-enacted in an Adelaide parade.

The 2,000-seat Festival Theatre is convertible, in three hours, from an opera house to a concert hall with outstanding acoustics. A drama theatre seats some 600 people, an experimental theatre 350. There are hourly backstage tours of the establishment. Outside, bold sculptures are strewn around the plaza. You can eat outdoors in a Festival Centre bistro overlooking the river, or make your own picnic on the lawn. Or take a sightseeing boat up the river to the century-old Adelaide **Zoo**, where you can pet the kangaroos and admire an outstanding collection of Australian birds, 365 days a year.

Behind the Festival Centre, the South Australian **Parliament House** is dignified by ten Corinthian columns and altogether so much expensive stonework it was nicknamed the "marble palace". However, the idea of a mighty dome to top it all off was abandoned. The foundation was laid in 1881 but work continued, on and off, over the following 58 years. Next door, the **Constitutional Museum** occupies the Old Parliament House. Australia's only museum of political history cheerfully reports the story of the building itself and of democracy in South Australia, using documents of the day and modern audiovisual techniques. To keep grass-roots democracy dynamic, a bulletin board invites "vox pop" opinions on controversial issues.

Glamorous Games

A startling change of pace lies in ambush just next door: **Adelaide Casino** is the new name of the game in a dazzling conversion of the vastly cupolated old railway station. They've created an uncompromisingly plush gambling den which, despite the potted palms, marble floors and stupendous chandeliers, is open (until 4.00 a.m. weekdays, 24 hours on weekends) to ordinary people. Most of the clients seem to favour keno, a bingo-esque game, and lines of coin-operated video games to the complexities of blackjack, roulette, baccarat and other international pastimes on offer.

Elsewhere along North Terrace, the **University of Adelaide** is at the heart of a cluster of cultural institutions. Whale skeletons fill the show windows of the **South Australian Museum** as a come-on. Inside, a monumental collection of Aboriginal artefacts include extraordinary sculptures collected in the Lake Eyre region by a turn-of-the-century Lutheran missionary. Among them: a group of bow-legged dogs modelled in resin extracted from the desert's spinifex grass. Other countries are well represented in a comprehensive survey of ceremonial masks, shields and sculptures from South Pacific islands. And you can see a traditional trading vessel from New Guinea, which remained in service until recent times, with a bamboo deck and a sail made of bark. The museum also features a didactic display of stuffed Australian animals, reptiles, birds and fish, contemporary as well as extinct.

The **Art Gallery of South Australia** covers centuries of the world's art, from ancient Chinese ceramics to contemporary Australian paintings and sculptures. The collection of prints and drawings, including old European works, is outstanding. Some of the modern items on show are staggeringly avant-garde.

History and Commerce
The **Migration Museum**, in the onetime Destitute Asylum next door, is subtitled "a social history of South Australian immigration and settlement". Displays document the hardships of the pioneers and the changing problems and policies leading up to the cultural mosaic of the modern state.

Two more of the historic buildings on North Terrace: **Holy Trinity Church**, the first Anglican church built in South Australia (begun in 1838); and **Ayers House**, a 45-room mansion furnished in opulent 19th-century style. The house was owned by a local businessman and statesman, Sir Henry Ayers, after whom an admiring explorer named Ayers Rock.

Parallel with North Terrace, **Rundle Mall**, a pedestrian mall, is the heart of Adelaide's shopping area. Its trademark is a towering sculpture comprising double-decked spheres of stainless steel reflecting the animation all around. The mall's merchants include big department stores, boutiques, cafés and restaurants. Street entertainers are usually on hand to sing, dance, play or mime in hopes of collecting a few coins. Rundle Street's westward extension, **Hindley Street**, is more cosmopolitan and slightly rakish, with restaurants of many nationalities, coffee bars, amusement arcades, and even strip clubs and "adult" bookstores.

For another kind of shopping experience, have a look at the **Central Market** in Grote Street, off Victoria Square. This carnival of fresh fruits and vegetables is said to be the biggest produce market in the southern hemisphere. Here you'll find coffee beans from New Guinea, Guatemala and Kenya; Australian Camembert and English Stilton; Spanish chorizos and Australian pepperoni; and every kind of bread from pitta to pretzels.

Light and Vision

The central hall of the **General Post Office**, at the north end of Victoria Square, has been in use since 1872. Inspirational sunlight pours in from above in this precocious atrium design, a strangely splendid place for buying stamps. Around the corner at 2 Franklin Street, the **Postal Museum** has photographs, equipment and costumes from the days when a letter from abroad was a thrill. The **Telecommunications Museum** at 131 King William Street fills three floors of a one-time Cable & Wireless telegraph office with ancient telexes, telephones and radio transmitters, plus plans for the future.

North of the city centre, **Light's Vision** is not a sound-and-light show, as its name may suggest. It's a monument to the foresight of Lieutenant-Colonel William Light, who was sent out in 1836 to find the ideal site for a model city, then devise the total plan for its development. Atop a pedestal on Montefiore Hill, his statue peers over the parklands, pointing at the city of Adelaide, which he created.

On the opposite side of the river, you can visit a lesser-known facet of "Swinging Adelaide". Over the years, 45 people were hanged in the Adelaide **Gaol**, a mid-19th-century institution that would seem to belie the theory that a convict-free society would attract only law-abiding people. It held prisoners until as recently as 1988. Notice the tricky "honeycomb brickwork" of the wall, designed to expose potential escapers. It's open for visits on the first and third Sunday of each month.

Nearby Places

Adelaide has an outstanding public transport system, including the last word in buses—a "bullet bus" that steers itself along its own smooth roadway. The Busway (formerly called the O'Bahn) has buses purring along at up to 100 km (60 miles) per hour from the centre through pleasant green countryside to the north-eastern suburbs.

Nostalgia persists: the state's last surviving tramcars still clatter along between the edge of Victoria Square and the seashore at suburban **Glenelg**. This old-fashioned beach resort, from which a fishing pier forges far out to sea, was the original landing place of the colonists who founded South Australia. An expensive full-size replica of their vessel, a converted freighter named HMS *Buffalo*, planted nearby, serves as a museum and restaurant. (The original ship was wrecked off New Zealand in 1840.) Another notable thing about Glenelg, of course, is its name, a palindrome that reads equally well from back to front. Few towns are so ambivalent.

A Streetcar Named Glenelg

Riding a tramcar more than 60 years old on the route between Adelaide and Glenelg is one of those fun runs, like the San Francisco cable-cars, that only improve with age. If it all makes you yearn for the clang of the trolley, find your way to the seaside suburb of St Kilda and the **Tramway Museum**. The exhibits include "No. 1", Adelaide's first electric tram, dating from 1908, and "No. 381", the last word in streetcars, built in 1953. The museum operates its own 2-km (1¼ -mile) tramline to the beach front—just for fun.

Among other **beaches** near Adelaide, from north to south along the Gulf of St Vincent: Semaphore, Grange, Henley Beach, West Beach, Somerton, Brighton and Seacliff.

Port Adelaide, originally known unaffectionately as Port Misery, has exploited its history in a big, serious redevelopment project. The result is an outstanding array of restored 19th-century institutions, topped by the lighthouse, now in its third location since 1869. For a start you can climb up for the overall view. The "Heritage Walking Tour"—a brochure with a map is available at several locations—goes to 21 other points on or near the waterfront. Much of this comes under the aegis of the highly regarded South Australian **Maritime Museum.**

Port Adelaide has two museums for transport specialists: the Port Dock Station Railway Museum operates steam locomotives of various ages and gauges, and a model railway line. The aviation equivalent may be found at the South Australian Historical Aviation Museum at 11 Mundy Street, with military and civilian planes on view.

Adelaide Hills

When it's hot in summer or gloomy in winter, Adelaide takes to the hills. The last manifestation of the Flinders Ranges, south and east of the city, the Adelaide Hills provide a background of forests, orchards and vineyards. There are pleasant drives, walks, views and picnic possibilities. The highest of the hills, **Mount Lofty** (770 m or 2,500 ft) is only half an hour out of town by car. From the Mount Lofty Summit Lookout you can see all of the city, the suburbs and nearby beaches,

and look down on the hang-gliding enthusiasts riding the hot air currents on the leisurely route back to sea level.

Hahndorf, a hill village just off the South Eastern freeway about 30 km (less than 20 miles) from Adelaide, has changed little since it was settled in 1839 by German refugees. To the delight of sightseers, many of the original buildings, with their high-pitched roofs, have been restored. Tree-shaded Main Street is lined with quaint handicrafts shops, cafés, restaurants and other historic charms. The Hahndorf Antique Clock Museum is said to possess the world's largest cuckoo clock. A number of folklore events brighten the tourist calendar, especially a marksmanship and beer-drinking festival every January. Hahndorf was named in honour of a Captain Hahn, who commanded the ship that brought the original Prussian settlers to Australia and helped them find this place. In World War I, as part of a campaign to purge any German traces from the map of Australia, the government abruptly changed the name of Hahndorf to Ambleside.

Up the River

When it comes to the **Murray River**, the Australians go into transports of delight. Having few rivers, they are thrilled by the local equivalent of the Mississippi. The Murray begins in the Snowy Mountains (the Australian Alps), becomes the frontier between Victoria and New South Wales, and enjoys its last meanderings through the state of South Australia. The river accounts for the beautiful vineyards, orchards and pastures along the way, not to mention the boating, fishing and water-skiing. In the 19th century the river was a main highway for passengers and cargo, but the advent of railroads and highways left the Murray more of a pleasure route.

Paddle-steamers churn up nostalgia along the lower Murray, only an hour's drive from Adelaide. A variety of boats, big and small, ultramodern and old-fashioned, offer short excursions or voyages of several days. It's also possible to hire a houseboat and ply the river at your own pace. In that case you can fish for your own dinner. The Murray cod run to gargantuan sizes, and you can change your diet by catching yabbies, the big freshwater crustaceans akin to crayfish.

The biggest town along the river here, **Murray Bridge**, started as a crossing point for the cattle migrations. Stirring up the water nowadays are water-skiers. Up river, in the old town of **Mannum**, where the first paddle-boat was built in 1853, the restored paddle-steamer *Marion*, dating from 1898, is a museum. There's still a lot of comings and goings of paddle-boats and other craft down at the riverside.

Barossa Valley

For reputation and productivity, no wine-producing region of Australia can beat the Barossa Valley. A mere 30 km (about 20 miles) long and 8 km (5 miles) wide, it's small but beautiful.

The landscape is an appealing compound of soft hills, sheep-grazing land, cosy villages, and of course the rows of vines that produce some famous wines. Specialities of the region are a delicate white Riesling, reminiscent of the wine from along the Rhine River in Germany, and a hearty red.

Barossa was founded by Germans, who arrived in 1842 fleeing religious persecution at home. The German connection became a liability when Australia plunged into World War I. Some of the Teutonic place-names were changed for "patriotic" reasons, and the government shut down a German printing house for fear subversive leaflets would be produced.

Nowadays, the Germanic flavour pervading the valley is part of the charm. You'll see neat stone cottages with filigreed verandahs and decorous gardens; if the inhabitants came out wearing lederhosen it wouldn't be much of a shock. To the tune of oom-pah-pah music, you'll get to taste bratwurst as a change from the meat pies of Adelaide, with sauerkraut instead of overcooked cabbage.

The Barossa Valley is only about an hour's drive north-east of Adelaide, a perfect distance for an easy all-day excursion devoted to taking in the local colour and sampling the wines. Many of the wineries are geared to this transient trade, advertising guided tours of the premises and offering explanatory tastings. The vineyard route is so popular that the roads and cellars can get crowded on Sundays and bank holidays.

Every other year (the odd numbers) the Barossa Valley stages an ebullient Vintage Festival in March or April, a week-long carnival as earthy as the wines to be celebrated. The locals— and thousands of visitors from Australia and overseas—dance in the streets, sing, play games, eat, and even do a bit of drinking, as well.

Barossa Towns

The gateway to the district, **Gawler**, was laid out by the progressive town planner, Col. Light himself. Among the stately buildings are several old churches. In 1878, the post office clock struck 100 times, prompting some doomsday panic, but the world failed to end and now the clock is back on schedule.

Northward, **Bethany** was founded in 1842, under the name of New Silesia. There are quaint old cottages and a Lutheran church more than a century old and what's quite probably the country's smallest motel—with room for two.

The small town of **Tanunda**, surrounded by wineries, retains its old German air. The site of the first market, Goat Square or Ziegenmarkt, is protected as a national monument.

Rather more businesslike and less folkloric than some of the old German-style villages of the Barossa, **Nuriootpa** is an important centre of the wine industry. Just out of town on the Sturt Highway, two very big wineries rub shoulders—Penfold and Kaiser Stuhl, now under the same management. The Barossa Valley is well signposted, but if you need a map and a brochure, a good place to go is the tourist office in Nuriootpa (known as

Schnitzel, bratwurst, and maybe a yodel accompaniment in a typical Barossa Valley eating house.

"Nuri" to its friends). It has its headquarters in the mansion of William Coulthard, who designed the town in the mid-19th century.

Leaps and Bounds

Kangaroos hold a special place in the Australian consciousness. As a sort of national symbol, they are looked on fondly, though not by farmers whose crops they have devoured. Kangaroo stew, one of the favourite dishes of pioneer days, is on the menu in some Outback restaurants, but animal rights partisans and others take offence.

When Captain Cook first came to grips with Australia's novelties, he asked an Aborigine to tell him the name of the bizarre hopalong creature. "Kangaroo," said the expert. Cook duly informed the world. Much later, it turned out that in the native lingo "kangaroo" means "I don't know".

In the thick of the harvest season, a Barossa Valley winery starts the grapes on their way to the press.

Kangaroo Island

Yes, there are kangaroos on Kangaroo Island. And koalas, emus, echidnas, brush-tailed possums and more. South Australia's favourite escapist resort, Kangaroo Island, is so big you could spend a week finding the best places for swimming, fishing and sightseeing, let alone wildlife-watching.

About 145 km (90 miles) long and 30 km (20 miles) wide, this is the country's third largest island, after Tasmania and the Northern Territory's Melville Island. For tourists in a typical rush, though, there are one-day excursions; it's only half an hour by air from Adelaide.

The explorer Matthew Flinders, circumnavigating Australia at the beginning of the 19th century, chanced upon Kangaroo Island in a storm. His hungry crew, amazed to be met by a mob of fearless, friendly kangaroos, consigned some of the reception committee to the stew pot. Grateful for the sustenance, the great navigator named the place Kangaroo Island. Right behind the Flinders expedition came a French explorer, Nicolas Baudin. Having lost the territorial claim to the British, he contributed some French names to the island's features. They're still on the map: places like d'Estrees Bay, Cape du Couëdic and Cape d'Estaing. Later settlers acknowledged Baudin's effort and built a white-domed monument at Hog Bay, called **Frenchmans Rock**.

250

*O*n the south coast of Kangaroo Island, a couple of relaxed
sea lions turn their backs on the friendly tourists.

For newcomers, meeting a road train on a narrow Outback route can be a stressful driving experience. It's usually wise to yield the right of way.

Going Places

The capital of Kangaroo Island, **Kingscote**, has a permanent population of about 1,200 and an elongated pier. This is where the roll-on/roll-off ferry from Port Adelaide docks; the island's airfield is only a few kilometres inland. Dolphins, seals and penguins frolic just offshore.

In 1919 the western end of the island was designated a nature reserve. **Flinders Chase National Park** is South Australia's biggest. This is not a zoo; the animals are in their natural state, but in the absence of predators the kangaroos, koalas and emus have become extroverts, snuggling up to the visitors and trying to sponge or steal some food.

On the south coast, **Seal Bay** belongs to Australian sea lions. They are so unafraid of humans that you can wander among them at will, except in certain fenced-off areas. Bird-watchers thrill to local species which show clear differences from mainland relatives, and a noisy population of migratory birds from distant oceans.

Three Peninsulas

Aiming across the Southern Ocean toward Antarctica, three peninsulas protrude from the coast of South

Australia. As you read the map from east to west they grow bigger and wilder, offering a generous sample of the state's many facets, from vineyards and almond orchards to wheat fields and deserts.

Fleurieu Peninsula

An hour's drive south of Adelaide, the Fleurieu Peninsula is an easy-to-reach, easy-to-like holidayland of surfing beaches, vineyards and history. The history starts at the beginning of the 19th century when the French explorer Baudin named the peninsula after his Navy minister, Count Pierre de Fleurieu.

The first industry on the peninsula was whaling, based at **Victor Harbor**. Ironically, now that the whales are no longer endangered by human predators in this area, they have returned to Victor Harbor; it seems they like the atmosphere. This coincidence has created a new tourist attraction, whale-watching. You can also ride a vintage horse-drawn tram across the causeway to the sanctuary of Granite Island to see the resident wallabies and fairy penguins.

The old river port of **Goolwa**, to the east of Victor Harbor, was left behind by history and technology. Australia's first public railway opened here in 1854, linking Goolwa and Port Elliot. You can still travel on the Cockle train, steam-powered, to Victor Harbor.

Another somewhat historic place is **Maslin's Beach**, on the Gulf St Vincent coast. Here a new leaf was turned in the evolution of Australian social customs. This was the nation's first legal nudists' beach!

Inland, the peninsula's fame comes from scores of vineyards basking in the sunshine of the **Southern Vales**. They've been making wine here since 1838, to great effect. Many of the wineries encourage connoisseurs or rank-and-file wine-drinkers to stop in and try the vintages, though you needn't feel guilty if you taste and run. The best-known area of wine production is **McLaren Vale**, so close to the sea it's called the Wine Coast.

Yorke Peninsula

West of Adelaide, the Yorke Peninsula is shaped rather like the boot of Italy, but it's so narrow that you're never more than 25 km (15 miles) away from the sea. Swimming, fishing and sailing opportunities are infinite along an 800-km (500-mile) coastline of cliffs and sandy beaches.

The Yorke Peninsula is a wheat-and-barley breadbasket, but it first drew attention in the 19th century as a copper-mining district. Most of the miners were imported from Cornwall, England's copper-rich south-western peninsula, and the Cornish touch can still be seen in the design of the old cottages and churches. They've even kept up the homely tradition of baking Cornish pasties.

For an insight into the 60 years of the copper boom, see the ruins of the mine superstructures near **Moonta**, and the museum. Among Moonta's historic buildings are a couple of hotels, the state's first Masonic Hall, the post office and some cottages, all from the early years of prosperity. Another former copper centre, **Kadina**, the peninsula's biggest town, is surrounded by abandoned mines.

The resort of **Port Victoria**, on the peninsula's west coast, used to be crammed with windjammers being loaded with grain. Its history is all recorded in the local maritime museum. **Wardang Island**, which shelters the harbour, is an Aboriginal reserve.

Innes National Park, at the tip of the boot, is predictably unspoiled. The rarest animal living here is a tiny marsupial, the southern pygmy possum. If you're interested in shipwrecks, you don't even have to don your snorkel mask here, for the remains of the *Ethel*, grounded in 1904, stand on the beach near West Cape.

Eyre Peninsula

From beach resorts and fishing villages to wheat fields and bushland, the Eyre Peninsula has a bit of everything, including industrial centres and a prized wilderness, **Lincoln National Park**. Atop magnificent cliffs at the tip of the peninsula, the park is home to kangaroos and birds as diverse as emus, parrots and sea eagles.

Fishing boats big and small are anchored in the attractive deep-water harbour of **Port Lincoln**, the tuna-fishing capital of Australia. Founded in 1834, the town counts among its historical monuments a pub more than 150 years old.

The biggest city on the peninsula, **Whyalla**, grew on a solid base of heavy industry—as heavy as iron and steel. If a blast furnace is your cup of tea, you can join one of the daily tours of the local steelworks, which produces a million or more tonnes of steel per year; the public can also visit the iron-mining area.

The Eyre Peninsula reaches as far west as **Ceduna**, where the endless expanse of the **Nullarbor Plain** begins. Ceduna was first settled on the shores of Denial Bay, as the explorer Matthew Flinders gloomily named it. Some famed surfing beaches are nearby.

Westbound travellers stock up on just about everything before leaving Ceduna, for it's more than 1,200 km (some 750 miles) to the next town of any significance (Norseman, WA). Filling stations do occur, but the route is lonely and gruelling. *Nullarbor* is Latin for "treeless", an indication that the plain is also waterless. However, as the Aborigines were always aware, water is there if you know where to look: underground in limestone caverns. Route 1, the Eyre Highway, follows

The Highway Man

The Eyre Peninsula and the Eyre Highway are named after an indefatigable 19th-century Briton, John Edward Eyre, who discovered—you guessed it—Lake Eyre. Australia's largest salt lake, some 640 km (400 miles) north of Adelaide, goes below sea level. Though invitingly blue on the maps, Lake Eyre is normally so dry that its salty crust has been used as the track for world speed records. Very rarely, rain transforms the desert scene and flowers bloom.

Before there was a highway or anything else, John Eyre made the first overland trek from Adelaide to the south-west of Western Australia, 2,500 km (1,500 miles) across the desert as the airliners now fly. It took him more than a year. Arriving at the port of Albany, WA, he accepted congratulations, a glass of hot brandy, a bath, and a fresh suit of clothes.

the dunes and impressive cliffs along the **Great Australian Bight**, which forms the bulk of the continent's curving southern coast.

The South-East

Halfway between Adelaide and Melbourne, the south-east of South Australia is rich in natural curiosities of the most dramatic sort, with family-style beach resorts nearby.

Something extraordinary parallels the coast from the estuary of the Murray River down to the small town of Kingston SE (meaning south-east, to avoid confusion with the other Kingston, on the river): an inland sea so salty a swimmer can hardly sink. The phenomenon is named the **Coorong**, from an Aboriginal word meaning "long neck of water". Although the region, now a national park, is unusually rich in shellfish and sea birds, it's almost uninhabited. With dunes to left and to right, a likely stop for a drink is the settlement called Policeman's Point—with a population estimated at seven—site of notorious hangings in the 19th century; it's a long story.

Kingston SE itself is a crayfishing port, as announced on the edge of town by a fantastical lobster as big as a house. Inside the structure you'll find the tourist office, among other services. North-east of Kingston, **Jip Jip Conservation Park** is known for its huge granite boulders and wildlife.

Robe, a small vacation town with plenty of beaches, is another lobstering port. Many historic buildings from the middle of the 19th century are protected here by the National Trust.

Dreamy Volcano

Before you explore the regional centre of **Mt. Gambier**, near the Victorian border, stop at the Lady Nelson orientation centre on the Jubilee Highway for maps and brochures and an audio-visual show. Mt. Gambier is built on a volcano, happily extinct. Its most glorious feature is **Blue Lake**, which is at once beautiful, mystical and useful (as a reservoir). The lake, which fills the volcano's crater, changes colour according to the season. Other towns build skyscrapers or monuments to adorn their central business districts but at Commercial Street and Bay Road in Mt. Gambier there's a big hole in the ground. It's a spectacular cave-in, around which a park was built. At the bottom of the hole, at the entrance to the cavern, flourishes a veritable jungle of tropical plants and trees.

Inland, the **Coonawarra** wine region, north of Penola, takes full advantage of an ideal conjunction of terrain and climate. Although the wineries generally lack the charm of the Barossa Valley establishments, it's worth snooping around the cellar doors; the product, especially the Coonawarra red wine, is very highly regarded.

Flinders Ranges

Rising from a landscape as flat as the sea, the tinted peaks of the Flinders Ranges speak poetry to lovers of robust scenery. In the spring the rugged

*O*pal fans, including professionals, come to Coober Pedy
for a rich variety of stones.

wooded hillsides come to life with a flood of wild flowers, but at any time of year the scene is intriguing. The mountains, like the desert, are much more colourful close up.

The last big town on the way to the Flinders Ranges is **Port Augusta**, historically and to this day a most vital rail junction. The biggest thing in town turns out to be the electricity station, which burns more than 3 million tonnes of coal per year. They run tours for visitors.

Quorn, on the edge of the wilderness, used to be an important railway town but it's been bypassed by time and new routes. The town still attracts rail buffs with its vintage Pichi Richi Railway, which steams through dramatic countryside at holiday time. The round trip takes less than three hours.

Wilpena Pound

The top phenomenon of the Flinders Ranges is a huge natural basin called Wilpena Pound. Rimmed by sheer cliffs, the saucer is about 20 km (12 miles) long and 8 km (5 miles) wide. Wilpena Pound is not only spectacular as a scenic and geological curiosity; it wins admiring squawks from the birdwatchers. Here you can spot butcherbirds, wagtails, galahs, honeyeaters and wedge-tailed eagles.

The flat floor of the Pound is perfectly designed for bushwalks (suggested routes are signposted). But not in summer, when it's altogether too hot for unnecessary exertions. In any season it's essential to carry a supply of drinking water. There's only one way into the amphitheatre, through a narrow gorge occupied in rainy times by the Wilpena Creek.

An area of such grandeur was bound to inspire Aboriginal myths and art over thousands of years. Timeless rock paintings can be inspected near Wilpena at Arkaroo and at Yourambulla, south of the village of Hawker.

Farther north, Gammon Ranges National Park is even bigger than the Flinders Ranges park. It offers challenges to bushwalkers who appreciate the spectacle of ancient cliffs and gorges. The nearest civilization is the resort of Arkaroola, with its own wildlife sanctuary.

Outback South Australia

From an aeroplane, the South Australia Outback looks varied but menacing: an endless red desert, the nothingness broken here and there by dry riverbeds and tufts of brush and curious craters. Rarely the presence of intruders becomes visible: a narrow track as straight as a ruler, destination indeterminate.

Remarkably, the situation on the ground is less daunting than you might expect. A sealed road goes all the way from Adelaide to Alice Springs. The convenience of the Stuart Highway doesn't detract from the impact of the landscape—an awesome place to find yourself, even if you did remember to fill the fuel tank at the last hamlet. The highway is a literal lifeline; detours are very risky.

Woomera (appropriately, an Aboriginal word for "flying spear") used to be top secret when it was a pioneering test range for rockets, and a great area is still off limits. Since 1982 Woomera

Village has been open to tourists, who come to visit Missile Park and the Heritage Centre, featuring a selected history of the base.

An hour's drive along the desolate eastern edge of the Woomera Prohibited Area leads to **Roxby Downs**, the company town for a big mining operation. It's a startlingly comfortable oasis with a relatively lavish motel for visiting geologists or tourists. There are guided tours of the nearby **Olympic Dam** mining complex, which exploits rich reserves of copper, gold, silver and uranium.

Coober Pedy

The town the opals come from must rate as one of the most bizarre tourist attractions anywhere. From the air there's a devastated landscape, and only the regular gridwork frame of all the pockmarks indicates that the disaster is man-made. On closer inspection, the Swiss-cheese holes in the ground turn out to be mining shafts, mostly abandoned.

"Desert" means that in the summer the daytime temperature can reach 45°C (113°F) to 50°C (122°F). That's in the shade, which is extremely limited. In winter the nights become unpleasantly cold. Yet several thousand people, fortune-hunters of 48 nationalities, make their home in this far corner of the Outback.

The name Coober Pedy comes from an Aboriginal phrase meaning "white fellow's hole in the ground". And indeed many settlers have survived here by burrowing hobbit-like into the side of a low hill. Thus insulated, the temperatures within are constant and comfortable, regardless of the excesses outside. Among the dugouts are residences of some luxury, complete with electricity and wall-to-wall carpets. Also underground are an Anglican church and a Roman Catholic chapel, a bank and a luxurious air-conditioned motel.

Regular tours by bus or plane bring the curious crowds to Coober Pedy, about 850 km (530 miles) north-west of Adelaide. The tours visit the local opal fields, where most of the world's opals are produced, followed by demonstrations of opal cutting and polishing. Having learned the intricacies, you can buy finished stones and jewellery on the spot. Or try noodling in the mullock heaps: all you need is a rake or a strainer to sift through the rubble alongside a mineshaft, and if you're lucky you may find an overlooked opal. (The professionals now use ultraviolet scanners.) A word of warning since thousands of shafts are scattered over the desert here, great care must be taken not to fall into a hole (some are 20 m—65 feet—deep) or get in the way of machines or explosives. Amateur fortune-seekers require a permit (obtainable from the Mines Department in Adelaide) for serious fossicking.

If you can't make a fortune mining or selling opals in Coober Pedy you can dream about running a petrol station. The next fuel stop is 151 km (94 miles) in one direction, 252 km (156 miles) in the other. The town has seven stations, all on the main street. More unexpectedly, there is a car wash, although you'd never know it from the layer of desert covering local cars. Most of them look older than their drivers, and even dustier.

Surviving the Never-Never

In Australia, intrepid adventurers don't have to go far in search of a challenge. Questions of life or death can pop up anywhere in the Outback, even half an hour's drive beyond the zone of familiar comforts and conveniences.

Much of the continent is desert, described by Henry Lawson as "burning wastes of barren soil and sand". However, most of the vast empty spaces on the map are only vaguely comparable to desert of the Sahara type; the land can be less forbidding than it seems, for it supports vegetation—sometimes luxuriant—and fascinating wildlife. If you do want to venture off surfaced roads and follow the tracks into the unknown, you must take precautions, whether the terrain is red or golden desert, arid plains, rocky flatlands, or what the map shows as a lake but reality calls a salt flat.

When to go. Consider the season and the weather trends. Do not even think about driving into the Outback in mid-summer: the heat is unbearable. In the 1840s, explorer Charles Sturt recorded temperatures of 69.5°C (157° F) in the open and 55.5°C (132°F) in the shade. It was hot enough to melt the lead in his pencil and force screws out of wooden boxes. Just think what it could do to your car. Rain can also be a source of disaster: after many years of drought, it can suddenly pour down for a week, transforming the land into an enormous flood plain. Never camp in a dry river bed.

Four good wheels. Your vehicle should be a reliable four-wheel drive, with a complete set of spare parts: two spare tyres and tyre repair kit, two spare tubes, coil, condenser, fan belt, radiator hoses and distribution points, a tin of radiator leak fixative, spark plugs, an extra jack (with a large baseplate to prevent sinking in sand or mud), 5 litres (1 gal) of engine oil, a pump, a tool-kit, an axe and a small shovel. Fill the fuel tank at every opportunity and carry at least 20 litres (4½ gal) in reserve.

On the map. You will need good maps, and you should plan your route in detail—and stick to the plan relentlessly. In some areas you have to be equipped with two-way radio. At your point of departure, advise the police of your route, the estimated time of arrival at destination, and the amount of rations you are carrying. (Report to the police again when you arrive.) Always seek local advice about the best route available, the location of fuel and water sources, and of hazards you may encounter, and re-check your position on the map. In the event that you're totally lost, it's smarter to return to your starting point than to wander hopelessly on a hunch. If you wish to enter Aboriginal lands, you must obtain permission from the Aboriginal landowners, and at least four weeks' notice is required. Enquire at the tourist office for the appropriate address.

What to take. Heading into the bush is no picnic; you have to take adequate supplies. Most important is water. Humans can survive for weeks with no food at all, but without water it's a matter of a very few days. You will need up to 6 litres (1⅓ gal) per person per day, best carried in metal containers. Emergency rations should consist of non-perishable high-energy foods such as dried fruit, with canned meats, soups and fruit drinks. Invaluable components of your first-aid kit are aspirin, water-purifying tablets, salt tablets, diarrhoea pills, insect repellent, disinfectant, bandages and sun-block cream. Your personal survival kit, to be carried on your person at all times,

should contain a compass, map, whistle, waterproof matches, pocket knife, bandage and sticking plaster.

Other essentials: a set of billycans, several sheets of heavy-duty plastic, 2 m² (6.5 ft²), and a length of rubber or plastic tubing. And put a piece of nylon rope about 30 m (100 ft) long on your shopping list; it could come in handy, for instance, for towing.

Beating the heat. Wear loose, light cotton clothing and cover your head. Space blankets can prove a boon: the shiny aluminium side turned towards the sun reflects heat away from the body, keeping the temperature normal. To keep warm at night, turn the shiny side inwards.

The kangaroo factor. Anywhere off the beaten track, don't drive at night. Kangaroos are a real hazard, and you might collide with wild water buffalo. Animals are attracted to roads at night because the surface is warmer than the ground nearby.

In Case of the Worst

If your car breaks down in the bush, above all don't panic; it only wastes energy. Use your head to plan survival strategy. Stay with your vehicle, which will be a welcome source of shade, and more easily spotted by aircraft. If you do leave, mark your path so you can easily find your way back again.

Be seen. Make visible distress signals, using brightly coloured clothing, bedding or any other available material—anything that contrasts strongly with the colour of the earth around you. A smoking fire, day or night, is also a big help to searchers.

Back of Beyond, the landscape can be inspiring but the perils to human life can't be overlooked.

Keep cool. Move as little as possible to conserve body fluid; save all physical exertion for the cool night hours. Try to limit your drinking, as well, to the cool part of the day, when a few sips go farther.

In search of H₂O. Your main preoccupation must be dehydration. Ration your water, and set about finding additional supplies of your only really indispensable resource. If you see a patch of healthy vegetation and sizeable trees it could signal the location of a creek; even if it's dry, water might be unearthed by digging, most profitably at a bend; or if you find damp sand or mud, soak up the moisture with a rag and wring it out over a billycan. Another clue to a water source is animal tracks; wherever they converge is almost bound to be where they drink. A promising terrain for finding water is rocky; a passing rain shower can leave a pool of water in a boulder's cavity long after the surrounding soil has dried. At dawn you can wipe the dew from the grass, and your car. To extract water from the leaves of a tree, put a clear plastic bag over a branch; the tree's roots draw water from the earth, send it up to the leaves, and the sun condenses the moisture inside the bag. If you spy a bottle tree, you're in luck: it preserves water in its hollow trunk for months after the wet season. In an emergency you can also eat the rind of the bottle tree pods, chopped up and stirred with water.

Still waters. An enterprising project for the long haul is building a solar still. Dig a hole about 1 m (3 ft) square and 50 cm (20 in) deep, away from any shade. Place a large billycan in the bottom of the hole, and surround it with leafy foliage. Cover the hole with a sheet of plastic and seal the edges completely with earth, making sure that the plastic does not touch the interior walls of the hole. If you have a length of rubber or plastic tubing, place it in the bottom of the billycan before you seal the edges of the sheeting, leaving the other end outside to act as a siphon. Place a small stone in the centre of the plastic sheet, right over the billycan. Moisture from the ground will condense on the underside of the plastic sheet and will drip slowly into the billycan. In this way you can collect about 2 litres (3½ pints) of water per hole per day, so it's best to make several stills, at least 3 m (1 ft)

Rainwater often lingers in the hollows of rocks for a long time after it has evaporated elsewhere.

apart. You will have to change the position of the still every three or four days.

Clear, cool water. Whatever you do, drink only pure water; if it's tainted you could fall ill, adding dangerous complications to an already difficult situation. The first step is to filter muddy or questionable water through layers of sand, charcoal and tiny stones. Then boil it or add sterilization tablets.

Gourmet tips. Small animals—frogs, lizards and snakes—are attracted to your water supply; they could provide an extra source of food. In principle, anything that walks, crawls, swims, flies or grows from the soil is edible—or so they say. If you usually draw the line at snakes, you should know that all reptiles are edible. But be sure to discard the head and venom glands of any poisonous snake on your menu.

You'd be surprised what wholesome food can be made of the insects that abound in the bush. Termites seem to be the least repulsive of the offerings and ants are rich in nourishment. As for plants, many are edible but you have to know which. Avoid milky sap and bitter taste. When in doubt, rub a bit of the plant on your body to see if it irritates delicate skin. Tentatively taste a tiny bit for your mouth's reaction, then eat a minute portion and wait for developments. If there's no upset, you're ready to dig in. Incidentally, if you have no water, it's better to eat nothing at all.

Summing up, the prospects may seem harrowing, but, after all, the Aborigines have survived this forbidding land for 40,000 years.

For the parched traveller, the good news is that where there are trees there is moisture. And some shade.

Between Alps and Desert, a Historic Garden State

With roughly the same area and population as Minnesota, Victoria is the smallest state on the Australian mainland and the most densely populated. You won't feel crowded. Beyond the sophisticated capital, the scenery is so rich and pretty that the state's first name was *Australia Felix*—Latin for bountiful or lucky.

About seven out of ten Victorians live down south in metropolitan Melbourne, a state capital with old-fashioned charm in the shadow of the skyscrapers. A hub of finance, industry, fashion, culture and sports, Melbourne is within easy striking distance of the state's bushland and 19th-century boomtowns, as well as vineyards and ski-slopes, lakes and rivers, and some of the world's most thrilling coastline.

A dainty spire towering over the south bank of the Yarra marks the Victorian Arts Centre and its theatres, museums and concert hall.

After some exploration and tentative settlement, the colony really got its start in 1835 when John Batman, a far-sighted operator from Tasmania, bought 40,500 ha (100,000 acres) from the Aborigines. Even if Batman drove a mercilessly hard bargain, buying—rather than stealing—was a rare method of acquiring land from the traditional owners.

The gold rush broke out in Victoria in 1851, only a few months after the fever hit New South Wales. A gold strike at Ballarat so electrified the state that Melbourne itself risked becoming a ghost town; businessmen locked their offices or shops and rushed to the gold-fields, and ships were abandoned by their gold-crazed crews. Victoria's population increased sevenfold in ten

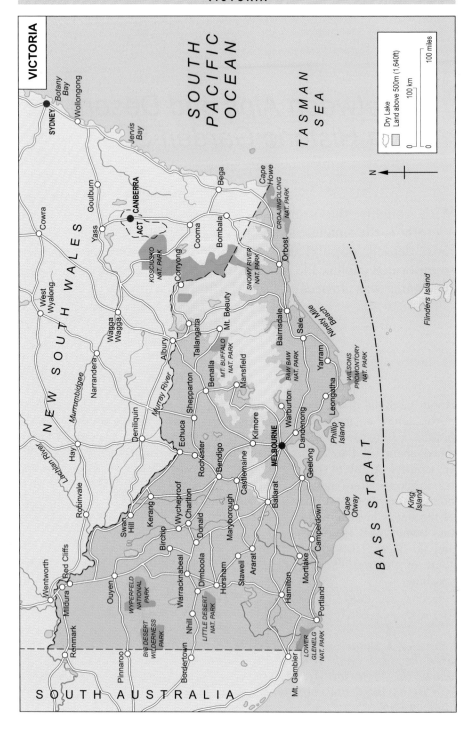

VICTORIA

SYDNEY
Botany Bay
Wollongong
Jervis Bay

SOUTH PACIFIC OCEAN

TASMAN SEA

Dry Lake
Land above 500m (1,640ft)

0   100 km
0   100 miles

N

Cowra
Goulburn
CANBERRA
ACT
Yass
Bega
Cape Howe
CROAJINGOLONG NAT. PARK

West Wyalong
KOSCIUSKO NAT. PARK
Corryong
Cooma
Bombala
Orbost
SNOWY RIVER NAT. PARK

NEW SOUTH WALES

Wagga Wagga
Narrandera
Albury
Tallangatta
Mt. Beauty
Bairnsdale
Ninety Mile Beach

Murrumbidgee
Murray River
Shepparton
Benalla
MT. BUFFALO NAT. PARK
Mansfield
Sale
Yarram
BAW BAW NAT. PARK

Hay
Deniliquin
Echuca
Rochester
Kilmore
Warburton
Leongatha
WILSONS PROMONTORY NAT. PARK

Lachlan River
Robinvale
Bendigo
Castlemaine
MELBOURNE
Dandenong
Phillip Island

Swan Hill
Kerang
Wycheproof
Charlton
Donald
Maryborough
Ballarat
Geelong

Wentworth
Red Cliffs
Birchip
Kerang
Cape Otway
King Island

Renmark
Mildura
Ouyen
WYPERFELD NATIONAL PARK
Warracknabeal
Dimboola
Horsham
Stawell
Ararat
Mortlake
Camperdown
Portland

Pinnaroo
BIG DESERT WILDERNESS PARK
Nhill
LITTLE DESERT NAT. PARK
Bordertown
LOWER GLENELG NAT. PARK
Hamilton
Mt. Gambier

SOUTH AUSTRALIA

BASS STRAIT

Flinders Island

266

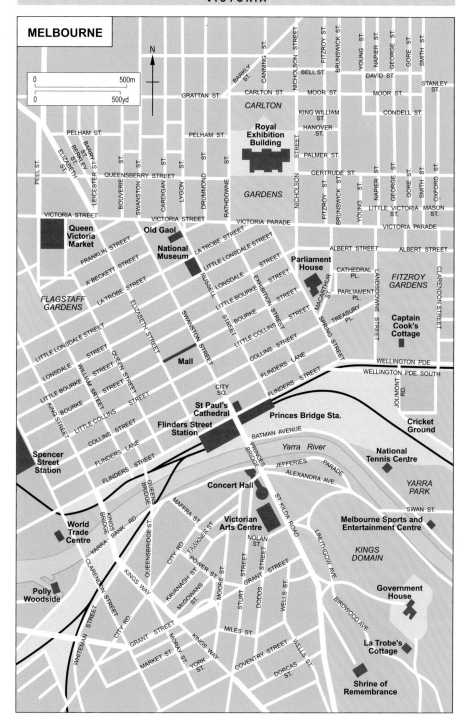

MELBOURNE

N

0 _____ 500m
0 _____ 500yd

PELHAM ST.

PEEL ST.

BARRY ST.
BERKLEY ST.
ELIZABETH ST.
LEICESTER ST.
BOUVERIE ST.
SWANSTON ST.
CARDIGAN ST.
LYGON ST.
DRUMMOND ST.
RATHDOWNE

QUEENSBERRY STREET

BARKLY ST.
CANNING ST.
NICHOLSON STREET
FITZROY ST.
BRUNSWICK ST.
YOUNG ST.
NAPIER ST.
GEORGE ST.
GORE ST.
SMITH ST.

BELL ST.

DAVID ST.

STANLEY ST.

GRATTAN ST.

CARLTON ST.

MOOR ST.

MOOR ST.

CARLTON

KING WILLIAM ST.

CONDELL ST.

PELHAM ST.

HANOVER ST.

Royal Exhibition Building

PALMER ST.

NICHOLSON STREET

GERTRUDE ST.

FITZROY ST.
BRUNSWICK ST.
YOUNG ST.
NAPIER ST.
GEORGE ST.
SMITH ST.
OXFORD ST.

LITTLE VICTORIA ST.
MASON ST.

GARDENS

VICTORIA STREET

VICTORIA STREET

VICTORIA PARADE

VICTORIA PARADE

Queen Victoria Market

Old Gaol

FRANKLIN STREET

A'BECKETT STREET

LA TROBE STREET

LA TROBE STREET

LITTLE LONSDALE STREET

RUSSELL STREET

EXHIBITION STREET

National Museum

ALBERT STREET

ALBERT STREET

FLAGSTAFF GARDENS

ELIZABETH STREET

LONSDALE

LITTLE BOURKE

BOURKE

LITTLE COLLINS STREET

Parliament House

CATHEDRAL PL.

PARLIAMENT PL.

LANSDOWNE STREET

FITZROY GARDENS

CLARENDON STREET

MACARTHUR ST.

TREASURY PL.

Captain Cook's Cottage

LITTLE LONSDALE STREET

LONSDALE

LITTLE BOURKE

WILLIAM STREET

QUEEN STREET

SWANSTON STREET

Mall

COLLINS STREET

FLINDERS LANE

SPRING STREET

WELLINGTON PDE.

WELLINGTON PDE. SOUTH

KING STREET

LITTLE COLLINS STREET

BOURKE

STREET

CITY SQ.

FLINDERS STREET

JOLIMONT RD.

St Paul's Cathedral

Princes Bridge Sta.

Cricket Ground

Flinders Street Station

BATMAN AVENUE

Spencer Street Station

FLINDERS LANE

FLINDERS STREET

QUEENS BRIDGE

PRINCES BRIDGE

JEFFERIES

PARADE

Yarra River

ALEXANDRA AVE.

National Tennis Centre

YARRA PARK

Concert Hall

ST. KILDA ROAD

SWAN ST.

World Trade Centre

KINGS BRIDGE

YARRA BANK RD.

MAFFRA ST.

CITY RD.

QUEENSBRIDGE ST.

Victorian Arts Centre

NOLAN ST.

POWER ST.

STREET

GRANT STREET

STREET

LINTHGOW AVE.

Melbourne Sports and Entertainment Centre

KINGS DOMAIN

Polly Woodside

CLARENDON STREET

CITY RD.

KINGS WAY

FAWKNER ST.

KAVANAGH ST.

McGOWANS ST.

MOORE ST.

STURT STREET

DODDS ST.

WELLS ST.

BIRDWOOD AVE.

Government House

WHITEMAN STREET

MORAY ST.

GRANT STREET

KINGS WAY

YORK ST.

MILES ST.

COVENTRY STREET

WELLS ST.

La Trobe's Cottage

MARKET ST.

DORCAS ST.

Shrine of Remembrance

years. Successful diggers descended on Melbourne with so much money to dispose of that morals loosened lustily.

Victoria, named to flatter the reigning monarch, was the earliest state to industrialize; Melbourne began producing cars in 1897. Today manufacturing—chemicals, motor vehicles, machinery, clothing—accounts for the bulk of the economy, thanks to a mostly benign climate, Victoria is a leading farming power, hence the nickname, "Garden State".

The agricultural potential was almost unexploited until the 1860s, after the gold rush fizzled out. Unemployed ex-prospectors eagerly fanned out as farmers, working land they could buy for one pound per acre. Immigrants in search of a figurative pot of gold followed in a steady flow that reached a tidal wave after World War II, with the policy of "populate or perish". This produced curious ethnic pockets around the state and the cosmopolitan effervescence of a multicultural society within the dignified confines of the capital city.

Melbourne

Look at the map of Melbourne and you might think the urban plan had been drawn on a piece of graph paper, so regimented are the central streets in their precise, logical grid pattern. The Victorian rigour is softened by

*M*ap of Victoria (page 266) and town plan of Melbourne (page 267).

splashes of green—translated as elegant parks and gardens offering merciful breathing space on the edges of the hubbub. This is a friendly but reserved city of *serious* buildings—banks that look as though they keep your money safe, and offices where bureaucrats are worthily enshrined.

This air of distinction may have something to do with the fact that Melbourne was founded not by prisoners (as was Sydney) but by adventurous free enterprisers with a vision of success. Early admirers of John Batman proposed naming the town Batmania, or alternatively Yarra Yarra. But in 1837 the town was officially and obsequiously named in honour of the head of the government in London, Lord Melbourne, a crony of Queen Victoria herself. It could have been worse. Among themselves the settlers called the place Bearbrass.

Don't believe what you hear about Melbourne, especially when it's Sydneysiders who say it. The long-running rivalry between Sydney and Melbourne is incurable. Snipers will remind you of a remark attributed to the actress Ava Gardner, who spent some months in Melbourne making the movie *On the Beach.* "Melbourne," she said, "is a good place to make a film about the end of the world in." (In the Gardner version, the world ends with a preposition instead of a whimper.) Sydney thinks Melbourne is boring, Melbourne thinks Sydney is superficial. Sydney blasts Melbourne's climate, Melbourne ridicules Sydney's self-satisfaction. Generally, Melbourne (with less than 3 million inhabitants) seems on the defensive, for instance on the subject of the unpredictable weather;

temperatures are subject to extremes. As for Sydney's celebrated Opera House, Melbourne was determined to outdo it, but in a "warm and welcoming" way, avoiding what was pointedly called "self-conscious grandeur". The result was the Victorian Arts Centre, a promising security blanket for local self-confidence.

Local Colour

If Melbourne is staid, as Sydneysiders allege, you'd never know it from the tramcars. Artists and cartoonists were commissioned to paint the sides of trams, creating an eclectic, electric gallery in motion. Another aspect of the Melbourne character that's anything but stuffy: the sports mania. "Footy"—high-scoring Australian Rules Football—rules here. Cricket is a passion (Melbourne holds the world's record for the biggest crowd ever at a cricket match—more than 90,000 fans, in 1961). And as for the horses, the Melbourne Cup is so all-engrossing that the first Tuesday in November, when the race is run, counts as a legal holiday.

Unlike Sydney, Melbourne is a city that empties after dark. Because local planners ruled that housing had to be low-rise, the suburbs sprawl for mile after middle-class mile of houses instead of apartments. Melbourne's night-life may be widely dispersed, but you can choose from opera and ballet, uninhibited discos and floor shows. In some categories, Melbourne more than holds its own; the city has always been the rock music capital of Australia. Melburnians also have a reputation as gourmets. Before deciding which of 1,300 restaurants to patronize they

M ore than just a suburban railway station, the Flinders Street Station is a monument to the optimism that reigned in turn-of-the-20th-century Melbourne.

diligently compare the ratings in the local epicure guidebooks, which are always best-sellers.

City Sights

Melbourne's river, the **Yarra,** embellishes the centre of the city while powering the mill of irony. "Too thick to drink, too thin to plough," say the wags, when they're not deriding "the only river in the country that runs upside down." Never mind. On the last

269

*D*ensely populated
Victoria is small in area but rich
in resources, including culture.

few miles of its journey from the Great
Dividing Range to the sea, laden with
red earth from farm country upstream,
the Yarra plays host to freighters, pleasure boats and rowing regattas. It
waters the gardens, reflects the
skyscrapers, and invites cyclists and
joggers to follow its course along pret-
tily landscaped paths. From river-level
you get a pleasant perspective of Melbourne. For a good look up at the
skyline and a close-up of river commerce, take one of the sightseeing
cruise boats that leave from Princes
Walk, by Princes Bridge.

Aerial views over the river and the
city point up the ample acres of green
in the parks and gardens scattered
among the businesslike blocks. (In au-
tumn the green contrasts with yellow
and russet leaves, for many trees, like
many Melburnians, are immigrants
from Europe.) The roster of vantage

points begins with the top of the
Shrine of Remembrance and rises to
skyscraper class: for instance, the 35th
floor of the Regent Hotel, or the summit of the AMP Building.

An inescapable sight along the
waterfront is the **World Trade Centre**,
a huge 1980s building meant to house
international trade exhibitions. On the
opposite bank, the *Polly Woodside*, a
square-rigged sailing barque, recalls the
adventurous days of the last century.
Launched in Ireland in 1885, the restored ship now serves as part of a
maritime museum.

Serving the Arts

Near the river, just south of the very
heart of town, an Eiffel-tower-style
superstructure marks the modern **Victorian Arts Centre**. This airy silver,
gold and white spire rises from flow-
ing curves suggesting a ballet dancer's
tutu. Alight at night, the tower shim-
mers against the sky.

The first part of the complex opened
in 1968: the **National Gallery of Victoria**, now a high-priority stop for art
lovers from all the world. The big collection covers European and Asian art,

old and new, and of course a comprehensive look at Australian painting and sculpture. Among the choicest items on show: a vast, anecdotal Tiepolo painting from the 1740s, *The Banquet of Cleopatra*; sculptures by Rodin, Henry Moore and Barbara Hepworth; a first-class survey of classical Chinese porcelain; and a splendid sampling of Australian Aboriginal paintings. The Gallery, founded in 1861, is the oldest such institution in the country. In comfortable modern surroundings it hits its stride with the wealth of Australian paintings from 18th-century discoveries to living masters. Do tilt your head back to admire the immense, 10,000-piece stained-glass ceiling of the Great Hall, which it is claimed is the world's largest.

The **Theatres Building**, directly beneath the symbolic spire that identifies the Arts Centre, is the place to see opera, ballet and modern musicals. Under the same roof are a playhouse for drama, with 2,000 seats theatrically upholstered in raspberry plush velour, and a smaller studio theatre for experimental works. The adjoining **Concert Hall**, which seats 2,700 people, is used for symphony concerts, but the acoustics can be changed to suit other types of performance. If you're not going to a concert, nip in for a glance at the art work in the lobby, or take a guided backstage tour. The complex caters well for hungry patrons of the arts, with everything from snack bars to luxury-class restaurants.

North of the River

Just across Princes Bridge on the north side of the river, the spires of **St Paul's Cathedral** are not as old as they look.

They were added in the 1920s, several decades after the original Gothic-style structure was completed. The church is a refreshing hideaway in the midst of the busiest part of the business district, a few steps away from the Victorian mass of the main railway station and a less obvious historic landmark, **Young & Jackson's** pub. There are older pubs around the country but none with a work of art so celebrated. In the bar hangs a notorious oil painting of the nude "Chloe"—which has delighted generations of beer drinkers since it scandalized Melbourne's art exhibition of 1880.

City Square, just north of the cathedral, has modern fountains, waterfalls, flowerbeds and outdoor cafés but, according to its critics, not enough character to win the hearts of Melburnians. Built in the golden optimism of the late 1860s, the **Town Hall**, on the opposite side of Collins Street, is used for concerts and official happenings. It can hold 3,000 people.

Collins Street and the parallel Bourke Street are the reason Melburnians claim to have the best shopping in Australia. There are big department stores, small trendy shops, and a warren of arcades for making the most of those rainy hours. The outstanding example of an old-time Melbourne shopping institution, the glass-roofed **Block Arcade**, is an 1892 copy of a Milan landmark, the airy Vittorio Emmanuele Galleria. The architecture of medieval Venice inspired the neo-Gothic **ANZ Bank** building at 386 Collins Street, a surprising sight even in European-influenced Melbourne. The gold-leaf-spangled interior is just as intricate as the façade.

The Paris End

The eastern, hilly end of Collins Street used to be known as the Paris End because of the outdoor cafés shaded by plane trees and the European elegance of the shops. The **Collins Place** development here, attached to the Regent Hotel, features a conspicuously spacious atrium with stylish eating and drinking spots and a cinema at the bottom. Modern architecture fans won't want to miss the unusual **101 Collins** building, a neo-neoclassical extravaganza, with classic columns supporting nothing at all and yawning indoor open spaces.

The **Bourke Street Mall**, the other main shopping street, is a pleasure to roam. Diversions are provided by clowns, magicians, bagpipers and other hopeful talents. But don't get carried away by the relaxed atmosphere: although this is a pedestrians-only zone, there is one big exception: the trams rattle right down the middle of the mall. The **Royal Arcade**, at 331 Bourke Street, is Melbourne's oldest; the trademark is a clock incorporating the figures of the mythical giants Gog and Magog.

Historic Buildings

Begun in the 1850s, **Parliament House** stands majestically in its own park facing Spring Street. It's been called the finest legislative headquarters this side of London; in fact, many of the furnishings are copies of those in Britain's Palace of Westminster. The federal government used this as its lavish temporary headquarters before moving to Canberra. The building is open for guided tours when the state parliament is off duty.

Older than any of the well-preserved Victorian buildings is **Captain Cook's Cottage** in Fitzroy Gardens. The great discoverer never lived in Melbourne; the stone house was transplanted in 1934 from Great Ayton in Cook's native Yorkshire in England—shipped over in a couple of hundred crates and reassembled. Truthfully, it would be more accurate to call it Cook's *parents'* cottage: there's no evidence that the good captain did live under its tile roof in his 18th-century childhood. The only genuine Cook relic in the place is a small sea chest with the initials J.C. The lawns of Fitzroy Gardens, Melbourne's oldest, are shaded by exotic (for Australia) trees like elms and poplars.

Like many other Australian towns, Melbourne considers its old (1854) jail

---

On the Track

For more than a century, trams have been as much a part of the local scene as Victorian architecture, football and meat pies. When other cities switched to buses, sceptics scoffed at Melbourne's clattering trams as old-fashioned and slow. But tradition had the last laugh: the streetcars serve efficiently without contaminating the atmosphere. The modern trams are sleek, smooth-riding and fast.

For visiting motorists the trams are altogether less romantic. Cars can pass a stationary tram—at a maximum of 10 kph (6 mph)—only if a policeman or uniformed tramway employee gives the go-ahead. Trams have the right of way at crossroads. At certain main intersections, if you want to turn right, you have to drive into the left lane, after the trams have passed, then wait for the light to change before turning right. If it's all too complicated, ditch the car and take the tram.

a prime historical monument. Just across the street from the modern Police Headquarters on Russell Street, the three-storey **Old Melbourne Gaol** was the scene of more than 100 hangings. Death masks of the most famous prisoners are displayed, along with other penal memorabilia, such as a "lashing triangle" which was last used in the enlightened year of 1958. The best-known character on death row, Ned Kelly, the celebrated bushranger, was executed here on Melbourne Cup Day 1880. The jail displays the weird suit of improvised armour he was wearing when captured. And you can step inside the executive-sized cell that was his last residence on earth; it has a fine view of the gallows.

The **National Museum** looks not too promising if you enter through the Russell Street entrance, just down the street from the jail. Old-fashioned zoological exhibits are stuffed under glass. But it gets better and brighter as you proceed through rooms and labyrinthine corridors. Among the principal subjects are natural history, geology and anthropology, and there are imaginatively equipped rooms where children can get to grips with the exhibits. The museum's most visited display is an equine shrine: the taxidermist's version of Phar Lap, considered the greatest racehorse in the nation's history. He won the 1930 Melbourne Cup by three lengths. The chestnut gelding's heart suddenly failed

in 1932, after he won California's Agua Caliente Handicap. Phar Lap remains a national hero.

Human Interest

You can brush up your chopstick technique in Melbourne's **Chinatown**, centred on Little Bourke Street, east of Swanston Street. Special street lights and gates define the area, where Chinese restaurants are jammed shoulder to shoulder with cafés, a church, small factories and exotic shops. The area has had a unique flavour since the gold-rush days, when fortune-hunters from China crowded into this low-rent district before and after their efforts in the bush. Chinatown today glows on the maps of local gourmets.

The **Chinese Australian History Museum**, 22 Cohen Place, off Little Bourke Street, displays what's claimed to be the world's largest festive dragon. More seriously, it documents the trials of the Chinese community here, merchants and miners and their families, from boom times through the White Australia Policy to today's multiracial society.

Back to the gourmet beat, and **Queen Victoria Market**, which sums

*M*elbourne's cornucopia: at Queen Victoria Market all sorts of produce are always in season.

up the bounty of Australian agriculture. Here you can admire just about everything that grows on this continent, piled up in irresistibly fresh pyramids. It's as if the best fruit and vegetables had been creamed from every market from Sweden to Sicily. The best time to take in the atmosphere is early in the morning; Queen Victoria Market is closed Mondays and Wednesdays. On Sundays it becomes a flea market for cheap clothing and bric-a-brac.

Parks and Gardens

South of the river, the **Royal Botanic Gardens** are classed among the finest in the world. Some 36 ha (nearly 90 acres) of superb rolling landscape remind the visitor that Melbourne enjoys four seasons. Each time of year has its specialities, and seasonal leaflets are issued for guide-yourself walks. For Australians, some of the joy of this park is the selection of brightly tinted trees and plants from the northern hemisphere. A total of 13,000 botanical species, including century-old English elms and a giant American swamp cypress, are represented here, among the lovely lawns and lakes.

Between the Botanic Gardens and **Kings Domain** (a make-work project of the Great Depression) stands the imposing **Government House**, the state governor's mansion with an estimated 200 rooms, and **La Trobe's Cottage**, its early 19th-century predecessor. The timber cottage was shipped out from Britain as a prefabricated home for Charles La Trobe, who became Victoria's first Lieutenant-Governor in 1851. You have to cheer one of La Trobe's achievements: establishing a wine industry in Victoria.

Across from the cottage, the massive **Shrine of Remembrance** commemorates the Australians who fell in World War I; tragically, more than 60 per cent of all Australian troops were either killed or wounded in the "war to end all wars". Once a year, every Armistice Day, 11 November, at precisely 11 a.m., a beam of sunlight coming through an opening in the roof strikes the Rock of Remembrance. The shrine was built on a rise that is visible to Anzac Day paraders, straight ahead, throughout their march down Swanston Street.

The **Sidney Myer music bowl**, at the north end of the domain, is the setting for concerts and operas under the stars, with an audience of 20,000 on the grass. The soaring bowl's acoustics are as carefully calibrated as its storm-worthiness; the design was tested in a wind tunnel.

In Parkville, north of the city centre, the **Royal Melbourne Zoo** charms foreigners with kangaroos, koalas, platypuses and the like. What fascinates the locals is an all-star cast of elephants, giraffes, snow leopards, monkeys and other animals from afar. Altogether, more than 350 species reside among delightful gardens, and there's a walk-through aviary. The zoo is open 365 days a year, from 9.00 a.m. to 5.00 p.m.

Suburbs

The inner city suburb of **Carlton**, laid out as a roomy extension of Melbourne, combines the restored elegance of Victorian architecture with contemporary dynamism. The latter may be attributed to the area's large immigrant colony, mostly Italian. Hence the profusion of outdoor cafés, pizzerias, trattorias and gelaterias. **Lygon Street** is a festival of ethnic cafés and restaurants, where a doorman might importune you on behalf of some home-made lasagne.

In **South Yarra**, about 2 ha (5 acres) of lawns and gardens surround Melbourne's finest stately home, **Como House**, an Australian Regency and Italianate design. Now run by the National Trust, this example of the colonial era's high style was completed with the addition of a gold and white ballroom in the 1870s. For a breath of air, each of its two storeys was built with wide verandahs decorated with intricate ironwork.

Melbourne is considered Australia's most conservative society, and **Toorak** is the snootiest of its suburbs. They say Toorak harbours more money than any other suburb in the whole country. The mansions, nicely landscaped, make tourists and most other passers-by stop and gawk. Shopping on the Toorak Road is full of stylish delights, well worth gaping at, even if you can't face the price tags.

A totally different shopping experience awaits in the seaside suburb of **St Kilda**, traditionally a funfair kind of place with a late-20th-century cosmopolitan overlay. On Sundays its Esplanade is taken over by artists, antique dealers and flea market entrepreneurs of every sort. Ackland Street's restaurants, cafés and bakeries preserve a middle-European Jewish flavour. Elsewhere in St Kilda you will notice the traces and spices of dozens of other nationalities.

Excursions

A favourite day trip from Melbourne heads up to the **Dandenong Ranges**, volcanic mountains where flowered hillsides and eucalyptus forests set the scene for total relaxation. Aside from enjoying the fresh air, you can drop in on a rich variety of galleries, museums, nurseries, restaurants, tea shops and outright tourist attractions. Only an hour's drive from town (it's easier on a weekday when the recreational traffic is lighter), the hills are barely high enough to make your ears pop. Mount Dandenong itself claims an altitude of only 633 m (2,077 ft).

One highlight of a day among the small towns, farms, parks and gardens of the Dandenongs is a ride on **Puffing Billy**, a restored old steam train plying 13 km (8 miles) of narrow-gauge track. The line was seriously devoted to passenger operations from 1900 to 1958. Four years later it was converted to the tourism business. The train never achieves great speed. In fact, an annual race pits Puffing Billy against hundreds of runners.

The **William Ricketts Sanctuary** is an extraordinary collection of sculpture by a loner who was obsessed with Aboriginal culture and its near-destruction by his fellow whites. Ricketts carved the most lifelike faces of Aborigines, accompanied by their spiritual symbols. The result is unorthodox, even unnerving.

Flora and Fauna
In **Sherbrooke Forest Park** you can give your lungs a treat, savouring the elixir of ferns and mountain ash and whatever flowers happen to be in

bloom. The forest is immensely tall, with mountain ash monuments as high as 20-storey buildings and ferns as big as palm trees. This is the place to see, or at least hear, the lyrebird, a great mimic; it imitates other birds, human voices and even inanimate objects like passing cars. Among the animal

M ountain ash reach colossal proportions in Sherbrooke Forest Park.

residents of the park is the echidna, alias the spiny anteater.

Healesville, less than 60 km (40 miles) east of Melbourne, is the place to go for an intimate look at Australian animals on their home ground. The **Wildlife Sanctuary**, nearby in the Yarra Valley, contains more than 200 native species, such as kangaroos, wombats and emus. The animals feel quite comfortable with humans about, and many come up to mingle with the visitors, hoping to share a picnic. The sanctuary was founded in 1921 as a

research establishment for the study of the local fauna.

The Yarra Valley was the site of the first commercial winery in the state, dating back to the middle of the 19th century. After drastic ups and downs, the region's vineyards are again doing well, and are worth a wine-tasting outing. The reds and whites rate highly, and sparkling wines and port are also available. The only problem here is propinquity: Melbourne is so close that there's always the threat of new suburban homes encroaching on the vines.

Penguin Parade

It's a long, exhausting day-trip, but a magical experience for adults and children, to **Phillip Island**, home of the fairy penguins. These lovable mini-penguins have always used the island as their base. Hundreds of them come home at sunset; the number varies depending on activities at sea, where they spend most of their time fishing for squid, pilchard and anchovy. For reasons of their own, perhaps sensing danger, they tread water offshore until night falls before venturing onto the beach. After decades of being stared at by visitors they still feel insecure arriving on the island.

Before dusk, hundreds of tourists gather behind ropes on Summerland Beach and in viewing stands on the sandhills above. As the spotlights are turned on, announcements in English and Japanese warn the visitors not to touch or upset the penguins: no flash cameras, no running, no violent movements. The penguins observe all this and wait for the first star to appear in the sky.

The first brave penguin scout, no bigger than a seagull, scrambles onto dry land and, looking around suspiciously, lurches across the beach and up the hill to his burrow. (Penguins swim better than they walk; at sea they've been clocked at 40 kph or 25 mph.) It can take half an hour or more for all the birds that are coming ashore to arrive. As they feed the young and settle down, long conversations, perhaps even quarrels, go on into the night, within families and from burrow to burrow.

Phillip Island, which is 120 km (75 miles) south-east of Melbourne,

Smallest of all penguins, the fairy penguins of Phillip Island are intrepid fishermen, but they also eat out of the hand of their keeper.

receives about 2 million visitors a year. It is linked to the mainland by a bridge at San Remo. The fairy penguins (the only species that breed in Australia) are the stars, but the supporting cast is also worth seeing: thousands of fur seals residing on tall rocks on the west coast; clouds of mutton birds arriving every November; and a colony of koalas, vegetating in the high branches of the gum trees. Take a sweater or coat with you for the penguin parade, for the night breeze here can be very chill, even in summer.

The Gold-fields

In 1851, the only word that generated more excitement than the warning of "Fire!" was the cry of "Gold!", and **Ballarat** is one of the first places the happy shout was heard. Driving about 110 km (70 miles) westward from Melbourne takes you back in time to this attractive town, rich with the history of Australia's golden age. It's still a golden destination for tourists.

Ballarat has a bitter-sweet history. As soon as word spread that an old-timer named John Dunlop had hit pay dirt, thousands of miners trekked to the fields. They came from as far away as England, America and China. The early arrivals simply scooped up a fortune, but latecomers had to work harder, following the ore ever deeper.

Almost from the outset the government collected a licence fee from the miners. Many newcomers couldn't afford to pay a tax on hope, so they tended to lie low when the licence inspectors swooped. In the midst of growing antagonism between the authorities and the miners, charges of murder and official corruption pushed the diggers to revolt. In the Eureka Rebellion, Australia's first and only uprising, insurgent miners were besieged in their stockade. An uneven battle cost many lives, mostly diggers. The nation was stunned. The anguish endured for years, inspiring poets and politicians.

When peace returned to the gold-fields, and many of the miners' grievances were answered, Ballarat went back to the business of making a fortune. In 1858 a group of lucky Cornishmen came upon what they called the Welcome Nugget: 63,000 grammes (139 lb). It was eventually put on show in the Crystal Palace in London before being minted. Parallel with the discovery of wealth, Ballarat grew into a stately town where even art and good taste had their day.

The Way It Was

To see what Ballarat was like in the 1850s, visit **Sovereign Hill**, an open-air museum on the edge of town, where the sights, sounds and smells of the gold rush are reconstituted. Local folk, dressed in Victorian-era clothing, operate the shops, post office, bakery and printing office of what appears to be a real town. For authenticity, the admirable workhorses pull wagons along streets that are truly muddy on damp days. And wood is the fuel for the steam generators in the boiler House. Tourists are invited to try their

---

A Long Way from Home

The Chinese Village, one of the poignant reconstructions at Sovereign Hill, shows the scale and harshness of a tent camp set up to accommodate diggers who came all the way from Canton. Crammed into their comfortless ghetto, the coolies worked hard and kept to themselves, and were ostracized or at least resented by many European immigrants. Xenophobia gripped Australians, who feared a flood-tide of cut-price oriental immigrants—the Yellow Peril. To slow the flow, the government levied a discriminatory tax on Chinese who landed in Victorian ports. So a great many of them arranged to arrive in South Australia instead and *walk* the rest of the way to the "New Gold Mountain" in Bendigo.

hand with a digger's pan, under expert instruction. The **Gold Museum** traces the history of the mineral since biblical times and displays notable nuggets and gold coins. Ballarat produced, all told, some 567,500 kg (20 million ounces) of gold.

In the real Ballarat, the largest inland city in Victoria, the principal public buildings on the wide, tree-lined streets add up to a long-lasting monument to the good old days. Some of those who got rich quick had the good taste to spend their money on the finer things. Hence the statues of mythological subjects in Carrara marble among the begonias in the **Botanical Gardens**, and the admirable collection of early Australian art in the **Ballarat Fine Art Gallery**.

Bendigo

The name is a very roundabout corruption of Abednego, the Old Testament companion of Shadrach and Meshach. In the 1850s, Bendigo Creek, running through the centre of town, was awash with panning miners and Bendigo was known as "queen city of the central gold-fields". Today the sizeable city, with a couple of dozen buildings under the protection of the National Trust, is another excursion glowing with nostalgia. It's 150 km (93 miles) north-west of Melbourne.

The **Central Deborah Mine** is now a museum of 19th-century mining technology. From there you can take a "Talking" Tram, an antique vehicle rigged up for tourists, on an 8-km (5-mile) historic itinerary. The last stop is the Chinese temple or **joss house** (the expression is derived, it's thought, from the Portuguese *deus,* god). Chinese miners, who comprised 20 per cent of the Bendigo work force, worshipped in a prayer house constructed of timber and hand-made bricks. It's filled with relics of the early Chinese fortune-hunters.

Among the impressive Victorian-era buildings in Bendigo is the **Shamrock Hotel**, lavishly restored to its old verandahed grandeur. Dame Nellie Melba, the fabled opera singer, once stayed there. Her real name was Helen Porter Mitchell. Born near Melbourne in 1861, the coloratura soprano honoured her home town by adapting its name for her stage name. Admirers were inspired to perpetuate the fame of Dame Nellie with creations as earth-shaking as Melba toast and peach Melba.

South-East Victoria

Lakes and dairyland, beaches and rugged cliffs are the mixture in the south-east region of Victoria. From the Bass Strait up into the hills and beyond to real mountains, the area is rich in recreational potential.

Wilsons Promontory

Geologists have a field-day with Wilsons Promontory, but that's only the first of many fascinations. Until the Ice Age, the southernmost tip of the Australian mainland was connected to Tasmania. When the ice melted the heights became an island. Since then the dunes built up, linking the massive promontory to the rest of Victoria. The scenery is varied and spectacular, making Wilsons Promontory the state's most popular national park.

The 130 km (80 miles) of coastline ranges from magnificent granite headlands to peaceful sandy beaches. Walking tracks go through forests and moorland, and flower-covered heathland. Koalas live here, as do kangaroos and emus, and they all tend to be less shy than in most other places that you might meet them. The promontory, known locally as "The Prom", is about 240 km (150 miles) south-east of Melbourne.

Gourmet Detour

In West Gippsland, within easy day-trip distance of Melbourne, they've concocted the gourmet's version of a wine-tasting tour. Among the orchards and dairylands you can zoom in on the sources of some exquisite delicatessen meats as well as luscious fruit products. Meanwhile, all those cows you see are busy supplying the cheese factories along the Princes Highway. Go to the cheesy equivalent of the winery cellar door and try the Tambo cheese, Trafalgar cheese, Gippsland blue, Moe camembert and Drouin cheddar. The public relations idea-men have dubbed the itinerary "Chasing Gippsland Cheeses".

Gippsland

Near Wilsons Promontory, a tourist base for South Gippsland is the small town of **Yarram**, once a swamp. Indeed "yarram yarram" is an Aboriginal expression for "much water". Nearby **Tarra-Bulga National Park** preserves, in two enclaves, the rainforest that once covered all of South Gippsland. Nearly 40 species of ferns flourish beneath giant mountain ash trees. And the wildlife includes a dozen kinds of lizards and 13 species of frogs.

One of the more concise entries in the Victorian gazetteer belongs to **Moe**, the biggest town in the Latrobe Valley. Coalmining is Moe's business, but tourists stop by to see **Old Gippstown**, an outdoor folk museum in which dozens of authentic historical buildings from the region and beyond have been assembled. An iron house that wound up here was prefabricated in England and erected in what was, in the 1850s, the wilderness of North Melbourne.

For some ghost town atmosphere, head north from Moe to **Walhalla**, where gold fired the enthusiasm of thousands of settlers late in the 19th century. The place is almost abandoned except for the nostalgia industry, which runs tours of the Long Tunnel Extended Mine, which produced tons of gold in the good old days. Some old houses, the bakery, the fire station and the cemetery are also worth a look.

Sale, the metropolis of Gippsland, owes its success to oil and gas discoveries offshore in the Bass Strait. Find out all about it at the Oil and Gas Display Centre. The refineries are out of town, so Sale can pursue the finer things, such as plenty of art, indoors and outdoors, and a local wildlife refuge.

The nicely gardened town of **Bairnsdale** is the gateway to what the tourist industry is calling the Victorian Riviera, a reference to the Mediterranean microclimate. Unusual here is St Mary's Roman Catholic Church, an early 20th-century church with intricate murals decorating the walls and the barrel-vaulted ceiling.

The name of **Lakes Entrance** says it all in a straightforward Australian

*B*ushrangers like Ned Kelly kept Victoria police on their toes in the 19th century. This exhibit adds a note of realism to Death Row of the Old Melbourne Gaol.

way: this is where the Gippsland Lakes meet the sea, a happy conjunction for water sports fans. Lakes Entrance, an important summer resort, is also the home port of a big-time fishing fleet. The elaborate Gippsland network of lagoons has an abundant population of fish, seafood and birds to interest tourists on several levels.

The North-East

Historic towns, national parks and the Victorian Alps are the touristic credentials of the north-east region. If it's skiing you're after, the locals will tell you there's more ski-worthy snow in Victoria than in all of Switzerland.

Ned Kelly Was Here

You can't miss the marble monument in the main street of the pre-Alpine town of **Mansfield**, commemorating "three brave men who lost their lives while endeavouring to capture a band of armed criminals". The victims were mounted policemen shot by Ned Kelly, the notorious bushranger, and they are buried in the Mansfield cemetery.

The story's beginning, as well as the inevitable sequel, was written less than 100 km (60 miles) to the north, in and around **Glenrowan**, population approximately 200. Ned Kelly grew up in the district, and returned after killing the troopers and robbing a couple of banks. As a police dragnet closed in, Kelly cut the telegraph wires and took the town hostage. During the ensuing siege all the members of the Kelly gang were killed, but Ned, clad in a punishingly heavy set of home-made armour, was taken alive. Find out all about it at the Ned Kelly Memorial Museum and the Glenrowan Tourist Centre, where visitors are thrust into a computerized, animated re-enactment of the saga. They sell all kinds of Kelly souvenirs.

The garden city of **Wangaratta** has a number of attractions, including a couple of historic churches, but tourists on the Kelly trail may be more interested in the local **cemetery**, and the grave of Mad Dan Morgan. Compared with this 1860s bushranger, Ned Kelly looked like a model citizen. Morgan is credited with killing 70 people.

In its heyday, **Beechworth** was such a prosperous gold-mining town that in 1855 a local dignitary's horse wore gold horseshoes. More than 30 historic buildings are classified, among them the courthouse where Ned Kelly stood trial. Beechworth Gaol held Kelly twice, and his mother once.

Ski Vistas

Wombats, wallabies, lyrebirds and orange-tinted gang-gang cockatoos inhabit **Mount Buffalo**, a 35 km^2 (14 mile^2) granite plateau at the centre of a national park. The hard way up is a vertical wall 435 m (more than 1,400 ft) high, a favourite pursuit of expert rock-climbers. The easy way is driving. Australia's first ski-lift was built here in the 1930s.

Serious skiers will want to go higher into the Victorian Alps. **Mount Buller**, 1,600 m (5,250 ft) (nearly a mile high), is the closest ski resort to Melbourne, hence the frequent crowding in spite of the multiplicity of lifts. The village of **Falls Creek**, in the midst of a most scenic area, has become an important ski station, with runs for all grades, including champions. Another popular resort, **Mount Hotham** (1,750 m or 5,742 ft), offers skiing for all levels of attainment, with challenging cross-country runs, as well. When the snow melts, the whole area of the Victorian Alps comes alive with spectacular wild flowers.

South-West Coast

To the list of the world's most thrilling seacoast drives—think of California's Highway 101, the Amalfi Drive in Italy or the Nice-to-Monaco Corniche—add the Great Ocean Road snaking along Victoria's south-west coast. The twists and turns will exhilarate you, but the heart of the experience is the clifftop view of the raging Southern Ocean and what it has wrecked.

Second City

Heading south-west from Melbourne toward the open ocean, you can't avoid—nor would you want to—Victoria's second largest city. With less than 100,000 inhabitants, the seaport of **Geelong** is no competition for Melbourne, though in gold rush days it was touch and go which town would become the state capital.

Before and after the excitement of the gold discoveries, the backbone of the Geelong economy was the wool trade. An 1872 woolstore, a spacious and agreeable meeting place for farmers and buyers, has been restored as the **National Wool Museum**. This is the definitive story of the pastoral life in Australia, from sheep on the hoof to the finished product of their fleece. Everything you might want to know about shearing, selecting, washing, dyeing, carding, spinning and weaving wool is explained in a first-class array of displays and demonstrations in three galleries. If the subliminal message has been effective and you find that you desperately need a pullover—or at least a T-shirt—there are several shops on the premises.

The city of Geelong is also proud of its **Botanic Gardens**, in Eastern Park. Founded in the middle of the 19th century, they are noted for the colourful flowers and shrubs and venerable trees, including the only Chinese ginko tree in an Australian botanical garden.

Bellarine Peninsula

Shipping for Melbourne has to venture through the Rip, a narrow, agitated stretch of water between the Bellarine Peninsula and the Mornington Peninsula, the arms embracing Port Phillip Bay. A pair of lighthouses, one white and one black, are provided here for skippers to aim at. No such navigational aids awaited John Batman when he came from Tasmania and landed at **Indented Head** in 1835 to colonize what became Victoria. Today it's a quiet beach resort.

Actually, crossing the Rip is so difficult—a tourist brochure vaunts it as one of the ten most treacherous navigable passages of water in the world—that ships have to be guided by pilot boats from **Queenscliff**. Overlooking this drama, a vast redbrick fortress occupies some of the most valuable land in town; the strategic significance of Queenscliff has always been obvious, and at one time this was the British Empire's most heavily fortified post south of the equator. Otherwise, the Queen of Watering Places was a favourite weekend retreat for prosperous Melburnians in Queen Victoria's day, as witness the atmospheric old hotels still in use.

Surf Coast

Along the south coast of the Bellerine peninsula, and on down to Apollo

Bay, the Bass Strait provides powerful waves for some international surfing competitions. Surfers who can deal with waves as tall as a two-storey house head for Ocean Grove, 13th Beach, Jan Juc and Bell's beaches. The popular resort of **Torquay** calls itself the Surf Capital of Australia—and not just for fun, for they manufacture the equipment, too. (Nobody here claims to have invented surfing; the honour goes to a Hawaiian sportsman of noble descent, Duke Kahanamoko, who brought his skills to Australia in 1915.)

The Diggers' Road

With the giant earth-moving machinery of our day, building a clifftop road is a relative snip. But in 1918, when construction began on the Great Ocean Road, the equipment was picks and shovels, dynamite and raw courage. This 300-km (186-mile) highway over the riskiest but most spectacular of terrains was aimed at making work for unemployed veterans of World War I. After all, they were experts with picks and shovels, explosives and raw courage.

When the first stretch opened in 1922 a newspaper report concluded, "...admittedly it has beauty, but at present there is too much danger in it". Happily, some of the terrors have been ironed out by now. But from cliff's edge to beachside, there's never a dull moment.

Great Ocean Highway

Breathtaking is the least you can say about the Great Ocean Highway, an engineering achievement in its day and still an aesthetic triumph. A test for drivers and a treat for passengers, it teeters on clifftops, prowls through rainforest and zips along beaches.

Heading southwest from Torquay, the spectacular part begins when the road rejoins the ocean at the resort and artists' colony of **Anglesea**. The 18-hole golf-course at Anglesea is noted for the kangaroos grazing on the fairways. The road follows the headlands bush to the dramatically sited village of **Aireys Inlet**, with its giant white lighthouse. Nearby caves are supposed to have harboured pirates.

Lorne, an old-fashioned family resort with touches of sophistication, is separated from its splendid beach by a waterfront park. Behind the town are the cliffs, rainforests and waterfalls of the Otway Ranges.

Apollo Bay is a one-time whaling station that grew into a relaxed beach resort. Professional fishermen here specialize in shark, which you may inadvertently eat almost anywhere in Australia as a bland fish going under the alias of flake.

The highway turns inland through the rainy Otway National Park, rich in ferns and forests, though a track goes to the southernmost point on this coast, **Cape Otway.** The lighthouse here, atop a heart-stopping promontory, was built in the middle of the 19th century as a reaction to a rash of shipwrecks.

The Shipwreck Coast

Aeons before the first sailors learned the hard way, the Southern Ocean was an awesome rage of nature. The battered limestone cliffs of **Port Campbell National Park** tell the story. So does the record of shipwrecks up and down this coast, though most of the relics are visible today only to brave scuba-divers.

The cliffs have been so relentlessly hammered that they have simply surrendered in some dramatic places. The phenomenon called the **Twelve Apostles** consists of the pillars that survived, spookily braving unending torture.

At **Loch Ard Gorge**, terrifying waves meet cross-tides and undertow. It's the last place you'd want to be shipwrecked, for only cruel cliffs and flooded caves meet you. Even a fish wouldn't want to be caught in a spot like this, where the iron sailing ship *Loch Ard*, *en route* from England to Melbourne, went down in 1878. With the loss of about 50 lives, it was the worst maritime disaster in the history of Victoria. There were two survivors: an apprentice seaman, Tom Pierce; and 19-year-old Eva Carmichael, whom he swam back to rescue. A plaque on the clifftop above tells the whole heroic, romantic story, which, incidentally, doesn't seem to have ended in marriage.

The town at the western end of the park, **Peterborough**, was founded, ironically, because of a shipwreck. Some of the sightseers who came to look at the clipper ship Schomberg aground on her maiden voyage in 1855 decided the area was nice enough to settle in.

Whale Country

What has become the busy town of **Warrnambool**, where two rivers meet the ocean, used to be the stamping ground of early 18th-century whalers. Now that the whales don't have to worry about ambushes any more, they often come back to their old haunts in winter. There's a lookout spot for whale-watchers at Logans Beach, with pictures and diagrams posted to help.

Warrnambol's **Flagstaff Hill**, an indoor-and-outdoor museum, re-creates 19th-century port life. The "maritime village" is like a film set, and historical films have been shot here; even the "harbour" is artificial—a pond disguised with reeds. Authentic, though, are the lighthouse and an old fort on the hill above.

Port Fairy has such unaffected historic charm that even a sign like "Ye Olde drive-in bottle shop" doesn't feel phoney. This picturesque port began in the days of seal-hunters and whalers, long before Victoria was founded. Fishermans Wharf is always a dynamic scene when the boats arrive to unload their crayfish and abalone. The tourist authorities also promote a "shipwreck walk" along the beach, with a map pointing out the last resting places of a few of the 30 vessels that perished here. Bird-watchers flock to Port Fairy for the short-tailed shearwaters, or mutton birds (*Puffinus tenuirostris*).

The city of **Portland**, founded in 1834, has retained about 100 antique buildings, including a fort, a courthouse and a prefabricated hotel. But Victoria's westernmost deep-water port has to make a living, and all the bustle clashes with the atmosphere of an old whaling port. Among the distractions: a fleet of ocean-going trawlers, big tankers and grain and ore carriers, and the occasional multistorey sheep transporter. And Portland has a huge aluminium smelter. If you want to sniff the smelter up close, there's a viewing platform and explanatory signs. If you'd rather sniff the flowers, try the Portland Botanical Gardens, founded in 1857.

Of Crime, Punishment and Pioneers

You see them mingling awkwardly among the scholars hunched over their history in the splendid Mitchell Library in Sydney. Uneasy among books, these

Women made up only a small proportion of the passengers on the First Fleet. In a hungry colony, music was a luxury.

homespun researchers pursue the very narrowest field of investigation. They've come to plumb the archives in search of their roots.

A generation or two ago, very few Australians took an interest in genealogy. It might be nice to discover that one's great-great-great-grandfather had been a courageous British pioneer who helped build a new country. On the other hand, what if he turned out to be a convict, one of more than 160,000 unfortunates transported to Australia between 1788 and 1868? Maybe it was better not to dig too deeply. A petty swindler might be forgivable, even amusing, but suppose he were a murderer?

Nowadays, finding a felon in the family tree adds a bit of spice to the all too respectable life of the average suburban Australian, and the odds are good that

cheerful facts may emerge. A high proportion of the transported convicts had been found guilty of quite trivial offences, so the discoveries may ease or erase any trauma.

Amateur genealogists start digging in hopes that the ancestor will turn out to be one of those pitiful cases, convicts who by modern standards of justice seem to be martyrs. In his classic study, *The Fatal Shore*, Robert Hughes cites the tragic fate of William Francis, who was exiled for stealing a book (about the island of Tobago), and James Grace, aged 11, who was doomed for stealing 9 m (10 yds) of ribbon and a pair of silk stockings. Hughes notes that the majority of First Fleet convicts were transported for minor thefts and that there were no murderers or rapists aboard, but it seems the earlier the conviction the better the chance that the ancestor will turn out to be more victim than villain. The historian points out that after 1815 the arrivals tended to have been convicted of more serious crimes. He refers to a spot check showing statistically that more than half were second offenders and 80 per cent were thieves. Very few were sent to England's gulag for political offences.

In her book, *How to Trace Your Convict Ancestors,* Janet Reakes advises Australians where to start—perhaps in the Mitchell Library, which keeps all the Old Bailey trial transcripts. Then there are the rosters of the prison hulks, floating jails in the Thames Estuary or Plymouth Harbour, aboard which the unfortunates were held until their long journey began. After their arrival Down Under, luckily for genealogists, there was a lot of census-taking. And if the ancestor were charged with a new crime in the colony, or pardoned, or married, or granted land, somewhere in an archive the facts are waiting to be seized.

The author lists a score of contemporary organizations that might be helpful to amateur researchers, among them the Descendants of Convicts Group of the Genealogical Society of Victoria. No stigma there.

Nostalgia for pioneer ancestors adds to the appeal of Old Sydney Town, a historical theme park.

On the Roaring 40s, a Holiday Isle with a Checkered Past

It's a long way to Tasmania, a triangular (romantics say heart-shaped) island suspended 240 km (150 miles) south of southernmost mainland Australia. You can get there by aeroplane, by overnight car ferry or by fast catamaran. If you'd been around, say, 20,000 years ago, you could have walked there, as the Aborigines did. Low tide meant the Bass Strait was dry until the Ice Age glaciers melted.

Tasmania's Aborigines, who developed differently from their mainland cousins, fared well, fishing, hunting and collecting wild fruit, until the colonists arrived to tame the land and the people. The Aborigines resisted, and the white men retaliated with their stupendous technological advantage. Annihilation ensued. That's not the only sorrow in the island's checkered past.

The state of the state of Tasmania today would evoke a bitter laugh,

In repose, a Tasmanian Devil would hardly frighten a rabbit, but it growls and snarls and kills big animals.

interspersed with an oath or two, if the early colonists could come back and see it. Tassie, as it is familiarly known, is promoted as the Holiday Isle, with vigorous development of tourism, a vital economic sector. In the beginning the island was the place the really incorrigible prisoners were sent. If humble embezzlers and petty larcenists were transported to Botany Bay, the murderers and escape artists tended to be tagged for the supreme punishment of the convict's hell, Tasmania.

There's no disputing Tasmania's remoteness. It's the last stop before the South Pole; the Antarctic expeditions take off from Hobart. No matter in what direction you're heading, it's a staging post you hate to leave. Tasmania's scenery owes more to solar than

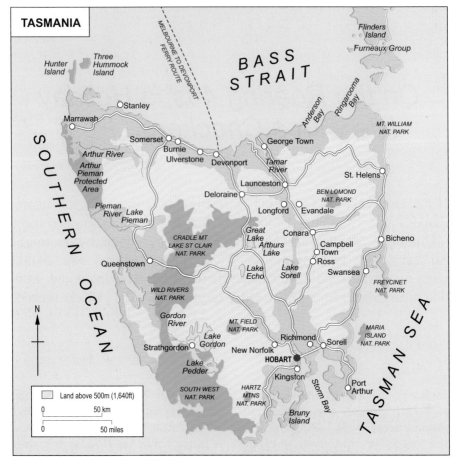

TASMANIA

Hunter Island

Three Hummock Island

Stanley

Marrawah

Somerset

Burnie

Arthur River

Ulverstone

Arthur Pieman Protected Area

Pieman River

Lake Pieman

Queenstown

CRADLE MT LAKE ST CLAIR NAT. PARK

WILD RIVERS NAT. PARK

Gordon River

Lake Gordon

Strathgordon

Lake Pedder

SOUTH WEST NAT. PARK

MELBOURNE TO DEVONPORT FERRY ROUTE

BASS STRAIT

Flinders Island

Furneaux Group

Anderson Bay

Ringarooma Bay

MT. WILLIAM NAT. PARK

George Town

Devonport

Tamar River

Launceston

Deloraine

Longford

Evandale

St. Helens

BEN LOMOND NAT. PARK

Great Lake

Conara

Arthurs Lake

Campbell Town

Ross

Lake Echo

Lake Sorell

Swansea

Bicheno

FREYCINET NAT. PARK

MT. FIELD NAT. PARK

Richmond

Sorell

New Norfolk

HOBART

Kingston

MARIA ISLAND NAT. PARK

Port Arthur

HARTZ MTNS NAT. PARK

Bruny Island

Storm Bay

TASMAN SEA

SOUTHERN OCEAN

N

Land above 500m (1,640ft)

0   50 km

0   50 miles

*M*ap of Tasmania.

Van Dieman's Land

polar influences. Although snow covers the hills in winter, it's a verdant island enjoying a temperate climate. Summer even brings shirt-sleeve weather, and for shade you can find palm trees as well as poplars and oaks. The terrain is a catalogue of contrasts—rainforests and moors, pastureland and orchards, lakes and raging rivers, cliffs and beaches. The historic towns are both inhabitable and lovable.

Early explorers happened upon Tasmania because it lies on the 40th parallel—the Roaring Forties, along which an unfailing westerly wind blows around the globe. Their sailing ships could hardly miss the place. The island is small only by the swollen standards of the Australian continent. With an area of about 68,000 km^2 (more than 26,000 miles^2), it's bigger than Sri Lanka or Switzerland.

However, that's not to diminish the achievement of the Dutch navigator,

Abel Tasman, who gets credit for discovering the island in 1642. He named it after his sponsor, Anton Van Diemen, the governor of the Dutch East Indies. The Dutch never saw a future for the island. Britain eventually claimed it only to cut out the French. Because of the cruel conditions inflicted on the British prisoners, Van Diemen's Land acquired a sinister reputation. The very name could send a shiver down a sinner's spine. The transportation of convicts was abolished in 1852, and three years later the name was changed to Tasmania in memory of its discoverer—though the

motivation was mostly to improve the image.

Since then it's been one triumph after another, as successive waves of free settlers developed an enviably amiable, relaxed way of life. If you like wild scenery, uncrowded towns, and open-hearted people, you could easily become a Tasmaniac.

H obart has something of the allure of a shipshape Scandinavian port, though snow is usually confined to the mountains. The "skyscraper" is the local casino.

Hobart

Australia's smallest capital city is a perfect ocean port on a dreamy river, happily overshadowed by soft green mountains. On the south-east corner of Tasmania, it might have been transplanted from quite another seafaring latitude, someplace as brisk and tidy as Bergen or Helsinki.

Obsequiously named after Lord Hobart, Secretary of State for the Colonies, the nation's second oldest capital city started in hardship and

hunger in 1803. Small comfort was the scenery, which reminded the settlers of the England they left behind. Hobart has kept a powerful array of historic monuments, from stately convict-built official buildings to quaint cottages. Best of all, they're spick and span and still in use.

Hobart's deep-water harbour may lack some of the glamour of Sydney Harbour, but it wins on charm. You never know what kind of ships you'll see here: freighters from Singapore, floating fish factories from Japan, or yachts from distant islands, perhaps Britain or Bermuda. The arrival of an ancient sealer, whaler or windjammer would be right in character. Sails still matter here: Hobart's Constitution Dock is the goal line of the gruelling Sydney-to-Hobart yacht race.

Returning to historical superlatives, Hobart was chosen as the site of Australia's first legal casino. The Wrest Point complex grew into an all-round recreation centre, topped by the almost inevitable provincial status symbol, a revolving rooftop restaurant.

With a population of 180,000 (suburbs included), unpolluted Hobart is small enough to get around and get to know, and as unsophisticated and satisfying as the local fish and chips.

City Sights

You can take a harbour cruise once you're in Hobart, but the only way to catch your first glimpse of the city from the sea is to arrive by cruise ship or your own yacht; the ferries and catamarans from the mainland go to more northerly Tasmanian ports. The waterfront, always colourful, is the place to start seeing the city on foot. In this port, ships from the sea come right up the river into the centre of town. You can watch crates of giant crabs and scallops come ashore, and follow their destiny to the floating fast-food restaurants moored here.

Just behind **Constitution Dock**, where the yacht race ends each New Year, the late Victorian-era **Customs House** stands out as one of the city's most imposing sandstone monuments. It was built at the turn of the 20th century on the site of one of the colony's original landmarks, the original customs house. There are statues of Britannia and Justice, the latter deprived of scales.

Also bordering the docks, **Salamanca Place** is a long row of sandstone warehouses from the 1830s, restored and proudly occupied by artisans' workshops, boutiques and restaurants. On Saturday mornings, cars are banned and the street becomes a bazaar: stalls selling arts and crafts, knick-knacks,

---

No Boomerangs

The saddest saga in Australia is the fate of Tasmania's Aborigines. When Van Dieman's Land was first settled, the indigenous people may have numbered between 3,000 and 7,000. Long isolated from mainland Australia, they had their own distinctive appearance and culture, and nothing so advanced as a boomerang, much less a gun.

After ambushes, massacres, manhunts, reprisals and counter-reprisals by the settlers, the surviving Aborigines were exiled to Flinders Island, hitherto known only for its shipwrecks. In spite of belated efforts to protect the race, the last full-blooded native Tasmanian died in 1876. Genocide is an emotive word, but try to find a more apt description.

flowers and vegetables cover the cobblestones; jugglers, mimes and minstrels perform and pass the hat.

The state's bicameral legislature meets in **Parliament House**, also facing the waterfront, built by convicts in the 1830s but with later additions and modifications. Confusingly, this long, low-rise stone building, which enjoys some admirable architectural details, was originally meant to be the customs house. The architect, John Lee Archer, had worked on the engineering for London's original Waterloo Bridge across the Thames.

More History

Another venerable structure still in use is the **Theatre Royal** on Campbell Street, Australia's oldest live theatre. Built in the most exquisitely luxurious style in the 1830s, it has featured stars like Noel Coward and Laurence Olivier. After a big fire in 1984 the "best little theatre in the world" (as Sir Laurence called it) was restored to its old glitter.

Overlooking Salamanca Place, **Battery Point** is the historic heart of Hobart, beautifully preserved as the nation's most complete colonial village. The battery in question was a set of coastal artillery guns installed in 1818. Ten years later signal flags were added, for relaying the big news of the day, such as ship arrivals or prison breaks. The area is worth an hour or two of exploration on foot, to absorb the atmosphere of the narrow, hilly streets, the mansions and cottages, churches and taverns. One of the upper-class colonial homes has been turned into the **Van Diemen's Land Memorial Folk Museum**. Called Australia's oldest folk museum, it is devoted to the colony's 19th-century way of life, from toys to farm equipment.

The oldest military establishment still in use in Australia, **Anglesea Barracks**, was built by convicts on a hill site chosen by Governor Lachlan Macquarie in 1811. The design and workmanship of the old buildings can be admired from outside, but to enter the original Officers' Mess or the centrally-heated military jail, for example, you have to make arrangements in advance. The oldest building still standing here is the hospital, completed in 1818; the morgue, behind it, was built 10 years later. The establishment is named in honour of the Marquis of Anglesea, who commanded the British cavalry. In a celebrated incident at the Battle of Waterloo, Anglesea put his foot down under, so to speak: when his leg was shot off, he had it buried with honours on the battlefield.

Down the River

Some commuters cross the Derwent River by ferry, which runs between the Brooke Street Pier and Bellerive. Motorists heading for the suburbs and the airport use the graceful **Tasman Bridge**. The prestressed concrete bridge ran into trouble in 1975; more accurately, trouble ran into the bridge. A bulk ore carrier, slightly off course, ploughed into the span; tragically, four cars tumbled into the river, killing all aboard, and the ship sank with six crew lost.

The **Botanical Gardens**, in the Queen's Domain, near the bridge, present more than 13 ha (33 acres) of Tasmanian vegetation in a nutshell. The exhibits also include greenhoused tropical trees and plants, as well as

Lady Franklin Remembered
The wife of Lieutenant-Governor Sir John Franklin, the dynamic and eccentric Lady Jane Franklin (1791–1875), is remembered most visibly in the Lady Franklin Museum, out of town on Lena Valley Road. The building, inspired by a Greek temple, was supposed to house an art museum but it wound up as an apple warehouse. Now it's spruced up again as the headquarters of the Art Society of Tasmania.

Lady Franklin upset hard-line Vandemonians by showing sympathy for female convicts; to get closer to the problem she once volunteered to have herself handcuffed, briefly. On another do-gooder front, she proposed to rid Tasmania of snakes by paying a bounty, but the snake-collecting enthusiasm of the convicts almost broke the bank.

Japanese gardens. The Domain's finest man-made monument is **Government House**, a 19th-century version of an English Tudor and Gothic mansion with 70 rooms, official residence of the governor.

At **Wrest Point**, the nation's first legal **casino** combines gambling, eating, drinking, dancing and floor shows in a one-stop entertainment centre. Gamblers have the choice of blackjack, roulette, *chemin-de-fer*, keno and the Australian favourite, two-up. The big prize is the view from the top of the circular mini-skyscraper encompassing the associated hotel.

Near Hobart

Protecting Hobart from cold southwest winds, in theory, at least, is **Mount Wellington**, named in appreciation of the Duke of Wellington, who toppled Napoleon at Waterloo. The view from the summit of the city's eternal landmark is an expansive panorama over Hobart and the valley of the Derwent. For this expedition you can forget your mountain-climbing equipment. A paved road goes all the way to Mount Wellington's summit, 1,270 m (4,167 ft) above the sea. Snow is a frequent visitor to the mountain during the winter—an exciting novelty for tourists from more northerly Australian climes—but it rarely blocks the road.

For an offbeat break on the drive out to Mount Wellington you can visit the **Cascade Brewery**, a historic monument in its own right. Founded in 1824, it is Australia's oldest brewery. The local beer owes its national reputation to the quality of the Derwent Valley hops and the mountain water.

An industrial excursion of another colour goes up the river to the old

Devilish Mascot
With its mouth open, eyes blazing and a warning snarl in its throat, the Tasmanian Devil can look as fierce as a hungry crocodile. But the pink-eared state mascot isn't looking for trouble. The big-mouthed little devil is a carnivorous marsupial with broad tastes: it eats just about anything from frogs and crabs to mice and poultry. Its only enemies are dingoes and foxes, which may explain its retreat to dingo- and fox-free Tasmania. Tasmanian Devils are relatively common in the countryside, though not very visible because they travel by night.

The Tasmanian Tiger, sometimes known as the Tasmanian Wolf, the largest pouched mammal anywhere, was thought to be extinct by the beginning of World War I. Like the abominable snowman, though, there are occasional reports of sightings. Keep looking.

Bottom of the world: a broad view of the wilderness wonderland of south-west Tasmania, near Port Davey.

ferry port of **Claremont**, where the major industry is a **chocolate factory** belonging to the Cadbury-Schweppes group. The chocolate's local ingredient is milk; all the rest is imported from the mainland or beyond. Guided tours of the assembly line attract sweet-toothed visitors of all ages, but children under eight have to be carried. Visitors can look forward to some samples from the 20,000 tonnes of annual production.

At **Taroona**, beyond Wrest Point, you can visit the remains of a different kind of factory, the **Shot Tower**, built in 1870. Although it looks like an ordinary smokestack, this tower 60 m

(nearly 200 ft) tall was used in the manufacture of gunshot and musket balls. Molten lead was dropped from the top of the tower into cold water, solidifying in perfectly spherical shape. The tower went out of business in 1904. You may climb the 291 steps up the internal spiral staircase to the very summit for a shot-putter's view of the countryside.

A complex of modern glass office buildings at **Kingston** is the working headquarters for Australia's extensive operations in the neighbourhood of the South Pole. The Antarctic Division of the Department of Science and Technology coordinates the logistics and the research in fields such as glaciology, botany, physics and medicine. Inside the main building are displays of sleds and faded flags from pioneering expeditions. Australia maintains four permanent stations in the Antarctic.

Port Arthur

Tasmania's most visited tourist attraction is as melancholy as a cry of despair carved on the wall of a prison cell. Just over 100 km (62 miles) southeast of Hobart, the old penal colony of Port Arthur is a matter of an hour-and-a-half drive. There was no road in convict times, so the condemned and their keepers had to go by sea. Some 200,000 visitors per year make the pilgrimage to these relics of the nation's grim beginnings, deemed so important they're protected by the National Parks and Wildlife Service.

Port Arthur was founded in 1830 as a prison within a prison, the place to punish convicts in the second degree. Having been exiled to Tasmania for a first crime, some of the prisoners were convicted of new crimes on the spot. These really hopeless cases would be sent to Port Arthur as the last resort. Tough discipline was common in all penal institutions at that time, but Port Arthur acquired a reputation as the nadir of brutality. Chain gangs, encouraged by the lash, built the solid stone buildings which have survived more than a century of abandonment, earthquake, fire, storm and looting.

The biggest building still standing, four storeys high, was designed to be a storehouse but became a penitentiary for 650 inmates. Other surviving buildings are the lunatic asylum and, next door, the "model" prison. Both have been restored. Convicts designed and built a large church, now in ruins. Its 13 spires represent Christ and the apostles. The church was never named or consecrated because it served several denominations, and also its record was marred by a murder committed on the premises during its construction. Then there is the mortuary, which did a lively business; nearly 2,000 graves occupy the nearby Isle of the Dead, in the middle of the bay. Other than that, Port Arthur was almost escape-proof, with sharks waiting on one side and killer dogs on the other. In total, approximately 12,500 prisoners did time at Port Arthur during its 47 years of operation.

Launceston

An unexpected Englishness pervades the commercial hub of northern Tasmania, a relaxed, roomy town of elm trees, rose bushes, and tidy squares and gardens sprinkled with patriotic statues and plaques. Launceston is a trove of Georgian and Victorian architecture. If you drive up from Hobart, you'll enjoy the sights along the road, skirting soft green hills studded with sheep. In the villages, to enliven the scene, the houses have roofs the colour of fire engines.

At the head of the Tamar River, Tasmania's second city was founded in 1805 as Patersonia. Soon afterwards, it became the namesake of the town of Launceston in Cornwall, birthplace of the colony's governor. The historic aspects of the town are enthusiastically preserved, starting in the very centre, the **City Square**. This ensemble challengingly groups together a modern pyramid-style state office building, a Japanese garden, and a building from 1830, **Macquarie House**. Restored to mint condition, this sometime warehouse, barracks and office building now serves as part of the local museum.

History and Nature

From stuffed platypuses to blunderbusses, from Aboriginal artefacts to prisoners' chains, the main building of the **Queen Victoria Museum**, on the edge of Royal Park, is crammed with unexpected insights into history and nature. You can examine an intact **joss**

Dawn over historic Launceston, Tasmania's second city, on the Tamar River.

house which originally served the Chinese tin miners in the Tasmanian town of Weldborough. The temple, rich in intricate gold leaf effects, was called the southernmost working joss house in the world. There's also an invigorating collection of modern art. Here, too, visitors can discover the mysteries of the southern night sky in the **planetarium**.

Life in early 19th-century Tasmania is recaptured in the enterprising **Penny Royal** development. A cornmill built in 1825 has been reconstituted, and a cannon foundry and arsenal created to demonstrate the stages of gunpowder

manufacture. You can follow the process from the distillation of saltpetre to the finished cannonballs: by way of quality control you can shoot a cannon. Transport relics here are a paddle-steamer, a naval sloop and an ancient tramcar, all in working order.

Just around the bend is the **Cataract Gorge**, a stirring geological feature, remarkably within walking distance of the centre of town. Here the South Esk River slices between steep cliffs on its route to the Tamar. There are hiking trails, boating opportunities, and a chair-lift spanning the canyon from on high. When built in 1972 it was hailed as containing "the longest single chair-lift span in the world"—an inspiring boast unless you suffer queasy spells dangling from great heights.

Round the Island

Tasmania has dozens of historic towns and villages full of colonial atmosphere—old churches and cemeteries and mansions, quaint pubs and arts-and-crafts shops. A sampler of sights, from north to south follows.

A couple of hundred thousand people arrive in **Devonport** every year on the Bass Strait ferry. Few realize how historic the big town is. Aboriginal rock carvings at Mersey Bluff reveal the lifestyle of the people who lived here for centuries before the island was explored. The Tasmanian Aboriginal Cultural and Art Centre here is called *Tiagarra,* the word for "keep" in the tribal language.

Low-rise Georgian buildings, well preserved from the middle of the 19th century, set the tone in **Evandale**,

south-east of Launceston. Nearby is Clarendon, an enormous, elegantly decorated mansion built in 1838. Among the historic figures who lived near Evandale: John Batman, the founder of Melbourne, and "Red" Kelly, father of the fabled Ned Kelly.

The streets of **Longford**, the site of the annual Tasmanian Folk Festival, are lined with European trees. Christ Church, a sandstone building with a stately clock tower, was constructed by convicts.

Bicheno, in the middle of the east coast, was used by sealers and whalers before it was exploited as a coal-exporting port. Now the tourists come to supervise the unloading of the fishing boats, and to dine out on it. Miles of unspoiled beaches add to the allure.

A stately home in **Campbell Town**, the Grange, belonged to Dr William Valentine, a science buff. Here in 1874 the southern hemisphere's first telephone conversation took place. Campbell Town remembers the convict labourers who contributed a brick bridge over the Elizabeth River.

More Bridgework

In **Ross,** too, the convict-built bridge is a landmark—long and graceful, with beautifully decorated arches; for his artistic efforts one of the stone-carvers was granted his freedom. The locals make a parable out of the main crossroads of Ross. On the four corners stand, or stood: Temptation (a pub), Salvation (a church), Recreation (the town hall) and Damnation (the jail).

A final bridge, the oldest stone bridge in Australia (1825), belongs in **Richmond**. It has six arches. St John's is the first Catholic church, begun in

1837. The courthouse, which is older than either monument, is still in business, too. The jail, now a tourist attraction, predates Port Arthur.

New Norfolk, up the Derwent River from Hobart, is one of those towns that wrestles over the title to the oldest licensed hotel in Australia. The Bush Inn has been restoring travellers' spirits since 1825. Even older is St Matthew's Church, though little of the original building has survived all the renovations and improvements.

Pining for Souvenirs

All over Australia the washed-out colours of the eucalyptus dominate the landscape. Tasmania has them, too, but only about 40 of the hundreds of species found on the mainland. Topping the list, the gigantic mountain ash grows here up to nearly 100 m (more than 300 ft).

What's special about Tasmanian forests is Huon pine, a slow starter that can reach a height of 30 m (about 100 ft)—if you can wait a few hundred years. Huon pine is an old favourite of shipbuilders, cabinet-makers and anyone else looking for a durable, easy-working wood. Souvenir shoppers in Tasmania are offered everything from fine-grained furniture to sniffable sachets of shavings.

Wilderness

Tasmania was lucky. Much of the island is so wild that settlers never gave it a second thought, leaving nature to get on with it. Now these wildernesses are World Heritage protectorates.

For many Australians from the other side of the Bass Strait, Tasmania is the closest they can get to European-style landscape. But reaching these wild places isn't so simple: four-wheel-drive vehicles, canoes, rafts, or just sturdy legs are the best way. In Tasmania a higher percentage of the total area has been set aside as national parks than in any other state.

South-West National Park covers nearly all of the south-western corner of Tasmania: rugged mountains, glacial lakes, icy rivers and forests of giant Antarctic beeches. There are walking tracks for experienced bushwalkers. One recent feature is the new Lake Pedder, flooded to 25 times its natural size for a hydroelectric project. For better or worse, the controversial scheme brought the first roads to the area.

Cradle Mountain–Lake St Clair National Park, a few hours' drive north-west of Hobart, is a savage wonderland of mountain peaks and waterfalls, temperate rainforests, and lakes astir with trout. Bushwalkers rave about the Overland Track, almost a week's worth of varied hiking thrills. The wildlife is all around: wallabies, possums, Tasmanian devils and wildcats. If the Tasmanian tiger wasn't thought to be extinct, this would probably be the place to find one.

A national park accessible to cars, non-bushwalkers and even the handicapped is **Mount Field National Park**. Just an hour's drive from Hobart, it is popular in winter as an easy-to-reach, no-fuss skiing area. In summer the heathlands beyond the giant forests break out in alpine flowers, though some areas are covered with pesky thickets of horizontal scrub, a Tasmanian speciality. At the entrance to the national park is a village with the engaging name of National Park.

The Bushrangers

A 19th-century Australian phenomenon that still hits close to the heart, the saga of the bushrangers began in Tasmania in the 1820s. You could say it ended in Melbourne Jail in 1880 when they hanged the most unforgettable outlaw of them all, Ned Kelly.

The earliest bushrangers were escaped convicts. In Van Diemen's Land, as it was called, conditions were ripe for banditry. Life was wretched for the prisoners and guns were plentiful for the stealing. Desperate men scavenged the countryside. Even the fugitives who barely survived the hardships of the bush were nourished by the thought that they had stolen their freedom.

The first of the bushrangers to attain heroic proportions, Matthew Brady arrived in Australia with seven years to serve and a predictable martyr's complex; he had been convicted for stealing

food. The authorities tried to nip his rebellious spirit—he endured hundreds of lashes—but at last he escaped from the dreaded penal colony at Macquarie Harbour on Tasmania's harsh west coast. Brady and the convicts who fled with him thrived at first in a Robin Hood sort of role; Brady was always uncommonly considerate of women and the poor. But the authorities, stung by his cheekiness, hunted them down with police, troops, spies, infiltrators, and dazzling rewards for informers. Caught, tried and condemned, Brady was widely mourned when he went to the scaffold, aged 27.

Better luck awaited another product of the Tasmanian penal system, Martin Cash. He set a record in the 1840s by escaping from Port Arthur four times. He wound up his hectic career as a free man, a farmer, in Tasmania.

Highway robbers, horse thieves and assorted outlaws fanned out across the Australian mainland in the 1850s. The gold rush made the stakes much more interesting. The exploits of the bushrangers, some of whom spared the poor while robbing banks or rich landowners or stagecoaches loaded with gold, gripped the nation's imagination and, in some cases, sympathy. Folk ballads commemorated specific desperadoes, their daring lives and cruel deaths—usually slain in ambush or swinging from the gallows. The songs eulogized notorious outlaws like Jack Donahoe ("this bold, undaunted highwayman"), Frank Gardiner ("the poor man's friend"), Ben Hall ("the widow's friend"), even "Mad Dog" Morgan ("the traveller's friend"), and

Like a knight's armour but heavier: Ned Kelly's iron suit saved his life, but the hangman won.

deplored their betrayal to the authorities. The bitter ballads, a substantial part of Australia's folk heritage, richly illuminate the formation of the national character.

Among the celebrity bushrangers was one "Captain Starlight", the prince of cattle rustlers. In 1870 he rounded up a thousand head of cattle in the Queensland outback and drove them about 1,500 miles to South Australia, where they fetched a fine price. Back in Queensland he was arrested, tried, but acquitted ... to the delight of anti-authoritarians everywhere.

And then there was Ned Kelly & Family. The son of a paroled convict, Ned was arrested for cattle rustling at the age of 16. In 1878 his widowed mother was jailed for wounding a policeman in the pursuance of his official duties, namely trying to arrest Ned's brother. This event inspired the establishment of the Kelly gang, which specialized in robbing banks and shooting constables, almost for the fun of it. The gang coveted a reputation as the scourge of the law and the ruling class, a consortium striving to redistribute the nation's wealth.

After two years on the run and a couple of spectacular bank robberies, the gang became the target for a massive counter-attack. From Melbourne the authorities despatched a special train with a crew of well-armed police and Aboriginal trackers to the Kelly zone of operations in northern Victoria. Forewarned, the gang launched a brazen pre-emptive strike. The Kellys took hostage the population of the small town of Glenrowan, cut the telegraph

wire to delay the news, and made plans to blow up the train. But one of the 60 inhabitants was able to slip away and tip off the police, who lay siege to the hostage-takers. For the ensuing shootout the gang donned their nightmarish homemade armour. All his cohorts were killed, but Ned, whose heavy iron contraption deflected most of the bullets, was captured while trying to escape.

The authorities had to move the trial to Melbourne to find a jury that didn't consider Kelly a hero. More than 30,000 people petitioned the government to grant him clemency. Sentenced to death, the bushranger impudently invited the judge to meet him in the hereafter. On the gallows, he is supposed to have shrugged, "Such is life." Two weeks after Kelly was hanged, the judge, indeed, died.

Contemporary view of a policeman engaged in the hunt for the infamous Kelly gang.

Beyond the Sightseeing: from Sports to Nightlife

With a continent's worth of sights to see, you will have to ration your energy to do justice to all the other activities. As you would imagine, Australia offers a generous variety of things to do, from the highbrow to the sybaritic, from opera to *haute cuisine,* to the flea market. Our survey starts in a particularly bountiful area, where the interests of almost all Australians converge: the world of sport.

Sports

There aren't enough hours in the day to satisfy the average Australian's passion for sports, outdoor and indoor, on land or water. When they're not playing it or watching it, they're reading about it, arguing about it or betting on it. You can weigh the impact of sports by the local newspapers, with their staggeringly comprehensive sports sections, and the television, which

*F*ishing in the wilds
*of the Northern Territory:
rewarding, but mind the
crocodiles.*

seems to devote half its time to live sports coverage and a lot of the rest to recapitulating the results.

Under the dependable sun, everything is possible, from skiing—on water or snow—to surfing to sailing. In a country so beautiful, with a climate so benign, you'll be tempted to join the crowds, either playing the game yourself or watching the professionals.

The sporting life in Australia is inescapable, almost around the clock, starting with the dawn jogger puffing past your hotel window and finishing with the football supporters celebrating late into the night with shouting, songs and car horns.

Only a sports-crazed country could possibly enthrone a racehorse as a national hero: Phar Lap, winner by three lengths of the 1930 Melbourne Cup. Having survived a couple of assassination attempts, he died in mysterious circumstances after a heroic victory in the United States; flags flew at half mast in Sydney. Today Phar Lap's body is the star attraction in Melbourne's National Museum, and his mighty heart is preserved in the Institute of Anatomy in Canberra. Every November the Melbourne Cup brings the nation to a temporary halt; everyone from prime minister to plumber tunes in to the race and almost everyone seems to take a flutter.

Tastes change. More than a century ago, a guidebook gloomily reported that very little hunting was available around Sydney, except when "occasionally parties are made up for rabbit, wallaby or kangaroo shooting". In 1903 the first car race was run in Australia. Three years later, daringly, surf bathing in the daytime became legal in Sydney. Water-skiing caught on in 1936. Australia won the Davis Cup in 1939. Melbourne held the Olympic games in 1956, and Aussie athletes seized 35 of the medals. The world was becoming aware of Australia as a foremost sporting power, a nation of hardy, aggressive competitors who became champions in fields as varied as tennis and swimming, cricket and golf.

In 1983 the yacht *Australia II*, with a revolutionary winged keel, captured the America's Cup. Hitherto a bolted-down fixture of the New York Yacht Club, the silver cup went on show behind bulletproof glass in the Royal Perth Yacht Club, shining brightly, like the local pride. The euphoria only lasted until 1987, when the Yanks recaptured the cup. But there is still plenty of nearby ocean to challenge sailing fans of ambitions big and small.

Water Sports

The easiest, most obvious of water pursuits, as convenient as the nearest beach, lake, river or pool, is swimming. Australians have been taking swimming seriously since 1894, when the first national championships were held. (About that time, Richard Cavill devised the Australian Crawl, based on the system of propulsion used by South Sea islanders.) Whatever your stroke, paddling about in the Indian Ocean, the Tasman Sea or the Coral Sea is the sort of sport or relaxation you'll long remember, but the surf can be as dangerous as it is invigorating. Most of the popular beaches are delineated by flags showing where it's safe to bathe. Beware of undertow or shifting currents, and always obey the instructions of lifeguards. Sharks are a tangible problem in some areas; when a shark alert is sounded, beat a retreat to the shore and ask questions later. In spite of their mild-sounding name, jellyfish are a very serious seasonal danger, especially in the north; elsewhere there may be Portuguese men-of-war, sea snakes or other silent menaces. Check locally before you put a foot in the surf. And a final cautionary reminder: protect yourself from the sun, which is more powerful than you think. Light complexions are particularly vulnerable to quick, painful sunburn and worse.

Snorkelling brings you into intimate contact with a brilliant new world of multicoloured fish and coral. The sport requires a minimum of equipment—a mask and breathing tube and,

306

You won't be the first to discover the attractions of Bondi Beach, but more isolated beaches are within easy reach.

optionally, flippers to expand your range of operations. Almost anyone who can do the dog-paddle can quickly learn to snorkel; no great skill or stamina is required.

The best place in Australia for **scuba-diving**—it's quite possibly the best place in the world—is the coral wonderland of the Great Barrier Reef. Some of the resort islands are equipped for all the needs of divers, though you may have to supply your own regulator and demand valves. If you want to learn the sport, the graduate version of snorkelling, your resort is likely to have weekly courses starting in the swimming pool or a quiet cove, leading up to an Open Water Certificate. Elsewhere along Australia's coasts, serious scuba-divers devote themselves to exploring submerged wrecks.

Surfing. Year-round surfing is a joy on several Australian coasts, with the biggest waves reserved for winter. The intrepid Captain Cook discovered surfing in Hawaii. He wrote: "The boldness and address with which we saw them perform these difficult and dangerous manoeuvres was altogether astonishing and scarce to be credited." It was nearly two centuries before the

As Australian as ice-cold beer, surfing is a year-round sport, thanks to wet suits and unbounded enthusiasm.

first world championships were held in Sydney. Surfboard riding areas are marked by signs, flags or discs. The best-known surfing zone in the country must be Sydney's Bondi Beach, but there are many more choice locations up and down the coast of New South Wales and beyond. Although Queensland's Surfers Paradise may be just that, many experts prefer the giant rollers farther north at Noosa; Gold Coast locations like Kirra Point and Lennox Head also supply world-class waves. Victoria's most popular surfing area is around Torquay; the aces go to Bell's Beach. On the west coast, there are easily accessible surfing beaches near Perth and Bunbury, with harder to reach challenges near Carnarvon.

Sailboarding (windsurfing) equipment is available in many resorts, with instructors on hand to encourage if you're a beginner or out of shape. The brilliantly-hued sails add to the spectacle as they whizz past many a sea-cove, and on lakes and rivers, too.

Boating. Hundreds of thousands of Australians are boating fans, and visiting yachts and their crews always get a warm welcome. At popular resorts, for instance along the Gold Coast or the Great Barrier Reef, sailing boats and powerboats can be chartered, with or without a professional skipper. Inland, you can command a sailing boat on one of the lakes or a houseboat on the relaxing Murray River. Or you might just settle for an hour's hire of a pedal boat.

Fishing. You'll need a licence to fish inland waters in some states, but the sea is free for all amateurs. Outstanding trout fishing is found in Tasmania and the Snowy Mountains. Seasons and bag limits vary with the district. As for game fishing, the challenge of the giant black marlin is best met off the northern coast of Queensland. If your catch weighs less than half a ton, it's polite to throw the little fellow back. Or settle for tuna, mackerel or sailfish. Good deep-sea fishing is also found off the coast of Western Australia, especially at Geraldton, and in the Spencer Gulf, near Adelaide. In the north, a coveted game fish is the barramundi, a great fighter prized for its delicate flesh.

Land of Champions

Overendowed with international sporting heroes, Australia basks in the glare of great names. A sampler from the hall of fame:

Tennis: Frank Sedgman, Ken Rosewall, Lew Hoad, Rod Laver, Roy Emerson, Evonne Goolagong, Margaret Court, Pat Cash.

Golf: Jim Ferrier, Peter Thompson, David Graham, Greg Norman.

Swimming: John Marshall, Dawn Fraser, Shane Gould.

Cricket: Don Bradman, Ian and Greg Chappell, Dennis Lillee, Rodney Marsh.

Track events: John Landy, Herb Elliott, Ron Clarke.

Motor racing: Jack Brabham, Alan Jones, Peter Brock.

Sports Ashore

For more than a century and a half they've been playing **golf** in Australia. Perhaps a million golfers, from the merest duffers to world champions, trek the nation's links at one time or another. For the visitor, the landscaping may be bizarre, the year-round climate may be better than you're accustomed to, but the game's the same. Melbourne considers itself the nation's golfing capital, with championship courses like Victoria and the Royal Melbourne. All the cities have golf clubs; they often operate under exchange agreements with clubs overseas, or you may have to be introduced by a local member. With no formality at all you can hire the equipment and play at one of the public courses found in all the sizeable towns. Golf is also a popular spectator sport in Australia. The Australian Open, rendezvous of champions since 1904, takes place in November.

Tennis. Whether the scene is Wimbledon, Flushing Meadow or the Australian Open, tennis players from Down Under have always won more than their share of championships. You'll find no shortage of courts, or partners. In towns and resorts some of the courts hire out rackets and shoes. If you're just watching, join the crowd. The biggest throng ever to watch a Davis Cup match was counted in Sydney in 1954: more than 25,000 fans. The world's top tennis stars usually tour Australia in December and January; the Australian Open in January puts Melbourne's splendid National Tennis Centre on the world map.

Rather more dignified than football, a friendly game of bowls offers a quiet day in the Australian sun.

Bowling (lawn bowls). All around Australia men and women, generally of a certain age, dressed in cream-coloured costumes spend hours in the sun decorously bowling on neatly trimmed grass. There are more than a quarter-million registered players. If you're a bowler you'll be able to find a game at almost any club. If you're just sightseeing, spare a few minutes to absorb the restful scene.

Skiing. Although Australia doesn't claim to have invented skiing, fur trappers in Tasmania were getting around on something similar to skis in the 1830s. Cross-country skiing is still popular, especially in the Snowy Mountains, the Bogong Plains and Dargo High Plains. The downhill season in the Australian Alps usually lasts from June to September, sometimes into November, which should be inducement enough for skiers from the northern hemisphere. The best-known and best-equipped resorts in the Snowy Mountains include Thredbo Village, Perisher Valley and Smiggin Holes (NSW) and Mount Buller, Falls Creek and Mount Hotham (Victoria). What's claimed to be the longest chairlift in the world runs 6 km (4 miles) above Thredbo. It can take more than an hour to reach the top.

The 'Footy' Craze

Australians are crazy about **football**—almost any of the four different sorts of football played here. The variety you play or go out to cheer tells a lot about who you are. A few definitions follow. Incidentally, whatever type of football is under discussion, the fans are likely to call it "footy".

Australian Rules Football, the most exotic of the games from a foreigner's viewpoint, was introduced in Melbourne in 1858. Its zone of influence is mostly Melbourne and the south. Crowds of 100,000 and more come out to watch the finals in September, which generate the excitement of an

American Super Bowl or an English Cup Final. The sport, combining elements of rugby, Gaelic football and other forms of the game, is characterized by long-distance kicks and passes and high scoring on an oversized but overpopulated field—with 18 players to a side.

Rugby Union, with teams of 15, is fast, rough and engrossing to the fans. Players from private schools add a posh aura to the violence of the tackles. American football can trace most of its roots to rugby (first played in England's Rugby School in 1823).

Rugby League, the professional, international version of the sport, is played mainly in Sydney and Brisbane. It's a rough-house game offering great physical challenges to the players, 13 to a side.

Soccer teams from Australia have had limited success in international competitions. At home the sport has benefited from the enthusiasm of recent waves of immigrants, and most clubs have ethnic connections. While soccer commands the biggest crowds in Europe and South America, its Australian audience is relatively restrained.

More Sports to Watch

Australians have been playing **cricket** since the early days of the penal colony at Sydney Cove. Purists deplore the innovations they've inflicted on it recently, but there's no stopping progress. In its classical form, the game goes on interminably—for as long as five days. In the television age the Aussies have had the temerity to make a showbiz spectacle out of a gentlemanly pursuit. Kerry Packer, the well-known billionaire, established World Series cricket in 1977, with teams in gaudy uniforms playing at night under the lights. Shockingly, too, they end the match decisively in a single day. Fortunately for conservative fans, the old-fashioned Test survives as well under the Australian sun. The season extends from October to the end of March.

The all-weather sport of **basketball** is gaining popularity on all levels, and draws impressive television audiences. **Netball,** originally known as women's basketball, has become the country's most popular competitive sport among women.

Horse-racing. In Australia, racing is more closely entwined with local life than almost anywhere else. Nearly every town, even in the Outback, has a racetrack, and the big cities have more than one. Saturdays and holidays are the best times to go to the races. Betting on horses, or most other things, is as Australian as ice-cold beer. Enthusiasts who can't make it to the race can participate in their own way through off-track betting facilities, legal and computerized and called TAB for Totalizator Agency Board. Illegal bookmakers, too, operate wherever races are under way. The biggest race of the year is the Melbourne Cup, a 3-km (2-mile) classic so obsessional that the day it is run—the first Tuesday in November—is a legal holiday in Victoria. This is just as well, for nothing would get done in any case while the state has horses on the brain.

Trotting (harness racing) can be seen in big cities and some provincial locations. In the capital cities the trotters run under floodlights. Some of the stakes are enormous.

311

Nearly every town in the country has a race-track: this one is in Townsville. Off-track betting facilities, legal and otherwise, are widely available.

Greyhound racing is another spectacle that draws crowds of punters. Spurred to speed by the unfulfillable promise of an artificial rabbit, the dogs usually run in the cool of the evening; the audience can be as fascinating as the sport itself.

Motor racing. Big races are run near Brisbane, Sydney and Melbourne. The biggest of all is the Australian Grand Prix, which has taken over the streets of Adelaide every year since 1985, with the big-name Formula One world championship contenders competing.

Entertainment

Characteristically, Sydneysiders claim to have a near-monopoly on Australian night-life, but Melburnians and others will tell you it's just not so. See for yourself. Most cities of any importance have a "what's on" magazine or brochure setting forth the local agenda, or check the local paper; you'll be impressed by the variety of events, from classical recitals to X-rated excesses.

The fact that a lot of racy entertainment is available should come as no great shock, considering Australia's lusty history. What may surprise you, though, is the rich store of "heavyweight" cultural attractions: opera, ballet, concerts, drama. Between the extremes there's something for everybody who just wants a relaxing evening out.

Theatre has been going strong in Australia since 1789, scarcely a year after New South Wales was founded. To help celebrate the birthday of King George III, a troupe of convicts put on a Restoration comedy (*The Recruiting Officer*) by George Farquhar. The first real theatre opened in Sydney in 1796. Drama today is at its liveliest in Sydney and Melbourne, where professional companies produce performances of the classics, recent British or American hits, and locally written plays. Some of the theatres themselves are works of art—architectural classics from a more opulent age, or modern showplaces. A typically Australian variation on the theatrical theme is the pub-theatre or theatre-restaurant, where dinner is served before or along with a cabaret, satirical review or musical comedy. (Flexible planners in Sydney should check the "Halftix" kiosk in Martin Place, which sells cut-rate tickets for some of the same evening's performances.)

Opera has attracted enthusiastic audiences Down Under since the days of Dame Nellie Melba, the greatest lyric soprano of the early 20th century. In modern times the coloratura brilliance of Dame Joan Sutherland has spread her fame, and that of Australia, around the world. Though you don't have to dress up, seeing grand opera in the Sydney Opera House makes a gala

You might stumble across a concert almost anywhere. This string quartet is warming up in Canberra.

occasion even more so; but opera-goers in other cities have their consolation in the way of acoustics and atmosphere in their newer theatres. The Australian Opera, the country's biggest performing arts company, is based in the Sydney Opera House.

Ballet. The country's prime classical dance company, the Australian Ballet, founded in 1962, has its headquarters in Melbourne but spends nearly half its time performing in Sydney. Among the foremost modern dance troupes are the Sydney Dance Company and the Australian Dance Theatre.

Concerts. What would musical Australia do without the ABC? The paramount patron of the arts, the Australian Broadcasting Commission operates a symphony orchestra in each state capital. Aside from their broadcasts, these orchestras criss-cross the country, bringing live, serious music to small towns as well as the great concert halls. The ABC also keeps up a steady stream of good recorded music on its ABC-FM radio network. Another influential promoter of serious music, called Musica Viva Australia, specializes in chamber concerts.

Jazz in Australia can be as traditional or avant-garde as you like. In the big cities there are jazz clubs, where you might hear a visiting immortal or an up-and-coming local band, and pubs featuring jazz, perhaps on weekends only. Indoor and outdoor jazz concerts are also advertised.

Other music—folk, pop, rock or beyond—can reveal something of a nation's soul. Listen to a bearded troubadour dishing out bush ballads in an Outback saloon. Or catch one of the flashy new pop groups, remarkable for their innovation. Australia gave the world John Farnham, Olivia Newton-John, Rick Springfield and John Paul Young, and bands like AC/DC, the Bee Gees, Divinyls, Easy Beats, INXS, Men at Work, Mental As Anything and Midnight Oil.

Night-life in the big cities flourishes in an array of conventional nightclubs, discos (trendy and otherwise), cocktail lounges, musical pubs and sing-along karaoke bars. Catering to minority tastes are comedy shops, transvestite spectacles and ethnic spots. Then there are the private clubs which provide all-round entertainment for their members; overseas visitors are usually admitted with a flash of a passport, but the dress regulations may be more formal than you would have expected. The clubs in many areas pay their way through the profits of their slot machines, called poker machines (more affectionately pokies), which provide endless fascination for Australians. For punters who prefer to wager folding money, gambling **casinos** are available in the bigger cities and resorts. Usually open very late into the night, they are equipped for, among other pursuits,

***

Games People Play

Everybody's doing it—betting on horses, on dogs, on numbers, long and short. Australians gamble more than just about anybody, and anywhere they can invest: at the track, at the off-track betting shop, at the club, at the casino. Wherever they are found, the casinos and the ever-more sophisticated coin machines attract far more money than the horses.

Among the explanations sociologists have given for Australia's gambling fever: the early influence of immigrants from wagering societies like Ireland and China, and the absence of a US-style anti-gambling lobby. The Australian states think gambling is a winner, for they take their cut, collecting billions of dollars for their budgets without having to raise visible taxes. Gamblers Anonymous is booming, too.

***

roulette, craps, keno, blackjack, baccarat and the backwoods game of two-up in a more refined, electronic version. They also have bars, restaurants and nightclubs.

Cinema. The Australian film industry, founded at the end of the 19th century, has been a major contributor to the art of moving pictures. Some of the big ones of modern times—*Picnic at Hanging Rock*, *My Brilliant Career*, *Breaker Morant*, the *Mad Max* series, *Crocodile Dundee*—have given the world a look at Australia's scenery as well as some insight into the national character and preoccupations. In spite of the inroads of television and home video, multi-screen cinemas are going strong, in the town centres as well as the suburbs. The big cities also have specialized cinemas for art films, foreign films and revivals.

Australia's Cinema

Australia sends the rest of the world two clashing images. Television soap operas—surprisingly successful export ventures—show a comfortable dream of suburbia. Serials like *Neighbours* and *Home and Away* bring into millions of overseas homes a sunny, apolitical corner of Australia, where the biggest problems are domestic infidelities. Almost everywhere the soaps from Down Under delight housewives who wish they could live like that.

For a picture of Australian life that's much closer to the reality, you have to go to the movies. Against backgrounds of extremes—either endless, parched horizons or claustrophobic urban sordidness—they often aim at the heart of a stressed modern society.

Considering that it's a country of only 16.5 million inhabitants, Australia projects a disproportionately big picture on the world's cinema screens. Its actors have won fame and all the trappings in Hollywood and beyond. Some of its directors, too, take their talent overseas to ring up international successes. Cinema aces like Bruce Beresford, Fred Schepisi and Peter Weir, are versatile enough to trade the Outback scenery for the landscapes of Pennsylvania, New England or Russia and retain their very Australian originality in big-budget productions of universal interest.

No Oscar-come-lately, the Australian movie industry has a distinguished history going back nearly a century. The first short film, produced in 1896, was what could be called a documentary. It showed ferry passengers going ashore in Manly, silently, of course. In those days any pictures that moved were fascinating, and the audiences and critics were impressed. Sports reels—a surefire hit in Australia—came next.

Curiously, the nation's earliest attempts at feature films were religious dramas. At the turn of the 20th century the Limelight Department of the Salvation Army produced long spectacles alternating between bits of home-made movie film and magic lantern slides, all backed by appropriate music. Rousers like *Soldiers of the Cross,* which drew big audiences, were doomed in 1906 when a new commandant took over the Army and abandoned showbiz.

Into the breach came the first full-length commercial dramatic film, and it developed a subject close to the Australian heart. *The Story of the Kelly Gang* was a 1906 hit by Charles Tait. When it was shown in England promoters pronounced it the longest feature film in the history of the world. In fact the length was flexible, depending on how fast the projectionist cranked his machine.

Other producers jumped on the bandwagon with films about famous outlaws, but the subject was banned in New South Wales in 1912. Luckily for the fans, World War I soon ensued, offering plenty of action without cops and robbers plots.

Between wars, and on into the 1950s, a dominant figure in the Australian film business was Charles Chauvel. He undertook projects rich in heroism and Outback landscapes. One early footnote: his historical swashbuckler, a 1933 talkie called *In the Wake of the Bounty,* was the first celluloid appearance of a young actor named Errol Flynn. There were two innovations in Chauvel's last feature film, *Jedda* (1955): it was Australia's first colour film, and it introduced Aboriginal actors in featured roles—in a love story. (In most films produced here, the love element is either tortured or secondary, a reflection of the gulf between men and women in contemporary Australian culture.)

Charles Chauvel's last feature film, Jedda, *was Australia's first colour film.*

A couple of films of the World War II era are still remembered. Chauvel's *Rats of Tobruk* showed wartime heroism by Australian troops in North Africa and New Guinea. Released just after the war, *The Overlanders,* written and directed by Harry Watt, was a documentary-style vision of heroism of another sort: the struggle to herd 85,000 head of cattle thousands of kilometres from the invasion-threatened Australian north to sanctuary in the south.

The national cinema began its march to global recognition in 1958 with the foundation of the Australian Film Institute. Three years later, parliament outlawed imported TV commercials in favour of home-grown spots, launching many technical and artistic careers. Next came big government financial aid to feature film finance, and the boom of the 1970s and '80s.

A whopping money-spinner of 1986 had the happy side-effect of luring many thousands of foreign tourists to Australia. It was the adventure comedy *Crocodile Dundee,* by Peter Faiman, with the unlikely star Paul Hogan, formerly a Sydney Harbour Bridge rigger. The enchantments of Kakadu National Park and Linda Kozlowski added to the film's commercial success, and a romantic sequel was soon in the cinemas.

Contemporary Directors

Before he went international, **Fred Schepisi** (born in Melbourne in 1939) brought to the screen profound revelations of Australian realities. His first full-length film, *The Devil's Playground* (1976), probed the pressures of a private school. *The Chant of Jimmy Blacksmith* (1978) won raves for its sensitive study of a young Aborigine's struggle for identity. After several Hollywood films Schepisi returned to Australia to do *A Cry in the Dark,* alias *Evil Angels* (1988), based on a sensational, socially significant criminal case. In 1990 he was back at the box office with the first glasnost-era thriller, *Russia House.*

Bruce Beresford (born in Sydney in 1940) can never be forgotten, or perhaps forgiven, for giving the world *The*

Jedda introduced Aboriginal actors in a love story for the first time.

Adventures of Barry McKenzie, based on a comic strip version of Australian vulgarity at its worst. Beresford went on to show his versatility with a tragic Boer War story, *"Breaker" Morant.* He is now best known for Hollywood successes like *Tender Mercies, Crimes of the Heart* and *Driving Miss Daisy.*

The first great success of **Peter Weir** (born in Sydney in 1944) was a haunting story of schoolgirls plunged into mystery and disaster, *Picnic at Hanging Rock* (released in 1975). Spooky, too, was *The Last Wave* (1977), a clash of white and Aboriginal cultures with apocalyptic results. Weir's 1981 saga, *Gallipoli,* considered Australia's most traumatic war story, the great disaster of World War I. Civil disorder and terrorism of more recent vintage provide an exciting backdrop for the 1982 production, *The Year of Living Dangerously.* Weir soon entered the big time, producing a parade of Hollywood-backed hits like *Witness, Dead Poets Society* and *Green Card.*

George Miller (born in Brisbane in 1945) was the mastermind behind the tremendously successful cult film series that began in 1979 with the futuristic extravaganza *Mad Max,* launching the stardom of Mel Gibson. (Although Gibson was born in the US, the film's very Australian soundtrack had to be dubbed into a more comprehensible dialect for American distribution.) Miller also directed the offbeat Jack Nicholson film *The Witches of Eastwick* (1987). Having studied medicine before movies, he is known as "Dr Miller" to distinguish him from another Australian director, George Miller, noted for the 1982 film *The Man from Snowy River.*

Gillian Armstrong (born in Melbourne in 1950) hit the big time in a hurry with her 1979 film *My Brilliant Career,* enhanced by a cast brimming with talent—Judy Davis, Sam Neill and Wendy Hughes. After an American film, *Mrs. Soffel,* Gillian Armstrong returned to Australia for *High Tide* (1987), a tale of small-town love and tension, and *Last Days of Chez Nous* (1991), a rich family drama.

The Right Place at the Right Price

Hotels

To help you choose a hotel, the following list is a selection based on the criteria of price, attraction and location. It is arranged by towns and cities in alphabetical order.

In each town the list begins with luxurious hotels and continues to moderately priced and finally more spartan accommodation. At the bottom end you may be pleasantly surprised to find air-conditioning and other comforts. We designate very expensive hotels, which normally meet the highest international standards, ▌▌▌▌. In premium hotels of Melbourne and Sydney, the rate for a double room can run from about A$240 up to four figures. In smaller cities the most luxurious hotels (still ▌▌▌▌) start at A$150. In Melbourne and Sydney expensive (▌▌▌) means A$120–240. Elsewhere, A$100–150. Moderate rooms (▌▌) cost about A$70–120 in the two biggest cities, A$60–100 elsewhere. Less than that rates ▌. (Backpackers' hostels, not listed here, start at about A$10 per night.)

Adelaide

Hilton International Adelaide ▌▌▌▌
233 Victoria Square, Adelaide
Tel. 08/217 0711
380 five-star rooms and 15 suites in the geographical heart of town.

Hyatt Regency Adelaide ▌▌▌▌
North Terrace, Adelaide
Tel. 08/231 1234
369 lavish rooms and 21 suites, atrium, pool, spa, gym—and the casino is next door.

Adelaide Meridien Lodge ▌▌▌▌
21 Melbourne St., North Adelaide
Tel. 08/267 3033
Modern luxury motel 2 km (1.2 miles) from city centre.

Hotel Adelaide ▌▌▌
62 Brougham Place, North Adelaide
Tel. 08/267 3444
In North Adelaide's gourmet district.

South Park Motor Inn ′ ▌▌▌
Centre South and West Terrace, Adelaide
Tel. 08/212 1277
On the edge of parklands.

Adelaide Travelodge ▌▌▌
208 South Terrace, Adelaide
Tel. 08/223 2744
195 rooms in Tower and low-rise wings, the latter less expensive.

Grosvenor Hotel ▌▌–▌▌▌
125 North Terrace, Adelaide
Tel. 08/231 2961
Opposite the casino, five floors divided into business and tourist class zones.

Festival Lodge ▌▌
140 North Terrace, Adelaide
Tel. 08/212 7877
Splendidly central small motel.

Ambassadors ▌
107 King William St., Adelaide
Tel. 08/231 4331
Small hotel opposite the tourist office.

Clarice ▌
220 Hutt St., Adelaide
Tel. 08/223 3560
Small hotel/motel near Victoria Park racecourse.

Albany, WA

Travel Inn ▌▌
191 Albany Highway, Albany
Tel. 098/41 4144
58-room motel.

Royal George ▌
Stirling Terrace, Albany
Tel. 098/41 1013
Hotel/motel in town.

Alice Springs, NT

Diplomat Motor Inn ▌▌▌
Hartley Street and Gregory Terrace, Alice Springs
Tel. 089/52 8977
93 units in town centre.

Four Seasons Alice Springs ▌▌▌
Stephens Road, Alice Springs
Tel. 089/52 6100
Comfort on the edge of town, opposite the casino.

Gapview Resort ▌▌▌
Corner Gap Road and South Terrace, Alice Springs
Tel. 089/52 6611
Tennis, pool, spa, etc.

Territory Motor Inn ▌▌
Leichhardt Terrace, Alice Springs
Tel. 089/52 2066
110 units in the bustle of town.

The Old Alice Inn ⏐
Todd Street, Alice Springs
Tel. 089/52 1255
Bargain accommodation in central Alice.

Apollo Bay, Vic.
Apollo International Motor Inn ⏐⏐
37 Great Ocean Road,
Apollo Bay
Tel. 052/37 6100
24-unit motel overlooking the beach.

Greenacres ⏐⏐
Great Ocean Road, Apollo Bay
Tel. 052/37 6309
Opposite the golf course, a 28-unit motel.

Ballarat, Vic.
Mid City Motel ⏐⏐
19 Doveton Street North,
Ballarat
Tel. 053/31 1222
Central location; heated pool.

Old Ballarat Village ⏐⏐
613 Main Road (Midland Highway), Ballarat East
Tel. 053/31 3588
Opposite Sovereign Hill.

Ballina, NSW
Ballina Beach Resort ⏐⏐⏐
Compton Drive, East Ballina
Tel. 066/86 8888
36-room motel in resort setting near surfing beaches.

Bathurst, NSW
Bathurst Motor Inn ⏐⏐
87 Durham Street, Bathurst
Tel. 063/31 2222
Pool, spa, gym, etc.

Governor Macquarie Motor Inn ⏐⏐
11 Charlotte Street, Bathurst
Tel. 063/31 2211
Quiet comfort in town centre.

Bendigo, Vic.
National Hotel/Motel ⏐⏐
186 High Street (Calder Highway), Bendigo
Tel. 054/41 5777
Opposite Central Deborah gold mine.

Shamrock ⏐⏐
Corner Pall Mall and Williamson Street, Bendigo
Tel. 054/43 0333
Historic hangout for gold miners and celebrities.

Brisbane, NSW
Sheraton Brisbane Hotel and Towers ⏐⏐⏐⏐
249 Turbot Street, Brisbane
Tel. 07/835 3535
410 rooms, 27 suites in skyscraper luxury atop a railway station.

Brisbane City Travelodge ⏐⏐⏐
Roma Street, Brisbane
Tel. 07/238 2222
18 storeys of comfort atop the busy Transit Centre.

Gazebo Hotel ⏐⏐⏐
345 Wickham Terrace, Brisbane
Tel. 07/831 6177
Overlooking the city, 11 floors, three for non-smokers.

Lennons Hotel Brisbane ⏐⏐⏐
66 Queens Street, Brisbane
Tel. 07/222 3222
For shoppers, the mall is at the door.

Mayfair Crest International ⏐⏐⏐
Ann and Roma Streets, Brisbane
Tel. 07/229 9111
Across the street from City Hall, 406 rooms, 36 suites.

Bellevue Hotel Brisbane ⏐⏐
103 George Street, Brisbane
Tel. 07/221 6044
Modern, central.

Embassy ⏐⏐
Edward and Elizabeth Streets, Brisbane
Tel. 07/221 7616
Small hotel, very central.

Gateway ⏐⏐
85 North Quay, Brisbane
Tel. 07/236 3300
Central with view of the river.

Marrs Town House ⏐⏐
391 Wickham Terrace, Brisbane
Tel. 07/831 5388
Small motel opposite Albert Park.

Metropolitan Motor Inn ⏐⏐
106 Leichhardt Street, Brisbane
Tel. 07/831 6000
North of the centre.

Parkview ⏐⏐
136 Alice Street, Brisbane
Tel. 07/229 6866
Near Botanic Gardens.

Soho ⏐
333 Wickham Terrace, Brisbane
Tel. 07/831 7722
Budget motel.

Broken Hill NSW
Broken Hill Overlander Motor Inn ⏐⏐
142 Iodide Street, Broken Hill
Tel. 080/88 5566
Small motel with all comforts, spa, pool.

Crystal ⏐⏐
326 Crystal Street, Broken Hill
Tel. 080/88 2344
Air conditioning and a pool table, too.

Broome, WA
Cable Beach Club ⏐⏐⏐⏐
Cable Beach Road, Broome
Tel. 091/92 2505
Super luxury on a paradise beach.

Quality Tropicana Inn ⏐⏐
Saville and Robinson Streets, Broome
Tel. 091/92 1204
Utilitarian, in town.

Bunbury, WA
The Lord Forrest ⏐⏐⏐
Symmons Street, Bunbury
Tel. 097/21 9966
102 rooms, 13 suites, spa, gym, etc.

Ocean Drive ⏐
562 Ocean Drive, Bunbury
Tel. 097/21 2033
70 rooms.

Busselton, WA
On the Vasse Resort ⏐⏐
70 Causeway Road, Busselton
Tel. 097/52 3000
Alongside the river, motel with 34 quiet rooms.

The Geographe ⏐⏐
Bussell Highway, West Busselton
Tel. 097/55 4166
37-room hotel-motel on the beach.

Cairns, Qld

Cairns Hilton ▮▮▮▮
Wharf Street, Cairns
Tel. 070/52 1599
259 international class rooms, five suites. Panoramic views of Trinity Bay.

Radisson Plaza ▮▮▮▮
Pierpoint Road, Cairns
Tel. 070/31 1411
202 luxury rooms, 18 suites. Harbour views, tropical gardens.

Matson Plaza Hotel ▮▮▮
The Esplanade, Cairns
Tel. 070/31 2211
Harbour views, all comforts. (Formerly Four Seasons).

Pacific International ▮▮▮
Corner Spence Street and Esplanade, Cairns
Tel. 070/51 7888
Overlooking the Marlin Jetty.

Lake Central Lodge ▮▮
137 Lake Street, Cairns
Tel. 070/51 4933
Motel with cheerful service in the centre of town.

Rainbow Motor Inn ▮▮
179 Sheridan Street, Cairns
Tel. 070/51 1022
Economical motel.

Canberra, ACT

Capital Parkroyal ▮▮▮▮
1 Binara Street, Canberra
Tel. 06/247 8999
Canberra's biggest, part of National Convention Centre.

The Hyatt Hotel ▮▮▮▮▮
Canberra
Commonwealth Avenue, Yarralumla
Tel. 06/270 1234
Elegant 1920s charm restored.

Canberra City Motor Inn ▮▮▮
Northbourne Avenue and Cooyong Street, Canberra
Tel. 06/249 6911
72 units, pool, etc.

Lakeside ▮▮▮
London Circuit, Canberra
Tel. 06/247 6244
On the shore of Lake Burley Griffin with 15th-floor restaurant.

Embassy ▮▮
Hopetoun Circuit and Adelaide Avenue, Deakin
Tel. 06/281 1322
In the diplomatic area, 1 km (½ mile) from Parliament House.

Forrest Motor Inn ▮▮
30 National Circuit, Forrest, ACT
Tel. 06/295 3433
77-room motel within walking distance of Parliament House.

Crest Motor Inn ▮
60 Crawford Street, Queanbeyan, NSW.
Tel. 06/297 1677
25 budget-priced rooms, short drive from Canberra.

Cessnock, NSW

Cessnock Motel ▮▮
13 Allandale Road, Cessnock
Tel. 049/90 2699
20 units, central.

Hunter Valley Motel ▮▮
30 Allandale Road, Cessnock
Tel. 049/90 1722
Closest motel to the vineyards.

Coober Pedy, SA

Desert Cave ▮▮▮
Hutchison Street, Coober Pedy
Tel. 086/72 5688
Underground rooms cost more than "ordinary" ones.

Opal Inn ▮▮
Hutchinson Street, Coober Pedy
Tel. 086/72 5054
Hangout of the opal traders.

Cooktown, Qld

The Sovereign Hotel ▮▮
Charlotte Street, Cooktown
Tel. 070/69 5400
A small tropical resort in itself.

Darwin, NT

Beaufort ▮▮▮▮
Esplanade, Darwin
Tel. 089/82 9911
Striking Post-modern architecture overlooking the bay.

Sheraton Darwin ▮▮▮▮▮
32 Mitchell Street, Darwin
Tel. 089/82 0000
12 storeys of luxury in central Darwin.

Atrium ▮▮▮
Peel Street and The Esplanade, Darwin
Tel. 089/41 0755
Pool, spa, etc.—and an atrium.

Darwin Travelodge ▮▮▮
Esplanade, Darwin
Tel. 089/81 5388
10-storey motel on the Esplanade.

Darwin Motor Inn ▮▮
97 Mitchell Street, Darwin
Tel. 089/81 1122
34-room motel.

Top End Frontier ▮▮
Corner Mitchell and Daly Streets, Darwin
Tel. 089/81 6511
Homey.

Cherry Blossom ▮
108 Esplanade, Darwin
Tel. 089/81 6734
Budget motel.

Darwin Transit ▮
69 Mitchell Street, Darwin
Tel. 089/81 9733
Where the backpackers meet.

Devonport, Tas.

Sunrise Motor Inn ▮▮
140 North Fenton Street, Devonport
Tel. 004/24 8411
Opposite Devonport Oval.

Formby ▮
82 Formby Road, Devonport
Tel. 004/24 1601
Opposite the ferry terminal.

Dubbo, NSW

Blue Lagoon Motor Inn ▮▮
81 Cobra Street, Dubbo
Tel. 068/82 4444
56 comfortable rooms on the Mitchell Highway.

Country Comfort Inn ▮▮
Peak Hill Road, Dubbo
Tel. 068/82 4777
Alongside the golf course.

Fremantle, WA

The Fremantle ▮▮▮▮
Esplanade
Marine Terrace and Essex Street, Fremantle
Tel. 09/430 4000
Historic building.

Tradewinds ▯▯
59 Canning Highway, Fremantle
Tel. 09/339 8188
Noted for value for money.

Geelong, Vic.
Eastern Sands ▯▯
1 Bellerine Street, Geelong
Tel. 052/21 5577
25-room motel opposite Eastern Beach.

Kangaroo ▯
16 The Esplanade, Geelong
Tel. 052/21 4022 or 052/21 4365
Overlooking the foreshore.

Geraldton, WA
Hacienda ▯▯
Durlacher Street, Geraldton
Tel. 099/21 2155
30-unit motel.

Ocean Centre ▯▯
Foreshore Drive and Cathedral
Avenue, Geraldton
Tel. 099/21 7777
New hotel overlooking the harbour.

Gladstone, Qld
Country Comfort ▯▯
100 Goondoon Street, Gladstone
Tel. 079/72 4499
Comfortable 5-storey motel.

Mid City Motor Inn ▯
26 Goondoon Street, Gladstone
Tel. 079/72 3000
Central location, as advertised.

Gosford, NSW
The Willows ▯▯
512 Pacific Highway, North
Gosford
Tel. 043/28 4666
50-room motel opposite Reptile Park.

Goulburn, NSW
Centretown Lagoon ▯▯
77 Lagoon Street, Goulburn
Tel, 048/21 2422
40-unit motel, indoor pool.

Posthouse Motor Lodge ▯▯
1 Lagoon Street, Goulburn
Tel. 048/21 5666
38-unit motel, outdoor pool.

Hobart, Tas.
Sheraton Hobart ▯▯▯▯
1 Davey Street, Hobart
Tel. 002/35 4535
Luxury in the heart of town.

Wrest Point ▯▯▯▯
410 Sandy Bay Road, Hobart
Tel. 002/25 0112
Luxury riverside hotel with its own casino, and vice versa.

Leisure Inns Hobart Macquarie Motor Inn ▯▯▯
167 Macquarie Street, corner
Harrington Street, Hobart
Tel. 002/34 4422
Central, with pool, sauna, etc.

Ambassador Motor Inn ▯▯
40 Brooker Avenue, Hobart
Tel. 002/34 2911
On the edge of Glebe.

Argyle Motor Lodge ▯▯
2 Lewis Street, corner Argyle
Street, Hobart
Tel. 002/34 2488
36-unit motel.

Barton Colonial Cottage ▯▯
72 Hampden Road, Hobart
Tel. 002/23 6808 or 002/28 7532
Colonial history plus charm in Battery Point.

Hobart Midcity ▯▯
96 Bathurst Street, Hobart
Tel. 002/34 6333
Hotel/motel opposite the post office.

Marquis of Hastings ▯
209 Brisbane Street, West Hobart
Tel. 002/34 3541
Small hotel/motel.

Jabiru, NT
Four Seasons Kakadu ▯▯▯
Flinders Street, Jabiru
Tel. 089/79 2800
Startling architecture for comfortable 110-room motel in Kakadu National Park.

Jim Jim, NT
Four Seasons Cooinda ▯▯▯
Jim Jim, NT
Tel. 089/79 0145
48-room motel in Kakadu National Park.

Kalgoorlie, WA
Quality Plaza ▯▯
50 Egan Street, Kalgoorlie
Tel. 090/21 4544
Comfortable, on a quiet street.

Exchange ▯
Hannan Street, Kalgoorlie
Tel. 090/ 21 2833
Historic.

Katherine, NT
Katherine ▯▯
Corner Katherine Terrace and
Giles Street, Katherine
Tel. 089/72 1622
Central hotel/motel.

Paraway ▯▯
Corner O'Shea Terrace and First
Street, Katherine
Tel. 089/72 2644
Overlooking the Katherine River.

Katoomba, NSW
Katoomba Town Centre ▯▯
224 Katoomba Street, Katoomba
Tel. 047/82 1266
In the heart of town.

Echo Point Motor Inn ▯
Echo Point Road, Katoomba
Tel. 047/82 2088
Near the lookout point.

Launceston, Tas.
Launceston International ▯▯▯▯
29 Cameron Street, Launceston
Tel. 003/34 3434
Central, modern and luxurious.

The Old Bakery Inn ▯▯
Corner York and Margaret
Streets, Launceston
Tel. 003/31 7900
Historic colonial complex.

Lithgow, NSW
Zig Zag Motel ▯▯
Chifley Road, Lithgow
Tel. 063/52 2477
30-room motel in Blue Mountains country.

Mackay, Qld
Alara Motor Inn ▯▯
52 Nebo Road, Mackay
Tel. 079/51 2699
On the Bruce Highway.

Hotel Whitsunday ▌
Corner MacAlister and Victoria
Streets, Mackay
Tel. 079/57 2811
34 rooms, central location.

Melbourne
Hyatt On Collins ▐▐▐▐
Corner Collins and Russell
Streets, Melbourne
Tel. 03/657 1234
Atrium, shopping centre and all.

Menzies at Rialto ▐▐▐▐
495 Collins Street, Melbourne
Tel. 03/620 9111
A historic architectural treat.

The Regent ▐▐▐▐▐
of Melbourne
25 Collins Street, Melbourne
Tel. 03/653 0000
Very posh skyscraper hotel.

Bryson Hotel ▐▐▐
186 Exhibition Street, Melbourne
Tel. 03/662 0511
Big, very central, popular.

Château Melbourne Hotel ▐▐
131 Lonsdale Street, Melbourne
Tel. 03/663 3161
Convenient location.

Downtowner ▐▐
66 Lygon Street, Carlton
Tel. 03/663 5555
*Modern motel, handy to lively
restaurant zone.*

George Powlett Lodge ▐▐
Corner George and Powlett
Streets, East Melbourne
Tel. 03/419 9488
Quiet yet handy location.

Kingsway ▐▐
Corner Park Street and Eastern
Road, South Melbourne
Tel. 03/699 2533
*6-storey motel near Botanic
Gardens.*

Magnolia Court ▐▐
101 Powlett Street, East
Melbourne
Tel. 03/419 4222
Close to Melbourne Cricket Ground.

Ramada Inn ▐▐
539 Royal Parade (Hume
Highway), Parkville
Tel. 03/380 8131
*40-unit motel opposite Princes
Park.*

Royal Parade Motor Inn ▐▐
441 Royal Parade (Hume
Highway), Parkville
Tel. 03/380 9221
Big comfortable motel, quiet.

The Victoria ▐▐
215 Lt Collins Street, Melbourne
Tel. 03/653 0441
*Old-fashioned hotel with modern
comforts.*

Miami ▌
13 Hawke Street, West
Melbourne
Tel. 03/329 8499
102 rooms, budget class.

Mildura, Vic.
Mildura Grand ▐▐
Seventh Street, Mildura
Tel. 050/23 0511
*Overlooking the majestic Murray
river.*

Kar-Rama Motor Inn ▌
153 Deakin Avenue, Mildura
Tel. 050/23 4221
34-unit motel.

Mount Gambier, SA
Red Carpet Inn ▐▐
Jubilee Highway East, Mount
Gambier
Tel. 087/25 4311
On the way into town.

Jens ▌
40 Commercial Street East,
Mount Gambier
Tel. 087/25 0188
22-room hotel in centre of town.

Newcastle, NSW
Newcastle Ambassador ▐▐▐
King and Steel Streets, Newcastle
Tel. 049/26 3777
6-storey motel in centre of town.

Noah's On The Beach ▐▐▐
Shortland Esplanade and Zaara
Street
Tel. 049/29 5181
Overlooking the South Pacific.

Noosa Heads, Qld
Sheraton Noosa Resort ▐▐▐▐
Hastings Street, Noosa Heads
Tel. 074/49 4888
*Modern luxury between Hastings
Street and the river.*

Beachcomber Resort ▐▐
8 Hastings Street, Noosa Heads
Tel. 074/47 3077
Small motel, central.

Parramatta, NSW
Parramatta Parkroyal ▐▐▐▐
30 Phillip Street, Parramatta
Tel. 02/689 3333
*Parramatta's first international
class hotel, 12 storeys tall.*

Parramatta City ▐▐
Corner Great Western Highway
and Marsden Street, Parramatta
Tel. 02/635 7266
Views over Parramatta Park.

Perth, WA
The Orchard ▐▐▐▐
707 Wellington Street, corner
Milligan Street, Perth
Tel. 09/327 7000
*258 rooms, 20 suites, 8
restaurants.*

The Perth International ▐▐▐▐
10 Irwin Street, Perth
Tel. 09/325 0481
15-storey luxury hotel.

Perth Parmelia Hilton ▐▐▐▐
Mill Street, Perth
Tel. 09/322 3622
*Tastefully furnished; some river
views.*

Château Commodore ▐▐▐
417 Hay Street, Perth
Tel. 09/325 0461
An old favourite; roomy layout.

Greetings Town Lodge ▐▐
134 Mill Point Road, South
Perth
Tel. 09/367 5655
Just across the Narrows Bridge.

Inntown ▐▐
70 Pier Street, corner Murray
Street, Perth
Tel. 09/325 2133
96-room hotel.

Kings Ambassador Perth ▐▐
517 Hay Street, Perth
Tel. 09/325 6555
Friendly, central.

Savoy Plaza ▐▐
636 Hay Street, Perth
Tel. 09/325 9588
In the mall.

Wentworth Plaza
300 Murray Street, Perth
Tel. 09/481 1000
96 rooms near bus and rail stations.

The Adelphi
130a Mounts Bay Road, Perth
Tel. 09/322 4666
Some rooms have river views.

Port Arthur, Tas.
Port Arthur Motor Inn
Historic Site, Port Arthur
Tel. 002/50 2101
35 rooms, situated among the historic remains.

Port Augusta, Vic.
Hi-way One Motel
National Highway 1, Port Augusta
Tel. 086/42 2755
45 rooms on the edge of the Flinders Ranges.

Port Douglas, Qld
Sheraton Mirage Port Douglas
Port Douglas Road, Port Douglas
Tel. 070/99 5888
Remarkably sumptuous—and pricey—tropical resort.

Lazy Lizard Motor Inn
121 Davidson Street, Port Douglas
Tel. 070/99 5900
Affordable 22-room motel.

Port Fairy, Vic.
Seacombe House Motor Inn
22 Sackville Street, Port Fairy
Tel. 055/68 1082
Historic atmosphere in National Trust buildings and others.

Port Hedland, WA
Hospitality Inn
Webster Street, Port Hedland
Tel. 091/73 1044
40-room motel, overlooking the ocean.

Port Macquarie, NSW
Country Comfort
Buller and Hollingworth Streets, Port Macquarie
Tel. 065/83 2955
60-unit riverside motel.

Mid Pacific
Clarence and Short Streets, Port Macquarie
Tel. 065/83 2166
On the riverside near post office.

Portland, Vic.
Richmond Henty Hotel Motel
101 Bentinck Street, Portland
Tel. 055/23 1032
Overlooking Portland Bay.

Proserpine, Qld
Proserpine Motor Lodge
184 Main Street, Proserpine
Tel. 079/45 1588
30-room motel on Bruce Highway, Restaurant, pool.

Queenscliff, Vic.
Ozone Hotel
42 Gellibrand Street, Queenscliff
Tel. 052/52 1011
24 rooms in historic building protected by National Trust.

Rockhampton, Qld
Country Comfort Inn
86 Victoria Parade, Rockhampton
Tel. 079/27 9933
On the riverside.

Criterion
Quay and Fitzroy Streets, Rockhampton
Tel. 079/22 1225
Fine old building.

Surfers Paradise, Qld
Quality Beachcomber
18 Hanlan Street, Surfers Paradise
Tel. 075/70 1000
Most rooms have ocean views.

Ramada
Gold Coast Highway and Hanlan Street, Surfers Paradise
Tel. 075/79 3499
Skyscraper luxury, 405 rooms.

Château of Surfers Paradise
The Esplanade and Elkhorn Avenue, Surfers Paradise
Tel. 075/38 1022
18 storeys, mostly suites.

Iluka
The Esplanade and Hanlan Street, Surfers Paradise
Tel. 075/39 9155
16 storeys, mostly suites.

Quality Islander
6 Beach Road, Surfers Paradise
Tel. 075/38 8000
In the heart of Surfers.

Silver Sands
Gold Coast Highway, corner Markwell Avenue, Surfers Paradise
Tel. 075/38 6041
Small, modestly-priced motel.

Sydney
Hilton International Sydney
259 Pitt Street, Sydney
Tel. 02/266 0610
At the monorail station, a central skyscraper, recently renovated.

Holiday Inn Menzies Sydney
14 Carrington Street, Sydney
Tel. 02/299 1000
Traditional favourite with spacious rooms, 4 restaurants, spa, etc.

Hyatt Kingsgate Sydney
Corner Victoria Street and Kings Cross Road, Kings Cross
Tel. 02/356 1234
33-storey landmark in lively area.

Inter-Continental Sydney
117 Macquarie Street, Sydney
Tel. 02/230 0200
A big, posh, modern hotel inside a historic building.

Hotel Nikko Darling Harbour
161 Sussex Street, Sydney
Tel. 02/299 1231
Called Australia's largest hotel, with 649 rooms overlooking Darling Harbour.

Park Hyatt Sydney
7 Hickson Road, The Rocks, Sydney
Tel. 02/241 1234
Understated low-rise luxury beautifully set on the waterfront.

Ramada Renaissance
30 Pitt Street, Sydney
Tel. 02/259 7000
Lavish version of "European elegance", 562 rooms.

The Regent Sydney ▮▮▮▮
199 George Street, Sydney
Tel. 02/238 0000
*Nearly 600 rooms in this
refurbished harbourfront winner.*

Sheraton Wentworth ▮▮▮▮
Sydney
61 Phillip Street, Sydney
Tel. 02/230 0700
*In the heart of the financial
district.*

Crest Hotel ▮▮▮
111 Darlinghurst Road, Kings
Cross
Tel. 02/358 2755
*Overlooking swinging Kings
Cross.*

Hyde Park Inn ▮▮▮
271 Elizabeth Street, Sydney
Tel. 02/264 6001
Overlooking Hyde Park.

Oxford Koala Hotel ▮▮▮
Oxford and Pelican Streets,
Sydney
Tel. 02/269 0645
Big, popular motel.

Macquarie Private Hotel ▮▮
Hughes and Tusculum Streets,
Potts Point
Tel. 02/358 4122
Small old-fashioned hotel.

The Manhattan ▮▮
8 Greenknowe Avenue, Potts
Point
Tel. 02/358 1288
Near Elizabeth Bay.

Oxford Towers Motor Inn ▮▮
13 Waine Street, Darlinghurst
Tel. 02/267 8066
Walking distance of city centre.

Park Regis ▮▮
Castlereagh and Park Streets,
Sydney
Tel. 02/267 6511
Reasonably priced, central.

The Russell ▮▮
George Street, Sydney
Tel. 02/241 3543
Quirky charmer on the Rocks.

Astoria ▮
9 Darlinghurst Road, Kings
Cross
Tel. 02/356 3666
Kings Cross on a budget.

Coronation ▮
7 Park Street, Sydney
Tel. 02/267 8362
*Around the corner from Town
Hall.*

Tamworth, NSW
Tamworth Motor Inn ▮▮
212 New England Highway,
Tamworth
Tel. 067/65 4633
29 rooms, pool, spa, etc.

Tennant Creek, NT
Bluestone Motor Inn ▮▮
1 Paterson Street, Tennant Creek
Tel. 089/62 2883
Comfortable 64-room motel.

Toowoomba, Qld
Glenfield Motor Lodge ▮▮
Ruthven and Stenner Streets,
Toowoomba
Tel. 076/35 4466
*In garden setting near golf course.
Restaurant.*

Townsville, Qld
Ambassador Townsville ▮▮▮
The Strand, Townsville
Tel. 077/72 4255
*14-storeys high-rise on the
beachfront.*

Townsville Reef International ▮▮
63 The Strand, Townsville
Tel. 077/21 1777
*Low-rise modern architecture on
the seafront.*

Yongala Lodge ▮▮
11 Fryer Street, Townsville
Tel. 077/72 4633
*Small motel alongside historic
building.*

Victor Harbor, SA
Apollon Motor Inn ▮▮
32 Torrens Street, Victor Harbor
Tel. 085/52 2777
Town centre, 31 rooms.

Grosvenor ▮
Corner Coral and Ocean Streets,
Victor Harbor
Tel. 085/52 1011
32 bargain-priced rooms.

Wagga Wagga, NSW
Pavilion Motor Inn ▮▮
22 Kincaid Street, Wagga Wagga
Tel. 069/21 6411
*45 rooms, central, enterprising
decor.*

Warrnambool, Vic.
Motel Warrnambool ▮▮▮
65 Raglan Parade, Warrnambool
Tel. 055/62 1222
Modern, near shopping plaza.

Olde Maritime Motor Inn ▮▮▮
Banyan and Merri Streets,
Warrnambool
Tel. 055/62 6488
Opposite Flagstaff Hill.

Warwick, Qld
Jackie Howe Motel ▮▮
Victoria Street, Warwick
Tel. 076/61 2111
32-room motel, central; two pools.

Whyalla, SA
Foreshore Motor Inn ▮▮
Foreshore at Watson Terrace,
Whyalla
Tel. 086/45 8877
39-room motel, some sea views.

York, WA
Settlers House ▮▮▮
125 Avon Terrace, York
Tel. 096/41 1096
Historic 1850's hotel.

Castle ▮▮
Avon Terrace, York
Tel. 096/41 1007
Historic 1850's hotel.

Yulara, NT
Four Seasons Ayers Rock ▮▮▮▮
Yulara Drive, Yulara.
Tel. 089/56 2100
100 rooms with all comforts.

Sheraton Ayers Rock ▮▮▮▮
Yulara Drive, Yulara
Tel. 089/56 2200
*Desert luxury in 226 luxurious
rooms, four suites.*

Red Centre Hotel ▮▮▮
Yulara Drive, Yulara
Tel. 089/56 2170
*Marginally most affordable of the
big three.*

Restaurants

Rating restaurants is risky anywhere, more so across an entire continent: chefs quit, owners change, prices rise. Here is a selection of restaurants recommended by recent travellers. "Expensive" in the big capital cities may mean A\$35–60 per person, A\$25–35 in small towns.

Adelaide

Beijing
73 Angus Street, Adelaide
Tel. 08/232 1388
Northern Chinese cuisine.
Inexpensive.

Mandarin Duck Bistro
110 Flinders Street, Adelaide
Tel. 08/223 2370
Favourite Chinese recipes well presented. Moderate to expensive.

Mistress Augustines
145 O'Connell Street, North Adelaide
Tel. 08/267 4479
The latest triumphs of nouvelle cuisine Australienne. Expensive.

Nediz Tu
170 Hutt Street, Adelaide
Tel. 08/223 2618.
High marks for innovative cuisine, good service. Expensive.

Paul's Cafe
79 Gouger Street, Adelaide
Cheap but good fish and chips and sophisticated dishes, too.
Inexpensive.

Albany, WA

Kooka's
204 Stirling Terrace, Albany
Tel. 098/41 5889
Country cooking, friendly service.
Moderate.

Alice Springs, NT

Overlander Steak House
72 Hartley Street, Alice Springs
Tel. 089/52 2159
Hearty Outback food surrounded by historic memorabilia.
Expensive.

Hindquarter Bistro
94 Todd Street, Alice Springs
Tel. 089/52 2233
Steaks. Moderate.

Angaston, SA

The Vintners Restaurant
Nuriootpa Road, Angaston
Tel. 085/64 2488
Stylishly-presented seasonal specialities for wine-route pilgrims.
Expensive.

Ballandean, Qld

Boxes Restaurant
Ballandean, NSW
Tel. 076/84 1130
Wholesome fare in the vineyards just north of NSW border.
Moderate.

Ballarat, Vic.

Alibis
10 Camp Street, Ballarat
Tel. 053/31 6680
Contemporary modern food in the historic gold-rush town.
Moderate.

Bendigo, Vic.

Copper Pot
2 Howard Place, Bendigo
Tel. 054/43 1362
French cuisine, nouvelle and traditional. Moderate.

Maxine's
15 Bath Lane, Bendigo
Tel. 054/42 2466
Casual dining on French and Italian themes. Moderate.

Brisbane

Daniel's Steakhouse
145 Eagle Street, Brisbane
Tel. 07/832 3444
Harbour view atmosphere, giant steaks nicely served. Moderate.

Jimmy's on the Mall
Queen Street Mall, Brisbane
Tel. 07/229 9468
Eat well while you watch the crowds stroll by. Moderate.

Kookaburra Queen I and II
The Pier, Eagle Street, Brisbane
Tel. 07/221 1300
On the river, lunch and dinner paddlewheeler cruises. Expensive.

Lyrebird
Performing Arts Complex, South Bank, Brisbane
Tel. 07/240 7575
Just the ticket before the opera.
Moderate.

Michael's Riverside
Riverside Centre, Eagle Street, Brisbane
Tel. 07/832 5522
Elegant modern atmosphere for luxury class Italian food.
Expensive.

Rumpole's Restaurant
North Quay and Turbot Street, Brisbane
Tel. 07/229 5922
Imaginative cooking in a tropical-style atmosphere. Expensive.

Canberra, ACT

Chifleys
Canberra Workers Club, Childers Street, Civic
Tel. 06/48 0399
Seafood specials and lively atmosphere. Live music weekends.
Moderate.

Comme Chez Soi
Ginninderra Village, Barton Highway
Tel. 06/30 2657
Belgian cuisine, of all things, in a very Australian atmosphere.
Moderate.

Fringe Benefits
54 Marcus Clarke Street, Canberra
Tel. 06/247 4042
Luxury meets haute cuisine in a friendly brasserie. Expensive.

Le Gourmet
4 Colby Court, Philip
Tel. 06/82 3363
French cuisine in elegant atmosphere. Expensive.

Imperial Court
40 Northbourne Avenue, Canberra
Tel 06/48 5547
Elegant atmosphere for tasty Cantonese cooking. Expensive.

Innovations Restaurant
35 Kennedy Street, Kingston
Tel. 06/95 7377
Australian food as authenic as wichetty grubs. Lavish decor.
Expensive.

Mama's Trattoria
Garema Place, Canberra
Tel. 06/48 0936
*Family-style pasta and Italian
cooking. Inexpensive.*

Mirrabook Restaurant
Sculpture Garden, Australian
National Gallery, Canberra
Tel. 06/273 2836
*For culture-lovers, lunch with a
view of the lake. Moderate.*

Terminus Tavern
9 East Row, Civic
Tel. 06/49 6990
*Do-it-yourself barbecues and home
cooking. Moderate.*

Cairns, Qld
Barra's
Conservatory Shopping Village,
Abbott Street, Cairns
Tel. 070/31 4343
*Family style seafood dinners.
Moderate.*

Fuji Japanese Restaurant
Minnie and Abbott Streets,
Cairns
Tel. 070/31 1134
*Sushi and other authentic
delicacies. Moderate.*

Verandah's
10 Shields Street, Cairns
Tel. 070/51 0111
*Most central location. Varied
menu stressing seafood. Moderate.*

Darwin, NT
Christo's
Mitchell Plaza, Mitchell Street,
Darwin
Tel. 089/81 8658
*Friendly service for Greek and
seafood specialities. Moderate.*

Genghis Khan Restaurant
44 East Point Road, Fannie Bay
Tel. 089/81 3883
*Choose the ingredients for your
own Mongolian barbecue.
Expensive.*

Lee Dynasty
21 Cavenagh Street, Darwin
Tel. 089/81 7808
*Well-presented Cantonese food;
yum cha Sundays. Moderate.*

Peppi's
84 Mitchell Street, Darwin
Tel. 089/81 3762
*Intimate upmarket dining,
international cuisine. Expensive.*

Fremantle, WA
The Left Bank
15 Riverside Drive, East
Fremantle
Tel. 09/319 1315
*Contemporary food in a historic
building. Moderate.*

Oyster Beds
6 Riverside Drive, East
Fremantle
Tel. 09/339 1611
*Seafood overlooking the Swan
River, an institution since 1932.
Moderate.*

Geelong, Vic.
Fishermen's Pier
Yarra Street, Geelong
Tel. 052/22 4100
*Fresh seafood, picture-window
harbour views. Moderate.*

The Source
310 Moorabool Street, Geelong
Tel. 052/21 1375
*Innovative cuisine, attentive
service, good wine list. Expensive.*

Ushers Restaurant
93 Yarra Street, Geelong
Tel. 052/29 7529
*French and continental cuisine.
Cozy. Expensive.*

Glenelg, Vic.
HMS Buffalo Seafood Restaurant
Adelphi Terrace, Glenelg North
Tel. 08/294 7000
*Well-prepared seafood aboard a
replica of S.A.'s equivalent of the
Mayflower. Expensive.*

Hobart, Tas.
Dear Friends
8 Brook Street, Hobart
Tel. 002/23 2646
*Elegant nouvelle cuisine in a
converted mill. Expensive.*

The Fish Caf
Elizabeth and Burnett Streets,
North Hobart
Tel. 002/34 3336
*Seafood in the liveliest of
atmospheres. Moderate.*

Sisco's
21 Macquarie Street, Hobart
Tel. 002/23 2059
*A long way from Spain, throbbing
guitars and cuisine to harmonize.
Expensive.*

The Upper Deck
Mures Fish Centre, Victoria
Dock, Hobart
Tel. 002/31 1999
*The freshest seafood overlooking
the harbour activity. Busy, noisy.
Expensive.*

Kurrajong Heights, NSW
Patrick's Pressoir
Kurrajong Heights
Tel. 045/67 7295
*Haute cuisine with a view
overlooking the Hawkesbury
Valley. Expensive.*

Launceston, Tas.
Shrimps
72 George Street, Launceston
Tel. 003/34 0584
*Classy seafood in a National
Trust building. Expensive.*

Victoria's
Cimitiere and Tamar Streets,
Launceston
Tel. 003/31 7433
*Tasmanian delicacies in historic
atmosphere. Expensive.*

Lorne, Vic.
Kosta's Taverna
48 Mountjoy Parade, Lorne
Tel. 052/89 1883
*Greek and international cuisine,
friendly service. Moderate.*

Maitland, NSW
Old George and Dragon
48 Melbourne Street, East
Maitland
Tel. 049/33 7272
*Elegant dining in the Hunter
Valley wine country. Expensive.*

Margaret River, WA
Leeuwin Estate
Gnarawary Road, Margaret
River
Tel. 097/57 6253
*Lovely fresh food in a beautiful
setting in the wine region.
Expensive.*

Melbourne

Colonial Tramcar
319 Clarendon Street, South
Melbourne
Tel. 03/696 4000
*Moveable feast: fine food on the
rails through scenic Melbourne.
Expensive.*

Diamond Dynasty
188 Little Bourke Street,
Melbourne
Tel. 03/663 3001
*Big restaurant in Chinatown
featuring lively yum cha sessions.
Moderate.*

Flower Drum
103 Little Bourke Street,
Melbourne
Tel. 03/663 2531
*Cantonese food at its best in the
heart of Chinatown.
Expensive.*

Fortuna Village
235 Little Bourke Street,
Melbourne
Tel. 03/663 3044
*Cantonese and Peking specialities.
Moderate.*

Ilyos
174 Lygon Street, Carlton
Tel. 03/663 6555
*A favourite Greek hangout
specializing in fish. Moderate.*

Jean Jacques by the Sea
40 Jacka Boulevard, St Kilda,
Melbourne
Tel. 03/534 8221
*Super seafood on the beach.
Expensive (except for cheap
takeaway department).*

Jimi's The Original
271 Victoria Street, Abbotsford,
Melbourne
Tel. 03/428 7531
*Big Greek-style seafood
restaurant. Music. Moderate.*

Malaya
30 Crossley Street, Melbourne
Tel. 03/662 1305
*Malaysian specialities.
Inexpensive.*

Mietta's
7 Alfred Place, Melbourne
Tel. 03/654 2366
Elegant French cuisine. Expensive.

Que Hong
176 Bridge Street, Richmond,
Melbourne
Tel. 03/429 1213
*Home cooking, Vietnamese style.
Inexpensive.*

Stephanie's
405 Tooronga Road, East
Hawthorn, Melbourne
Tel. 03/20 8944
*Outstanding French-based cuisine
in historic mansion. Expensive.*

Tansy's
555 Nicholson Street, North
Carlton
Tel. 03/380 5555
French-style cooking. Moderate.

Vlados Charcoal Grill
61 Bridge Road, Richmond,
Melbourne
Tel. 03/428 5833
*Huge steaks for the very hungry.
Moderate.*

Mt. Victoria, NSW

Bay Tree Tea Shop
26 Station Street, Mt. Victoria
Tel. 047/87 1275
*Light lunches in the Blue
Mountains. Closed midweek.
Inexpensive.*

Noosa Heads, Qld

Touché Restaurant
Hastings Street, Noosa Heads
Tel. 074/47 2222
*Overlooking the main street,
seafood in lively surroundings.
Moderate.*

Nuriootpa, SA

The Pheasant Farm
Samuel Road, Nuriootpa
Tel. 085/62 1286
*Gourmet lunch spot for Barossa
Valley winetasters, specializing in
game. Expensive.*

Perth

Botticelli
147 James Street, Northbridge,
Perth
Tel. 09/328 33763
*Just across the tracks from central
Perth, typical Italian food.
Moderate.*

Canton Restaurant
532 Hay Street, Perth
Tel. 09/325 8865
*Dependable Chinese food in the
heart of town. Moderate.*

Matilda Bay
3 Hackett Drive, Crawley, Perth
Tel. 09/386 5425
*Seafood and Swan River views
next to the yacht club. Expensive.*

Miss Maud
Murray and Pier Streets, Perth
Tel. 09/325 3900
*Swedish Smögasbord plus music.
Moderate.*

North Cott Cafe
149 Marine Parade, Cottesloe,
Perth
Tel. 09/385 1371
*Panoramic views and satisfying
food. Moderate.*

Pierre's
8 Outram Street, West Perth
Tel. 09/322 7648
*A major occasion for fans of
French cuisine. Expensive.*

The Plum
47 Lake Street, Northbridge,
Perth
Tel. 09/328 5920
*Candlelit cuisine with a European
accent. Expensive.*

Yugen Japanese Restaurant
566 Hay Street, Perth
Tel. 09/325 9093
*Down-to-earth Japanese food in
central Perth. Moderate.*

Pokolbin, NSW

Pokolbin Cellar
Hungerford Hill Wine Village,
Pokolbin
Tel. 049/98 7584
*Delightful atmosphere, cuisine and
wines for Hunter Valley explorers.
Expensive.*

Southport, Qld

Grumpy's
The Spit, Southport
Tel. 075/32 2900
*Cheerful wharfside atmosphere for
Gold Coast seafood. Moderate.*

Springton, SA

Cafe C
Craneford winery, Main Street,
Springton
Tel. 085/68 2220
*European and Asian tastes mingle
at the cellar door. Moderate.*

Surfers Paradise, Qld

Pellegrini Restaurant
3120 Gold Coast Highway,
Surfers Paradise
Tel. 075/38 7257
*Italian specialities in a cheerful
setting. Moderate.*

Sydney

The Art Gallery Restaurant
Art Gallery of NSW, Mezzanine
Level, Art Gallery Road, Sydney
Tel. 02/232 5425
*Australian cuisine and wines.
Lunch only, Sunday–Friday.
Moderate.*

The Bathers Pavilion
The Esplanade, Balmoral Beach
Tel. 02/968 1133
*Fabulous ocean view to
complement outstanding seafood
dishes. Expensive.*

Bennelong
Sydney Opera House, Circular
Quay
Tel. 02/250 7578
*A grand setting for a splurge
before or after the opera.
Expensive.*

Berowra Water Inn
Berowra Waters
Tel. 02/456 1027
*Nouvelle cuisine out in the
country, with a view. Very
expensive.*

Bilson's
Circular Quay West
Tel. 02/251 5600
*Views of harbour and opera house.
Excellent service, full wine list.
Expensive.*

China Sea
94 Hay Street, Haymarket
Tel. 02/211 1698
*Authentic Chinese restaurant in
the heart of Chinatown.
Inexpensive.*

Diethnes Greek Restaurant
336 Pitt Street, Sydney
Tel. 02/267 8956
*Old World atmosphere for
moussaka, lamb and Greek-style
seafood. Moderate.*

Doyle's On The Beach
11 Marine Parade, Watsons Bay
Tel. 02/337 2007
*On the beach, an old tradition.
Very big and very popular. Every
kind of seafood imaginable.
Expensive.*

Eliza's Garden Restaurant
29 Bay Street, Double Bay
Tel. 02/323 656
*Elegant celebrities' spot. Very
expensive.*

Fine Bouche
191 Palmer Street, East Sydney
Tel. 02/331 4821
*Highly regarded haute cuisine in
casual atmosphere. Expensive.*

Imperial Peking Harbourside
15 Circular Quay West, The
Rocks
Tel. 02/277 073
*Far from Chinatown, all the
traditional delights, especially
seafood. Expensive.*

Jordon's
197 Harbourside, Darling
Harbour
Tel. 02/281 3711
*Right on the harbour, seafood, of
course, outdoor dining. Music.
Expensive.*

Last Aussie Fishcaf
24 Bayswater Road, Kings Cross
Tel. 02/356 2911
*Fish and chips, char-grilled
octopus. Music, dancing. Can be
expensive.*

Oasis Seros
495 Oxford Street, Paddington
Tel. 02/33 3377
*Gourmet delights in dimly-lit
ambience—ambitious, original
cuisine. Expensive.*

Orient Hotel
89 George Street, The Rocks
Tel. 02/251 1255
*Cheerful ambience for barbecues
and salads. Inexpensive.*

Phantom of the Opera
17/21 Circular Quay West,
The Rocks
Tel. 02/247 2755
*Strong on seafood in gourmet
fashion. Glorious view. Open
terrace dining. Expensive.*

Rockpool
109 George Street, The Rocks
Tel. 02/252 1888
*Atmosphere, food and service
first-class. Seafood fantasies. Very
expensive.*

Siam
383 Oxford Street, Paddington
Tel. 02/331 2669
*All the spicy delights of Thai
cuisine. Moderate.*

Suntory
529 Kent Street, Sydney
Tel. 02/267 2900
*Fine Japanese cuisine based on
freshest seafood. Expensive.*

The Wharf Restaurant
Pier 4, Hickson Road,
Walsh Bay, Sydney
Tel. 02/247 9245
*Varied Australian cuisine, harbour
view but with back turned to the
Opera House, informal. Moderate.*

Tennant Creek, NT

Dolly Pot Inn
Davidson Street
Tel. 089/62 2824
*Several nationalities of cuisine in
a lively atmosphere. Inexpensive.*

Wollongong, NSW

Harbour Front Restaurant
Endeavour Drive, Wollongong
Tel. 042/27 2999
*Beautiful view. Seafood.
Moderate.*

Yulara, NT

**Four Seasons Ayers Rock Hotel,
Stuart Room**
Tel. 089/56 2156
*A chance to try bush tucker, like
sauteed wichetty grubs or
kangaroo meat. Expensive.*

Index

Page references in **bold** refer to main entries; those in *italic* refer to illustrations.